INDIGENOUS PEOPLES AND POLITICS

Edited by
Franke Wilmer
Montana State University

A ROUTLEDGE SERIES

Indigenous Peoples and Politics
Franke Wilmer, *General Editor*

Inventing Indigenous Knowledge
*Archaeology, Rural Development,
and the Raised Field Rehabilitation
Project in Bolivia*
Lynn Swartley

The Globalization of
Contentious Politics
*The Amazonian Indigenous
Rights Movement*
Pamela L. Martin

Cultural Intermarriage in
Southern Appalachia
*Cherokee Elements in Four Selected
Novels by Lee Smith*
Katerina Prajnerova

Storied Voices in Native
American Texts
*Harry Robinson, Thomas King,
James Welch, and Leslie Marmon Silko*
Blanca Schorcht

On the Streets and in the
State House
*American Indian and Hispanic Women
and Environmental Policymaking in
New Mexico*
Diane-Michele Prindeville

Chief Joseph, Yellow Wolf, and the
Creation of Nez Perce History in
the Pacific Northwest
Robert R. McCoy

National Identity and the
Conflict at Oka
*Native Belonging and Myths of
Postcolonial Nationhood in Canada*
Amelia Kalant

Native American and Chicano/a
Literature of the American
Southwest
Intersections of Indigenous Literature
Christina M. Hebebrand

THE PRESENT POLITICS OF THE PAST

Indigenous Legal Activism
and Resistance to
(Neo)Liberal Governmentality

Seán Patrick Eudaily

NEW YORK AND LONDON

Published in 2004 by
Routledge
711 Third Avenue,
New York, NY 10017

2 Park Square, Milton Park,
Abingdon, Oxfordshire OX14 4RN

First issued in paperback 2015

Routledge is an imprint of the Taylor & Francis Group, an informa business

Copyright © 2004 Routledge

All rights reserved. No part of this book may be printed or utilized in any form or by any electronic, mechanical or other means, now know or hereafter invented, including photocopying and recording, or any other information storage or retrieval system, without permission in writing from the publisher.

Eudaily, Seán Patrick, 1974–

The Present Politics of the Past: Indigenous Legal Activism and Resistance to (Neo)Liberal Governmentality / Seán Patrick Eudaily.

p. cm. — (Indigenous people and politics)
Includes bibliographical references and index.

ISBN 0-415-94960-2 (alk. paper)

1. Indigenous peoples—politics and government.
2. Indigenous peoples—Government relations.
3. Indigenous peoples—Legal status, laws, etc.

I. Title. II. Series.

GN380.E83 2004
323.11—dc22

2004001251

ISBN 13 : 978-0-415-65104-2 (pbk)
ISBN 13 : 978-0-415-94960-6 (hbk)

For Sara

Contents

Acknowledgments	ix
Chapter One Opening Statements: Clearing a Space for Thought	1
Chapter Two Interrogations: A Hauntology of Indigenous Peoples in World Politics	21
Chapter Three Governing "Free Subjects": A Genealogy of (Neo)Liberal Governmentality	35
Chapter Four Specters of Colonialism: Indigenous Legal Practice as Deconstructive Jurisprudence	59
Chapter Five Dossiers Introduction	77
Chapter Six Native Title in Australia	83
Chapter Seven Native Title in Canada	181
Chapter Eight Judgements: Indigenous Legal Claims Beyond the Limits of Liberalism	229

Notes	253
Bibliography	259
Table of Authorities	269
Index	275

Acknowledgments

As with any important endeavor in life, this project is the product of more than one person. My family, including those no longer with us, has always been my strength and my rock. Matt Stergios stirred my interest in history, and set me on the academic path that I have been on these last ten years. Orville Cope, Steve Maughan, Jasper LiCalzi, and Kerry Hunter all challenged me to be the better student and man that I already thought I was. Kirk Bowman taught that to teach was to inspire. Ron Terchek, Ted Gurr, Sangeeta Ray, Richard Brown, Christian Davenport, and Fred Alford all put up with me, and accepted this unorthodox research project. My "unofficial committee"—Steve Smith and Anthony Kammas—pushed my thought and my writing to a higher plane. Kath Sanders and my darling wife Sara spent countless hours troubleshooting the errors in the manuscript—any that remain are my responsibility alone.

Special thanks must go out to the Aboriginal and Torres Strait Islander Commission in Australia, the Assembly of First Nations in Canada, and *The Mining Journal,* London. All were kind enough to grant me permission to reprint at length their statements on native title in the dossiers contained within this work. I am also grateful to Lexington Books for permission to reprint in chapter three material originally appearing in my "The Kantian Peace Through a Radical Theoretic Lens," (with Kirk Bowman) *New Approaches to Comparative Politics: Insights from Political Theory,* Ed., Jennifer S. Holmes, Lanham, MD: Lexington Books, 2003, 111–123. Finally, I would like to thank the series editor, Franke Wilmer and my editors with Taylor & Francis, Kimberly Guinta and Joette Lynch. Without their encouragement and assistance, this work would not have come to fruition.

Seán Patrick Eudaily
Breckenridge, MN

Chapter One

Opening Statements: Clearing a Space for Thought

> Do not ask me who I am and do not ask me to remain the same: leave it to our bureaucrats and our police to see that our papers are in order. At least spare us their morality when we write.
> (Foucault, *The Archaeology of Knowledge* 17)

INTRODUCTION

Each phrase in the title of this work gives a clue as to its purpose and agenda. "The present politics of the past" refers to the conditions that have arisen in the recent politics of advanced liberal states with indigenous populations (such as the U.S., Canada, Aotearoa/New Zealand, and Australia) where "the past" is an issue or even at stake in contemporary struggles.

By invoking the activism of indigenous peoples, a concept of considerable slippage has been introduced. Many analyses of such subject areas either blindly accept or get bogged down in defining/defending terminology. For instance, in her study of American Indian activism in the U.S., Joane Nagel uses "the terms 'American Indian,' 'Indian,' 'Native American,' and 'native' interchangeably ... to refer to the descendents of the *aboriginal* inhabitants of North America [Emphasis added]," while seeming to accept the latter term as unproblematic (Nagel xii). Conversely, Guntram F. A. Werther reserves the term aboriginal to refer to only those peoples that "in their archaic polities ... were represented by non-state-organized-societies that were colonized as part of a European expansion that began in earnest in the fifteenth century"—a particular subset of *indigenous* peoples as "the sense of being the earliest known peoples of a place as expressed in the phrase 'since time immemorial'" (Werther xxvii, xxiv). And, as further

1

2 — The Present Politics of the Past

evidence that this debate has no end, Franke Wilmer defines indigenous peoples as those who:

> belong to the non-European, decentralized local communities that resisted the process of assimilation, national integration, and incorporation into areas of the world colonized and now controlled by descendents of Europeans. (Wilmer 7)

These are precisely the characteristics that Werther uses to distinguish aboriginal peoples from (merely) indigenous peoples. I, however, will not enter this semantic pit-of-no-return. First, one need not be a deconstructionist to recognize that all of these terms are negatively defined by the European norm. Therefore, I side with Russell Means of the American Indian Movement by not attaching much significance to the choice of terminology, all of which are European in origin (Means 25). The specific groups under study here self-identify as Aboriginal Australians, Torres Strait Islanders, Inuit, and First Nations or Indians—I have no desire to generalize my usage of "indigenous people" beyond the particulars at hand. However, with my use of "indigenous" I do have in mind a double entendre also alluding to peoples who are engaging in practices of resistance from within liberal legal regimes, and thus are indigenous to such power relations.

By my use of the terms "liberal" and "neoliberal" I have in mind a very particular and uncommon definition. I am not referring to either the American political discourse that designates the center-left as liberal, or to the discourse of traditional political theory that identifies liberalism with individual rights and limited government. Instead I am drawing on the Foucauldian literature that analyses the knowledges, power relations, and subjectivities emergent in the industrial West. That literature is centered upon the problematique of *biopower*, or the regulation of the life processes of a "natural" population and market (Foucault, *The History of Sexuality, Volume I: An Introduction* 139). An in-depth discussion of this usage will be undertaken in chapter three.

INTEGRATING THEORY AND METHODS

Commitment to the type of analysis of (post)coloniality and liberal regimes sketched above requires a corresponding shift in one's general approach to research. At the heart of this shift is the problematic relationship between theory and practice.

In this work I employ a poststructural research design. This form— which draws heavily upon the work of Michel Foucault, Gilles Deleuze,

Opening Statements 3

Jacques Derrida, and Michel de Certeau—is animated by a political motivation to support marginalized peoples against oppression under liberal government. However, unlike other forms of "critical theory," this approach contains no totalizing vision of a non-oppressive regime. Following Foucault, "I would rather oppose actual experiences" than provide a utopian blueprint (Foucault, "Revolutionary Action: 'until Now'" 231). Whereas this approach does entail a rejection of traditional modes of theorizing, it does so in order to improve them. A focus on practice, rather than ideal theory, allows the theorist to employ practical experience as a tool for innovation. As Deleuze writes,

> Practice is a set of relays from one theoretical point to another, and theory is a relay from one practice to another. No theory can develop without eventually encountering a wall, and practice is necessary for piercing this wall. (Deleuze and Foucault 206)

This move is ethical as well as intellectual. By allowing practice to "speak" to theory, one also "hears" the voice of the marginalized, often for the first time, without an intervening intellectual "speaking" for such people. Deleuze contends that the fundamental lesson Foucault has taught us is "the indignity of speaking for others" (Deleuze and Foucault 209). Thus, I will proceed with a focus on the direct practice of indigenous engagement with liberal regimes. Evidence of this engagement is best located in the archival sources of legal claims by indigenous peoples, judicial opinions about those claims, and public comment about such events. Although some secondary materials will be employed, the attempt will be to link the production of new theoretical insights to existing indigenous practice. There is much to learn from the practices of indigenous legal activism, particularly in the realm of developing non-liberal conceptions of democracy. How does one go about theorizing in this manner?

Before that question can be addressed, however, one would be remiss to neglect the strong critique Gayatri Chakravorty Spivak has leveled at the conception of the theoretical-practice-as-relay approach advanced by Foucault and Deleuze. Spivak detects a problematic silence below the talk of critical theory "beyond representation" (Spivak, *A Critique of Postcolonial Reason: Toward a History of the Vanishing Present* 257). The central question here is not so much "can the subaltern speak?" but rather what goes unsaid if we answer in the affirmative, as Foucault and Deleuze do? In abjuring representation, Foucault and Deleuze run together two different meanings of representation: "representation as 'speaking for,' as in politics [*vertreten*], and representation as 're-presentation,' as in art or philosophy [*darstellen*]" (Spivak, *A Critique of Postcolonial Reason: Toward a History of the Vanishing Present* 256). Does the Foucault/Deleuze formulation of theory-as-relay, in its desire to hear the voice of the subaltern, efface her silence all the more? Spivak certainly believes so; she writes:

> The ventriloquism of the speaking subaltern is the left intellectual's stock-in-trade "... The banality of leftist intellectuals' list of self-knowing, politically canny subalterns stands revealed; representing them, the intellectuals represent themselves as transparent." (Spivak, *A Critique of Postcolonial Reason: Toward a History of the Vanishing Present* 255-57)

In contrast to this "ventroloquism" Spivak harkens back to Marx's treatment of representation in the *Eighteenth Brumaire of Louis Bonaparte* as a better model of subjectivity. Marx's employment of class as both a descriptive and transformative category, on Spivak's reading, avoids essentialism. By focusing on the analysis of descriptive class as coming from difference (the cutting off of the proletarian mode of life from that of other classes), and class agency as "impersonal because it is systematic and heterogenous," Marx and Spivak retain a role for the intellectual denied by Foucault and Deleuze (Spivak, *A Critique of Postcolonial Reason: Toward a History of the Vanishing Present* 258). Spivak thus turns the arguments that the poststructuralists level at Marx on their feet:

> This sharpens the contrast Foucault and Deleuze slide over, the contrast, say, between a proxy and a portrait ... In the guise of a post-Marxist description of the scene of power, we thus encounter a much older debate: between representation or rhetoric as tropology and as persuasion. *Darstellen* belongs to the first constellation, *vertreten*—with stronger suggestions of substitution—to the second. Again, they are related, but running them together, especially to say that beyond both is where oppressed subjects speak, act, and know *for themselves,* leads to an essentialist, utopian politics. (Spivak, *A Critique of Postcolonial Reason: Toward a History of the Vanishing Present* 258-59)

At this point one must provisionally set aside Spivak's charge that the theory-as-relay approach "belongs to the exploiter's side of the international division of labor" in order to more fully explore what such a mode of theoretical practice may entail (Spivak, *A Critique of Postcolonial Reason: Toward a History of the Vanishing Present* 265).

In the essay "What is Enlightenment?" Foucault attempts to link his style of post-structuralism to the traditional forms of Western theorizing.

Opening Statements 5

Yet, this link is in the form of a mirror image—that of the counter-modern—which has existed as long as its modern counterpart.

> I have been seeking to stress that the thread that may connect us with the Enlightenment is not faithfulness to doctrinal elements, but rather the permanent reactivation of an attitude—that is, of a philosophical ethos that could be described as a permanent critique of our historical era. (Foucault, "'What Is Enlightenment?'" 42)

This form of critique must produce a "historical analysis of the limits imposed on us and an experiment with the possibility of going beyond them" (Foucault, "'What Is Enlightenment?'" 50). The intellectual and political rationale for this limit-attitude is no less than "to give new impetus, as far and wide as possible, to the undefined work of freedom" (Foucault, "'What Is Enlightenment?'" 46). Foucault (borrowing from Nietzsche) uses the term "genealogy" to refer to a type of research: 1) where the stakes are the "intensification of power relations"; 2) whose homogeneity results in the treatments of the "realm of practices, with their technological side and their strategic side"; 3) which finds systematicity in the analysis of how subjects are created through knowledge, power relations, and ethics; and finally, 4) derives its generality from addressing these issues within the framework of the dominant historical forms of the modern epoch (Foucault, "'What Is Enlightenment?'" 47–49). The following section will sketch out the form and implications of genealogical method.

The ethic of genealogy

What advantages does a genealogical approach have over traditional hermeneutic and empiricist research? The first difference is an explicit refusal to ground one's work on *a priori* assumptions of the "natural state of things." This applies especially to assumptions of human agency. Thus, instead of beginning with axiomatic assumptions and deriving hypotheses, genealogy begins with the event. The task is then to construct a counter-memory of the historical dispersion of forces, meaning-effects, and interconnections within which the event is located. This serves to sever the event from ties of "self-evidence" and "necessity" that we have learned to ascribe to the world (Foucault, "Two Lectures" 76). Therefore, a genealogical approach focuses on process, possibility, and discontinuities, rather than categorization, causality, and continuity. One seeks not to isolate particular variables while holding all others constant, as in empiricism, but to become aware of the delicate linkages between multiple statements, events, and practices in their interconnection. As Foucault writes,

> I would like to substitute the study of this whole play of dependencies for the uniform, simple activity of allocating causality; and by suspending the infinitely renewed privileges of cause, to render apparent the polymorphous interweaving of correlations. (Foucault, "Politics and the Study of Discourse" 58)

This approach will lead to a focus on details, practices, events—the whole workings of micropower in the minutia of history. By so doing one can localize an event or statement in its proper historical context, contra analyses which seek to lift themes, objects, and generalizable relationships as things-in-themselves. Thus genealogy focuses not on institutions or ideologies as objects, but rather on *practices*. Genealogy is concerned with questions of "how" instead of "what" or "why" (Foucault, "Questions of Method" 75).

Immediately an alarm will ring in the heads of some—how can genealogy ever aid in the accumulation of knowledge? What can we hope to gain by abandoning social *science*?

> What types of knowledge do you want to disqualify in the very instant of your demand: "Is it a science?" Which speaking, discoursing subjects—which subjects of experience and knowledge—do you want to "diminish" when you say: "I who conducts this discourse am conducting a scientific discourse, and I am a scientist?" (Foucault, "Two Lectures" 85)

Whereas scientific knowledge strives for a single metanarrative—necessary for the exercise of social control—genealogy locates itself as part of the "insurrection of subjected knowledges" (Foucault, "Two Lectures" 87).

Genealogy *is not* the refutation of theory with new facts (unlike empiricism), nor is it interpretation of new meanings for old events (unlike hermeneutics). Rather genealogy is an *ethos* of analysis that is in strategic alliance with practical resistance:

> Let us give the term *genealogy* to the union of erudite knowledge and local memories that allows us to establish a historical knowledge of struggles and to make use of this knowledge tactically today. (Foucault, "Two Lectures" 83)

Genealogy is also distinct from traditional history in two key ways: First, rather than being oriented towards the past, it is rather a "history of the present." Second, instead of investigating the "deep" meaning of events genealogy examines the "surface" created by placing those events in series, and in correlations with others series. Genealogy then seeks to de-couple events from the series that traditional history places then in and re-actualize

Opening Statements 7

them "along different and multiple series" (Colwell 27). Thus rather than a reinterpretation of meaning, genealogy produces a meaning-effect that is always linked to the creation of space that serves as the site of resistance to "self-evident" truths.

Power/Knowledge/Subjectivity: The Heideggerian Heritage of Poststructuralism

Foucault's definition of power differs greatly from the traditional "faces of power"(power over another, agenda setting, ideology) made familiar in political science by Dahl, Bachrach and Baratz, Marxists, and others. For Foucault, power is not a scarce substance to be held by an elite, but rather power represents diffuse flows of relational force—irreducibly plural in character. Deleuze describes the "Foucauldian" approach of power:

> Power is not essentially repressive (since it "incites, it induces, it seduces"); it is practiced before it is possessed (since it is possessed only in a determinable form, that of class, and a determined form, that of state); it passes through the hands of the mastered no less than through the hands of the masters (since it passes through every related force). (Deleuze, *Foucault* 71)

In addition to the view of power as an apparatus/form produced by an unformalized *diagram* of the relations of forces, Foucault links the exercise of power with the production of knowledge. He shows the linkage between *jurisdiction* (what is allowed under a diagram of power) and *verisdiction* (what is truthful within a discourse of knowledge). This "economy of discourses of truth" is both the *product* of power relations and subsequently becomes an essential *means* for the reproduction of the system of power that gave birth to it (Foucault, "Two Lectures" 93).

Spivak gives us another reading of Foucault's power/knowledge, by relating it to the distinctions (following Heidegger) of the ontological, ontic, and sub-individual states of being (Spivak, "More on Power/Knowledge" 30). Leslie Paul Thiele explains that Heidegger uses the *ontic* in "signifying that which does not directly address the ontological fundamentals of human being but rather pertains to its concrete possibility" (Thiele 52). If ontology is the description of being, then the ontic is the space of becoming, and the subindividual is the materiality that precedes being. Thus, in genealogy focus is turned to the ontic as the constitutive state of being, with the thought that there exists a subindividual level beyond even the constitution of subjects. Spivak attempts to name each of these levels of power/knowledge.

The homology I am about to draw, then, is, strictly speaking, an imperfect homology. It is between, on the one hand, *puissance* [capability], *pouvoir* [power], *force* and, on the other, *connaissance* [discipline/science], *savoir* [knowledge], *énoncé* [statement]. (Spivak, "More on Power/Knowledge" 36)

Thus, power/knowledge should be identified as constitutive practices located in the ontic, by an analysis of the apparati of *puissance/connaissance* in the ontological. Although such apparati are the result of their constitution (or "presencing [*Anwesen*]" to use the more Heideggerian term) in the ontic, they are not "caused" by said practices, at least not in the way that causation is usually conceived of in social science. Heidegger describes the constitution of (ontological) history as a "revealing, [or] *destining*"—where *destining* is the farthest thing from causation, much less fate "where 'fate' means the inevitableness of an unalterable course" (Heidegger 329-30). This schema can also be extended to include Foucault's third axis of inquiry, the formation of subjects. What results is a conceptual grid laid out with the Foucauldian themes of knowledge, power, and subjectivity marking the columns, and the Heideggerian divisions of the ontological, the ontic, and the sub-individual forming the rows (see Table 1).

In this light, the characterization of genealogy as the combination of "erudite knowledge and local memories" can be drawn out. It is the middle row in our chart that receives the most theoretical attention—the poststructural contribution to erudite knowledge. However, this attention to the ontic *in itself* is not aimed at theoretic advancement *for itself*. Rather, what genealogical studies seek to create is a new account of the emergence of ontological practices from distinct statements, forces, and bodies. It is because of the interest in such emergences that poststructuralism theorizes at the ontic level, for it is there that these transformations occur.[1]

In highlighting the manner in which Foucault's account of power plays in the space created by differentiating the ontological, ontic, and

Table 1 A Conceptual Grid with Foucauldian and Heideggerian Themes

CONCEPT MAP	Knowledge (objective)	Power (interested)	Subjectivity (subjective)
Ontological (ideal being)	Connaissance (discipline/sci.)	Puissance (capability)	Self
Ontic (becoming)	Savoir (knowledge)	Pouvoir (power)	Subject
Sub-Individual (material)	Énoncé (statement)	Force	Body

Opening Statements 9

sub-individual, Spivak ironically has pointed towards a response to her critique of Foucault and Deleuze's disavowal of representation. As Spivak suggests, "it might be useful to give the proper names of Foucault and Derrida *in* to each other, although such a move would not be endorsed by either" (Spivak, "More on Power/Knowledge" 25). Why highlight the linkages between the two thinkers? The answer given by Spivak (and seconded here) is that what connects the two, and in large measure defines poststructuralism, is the heritage of Heideggerian ont(ic)ology discussed above.

> For both Foucault and Derrida, in different ways, the ontico-ontological difference is a thinking through of the uses and limits of a critical philosophy. Their catachrestic nominalism may be trying to touch the ontic with the thought that there is a subindividual (or random for Derrida) space even under, or below, or before ... the "preontological Being as [Dasein's] ontologically constitutive state [Heidegger]." (Spivak, "More on Power/Knowledge" 30)

This is the theoretical "clearing" to be done before one can treat ontological subjectivity as the *subject-effect*. By employing the tripartite Heidegerrian categories, and in paying particular attention to the ontic as the space between the ontological and the subindividual, the eternal ping-pong of the dialectic between Hegelian idealism (the ontological) and Marxian materialism (the subindividual) can be avoided. However, Spivak only takes one halfway down this path; for even if the subject-effect is constituted in the ontic out of subindividual material, must subjectivity remain only the byproduct of practices of power/knowledge, or does it constitute a unique realm of practice? One may turn to Deleuze and de Certeau, two of Foucault's strongest readers, as guides for the rest of this journey.

In his reading of Foucault, Deleuze suggests the importance of Heideggerian patrimony. Yet, looking over the now completed body of Foucault's work, Deleuze has suggested that the notion of power/knowledge be supplemented by subjectivity.

The new triplet, power/knowledge/subjectivity, defines the scope of Foucauldian analysis. Deleuze writes:

> In truth, one thing haunts Foucault—thought. The question: "what does thinking signify? What do we call thinking?" is the arrow first fired by Heidegger and then again by Foucault. He writes a history, but a history of thought as such. To think means to experiment and to problematize. Knowledge, power, and the self are the triple root of thought. (Deleuze, *Foucault* 116)

Thus, one now may see the brief genealogy of the conceptual map outlined above. Placing power "between" knowledge and subjectivity allows it to fill a similar role as the ontic in Heidegger's schema. By placing power at the center of our analysis we reduce the tendency towards either objective (knowledge) or subjective reductionism. The Foucauldian concept of power allows one to investigate historical games of truth and of will, without a prior commitment to either as a foundation for thought. Therefore, if power is central to Foucault's thought, this implies not determinism, but its opposite. Power is the medium that makes decision/action possible between the "truth" of what is and the "will" to be otherwise. As de Certeau writes:

> Ethics is articulated through effective operations, and it defines a distance between what is and what ought to be. This distance designates a space where we have something to do. On the other hand, dogmatism is authorized by a reality that it claims to represent [*darstellen*] and in the name of this reality [*vertreten*], it imposes laws. [Genealogy] functions midway between these two poles: but whenever it attempts to break away from ethics, it returns towards a dogmatism. (de Certeau, "History: Science and Fiction" 199)

This returns one to the question of representation. Foucault and Deleuze are not so much running together the two meanings of representation, as Spivak suggests, but rather are distancing themselves from the dogmatic senses of "to represent." In the place of an epistemic realism and a political vanguardism, poststructuralism offers a catachrestic nominalism and an ethical responsibility—a "speaking of" and a "speaking with." In addition to answering Spivak's challenge, this formulation helps to connect the thought of Foucault, Derrida, Deleuze, and de Certeau to a common field of inquiry defined by their debt to Heidegger.

RESISTANCE TO POWER/KNOWLEDGE/SUBJECTIVITY

Although one might get the impression that power is omnipresent and thus domination is inescapable on such an account, Foucault comes to a very different conclusion. The encompassing flows of power do not negate the possibility of resistance. Indeed, even though Foucault rejects the notion that one could ever get "outside" of power, he theorized that the very sites of power's exercise are also sites of resistance (Foucault, "Power and Strategies" 141). However, for all of the references to resistance in Foucault's texts, the concept never gets the sustained treatment akin to the "tripartite axis of power-knowledge-pleasure" (Bartowski 44).

Opening Statements 11

This section lays out a sketch of a poststructural framework for approaching collective resistance. Such a framework, while eschewing foundational claims, is attentive to the four main aspects of contention as outlined by McAdam, Tarrow, and Tilly—that contention entails collective action, is episodic, affects interests, and involves the government (McAdam, Tarrow and Tilly 2). Resistance is collective in as much as it is conducted "in the name of" some social group; whether or not the action or statement is made by an individual (May). Episodes count as resistance events if they are clashes of bodies on bodies, statements on statements, or discourses on discourses—where the events are the points of contact, not a state of the bodies, statements, or discourses themselves (Foucault, "Theatrum Philisophicum" 173–75). Such clashes not only involve existing interests, but also the creation and/or transformation of interests. Finally, a genealogy of resistance can only be elucidated in opposition to existing forms of government, if employed in the broader sense of the term outlined in chapter three (Burchell, Gordon and Miller; Dean, *Governmentality: Power and Rule in Modern Society*). This follows from James C. Scott's dictum that once one has analyzed "a specific form of domination, one has gone far to specify precisely what a subversive act in this context would look like" (Scott 105).

An analytics of resistance

In order to analyze events of collective resistance, one must expand upon Foucault's elliptical description of resistance. Foucault writes that resistance is engendered by the very exercise of power:

> There are no relations of power without resistances; the latter are all the more real and effective because they are formed right at the point where relations of power are exercised. (Foucault, "Power and Strategies" 142)

However, if one is to connect this broad conception of resistance with the types of resistance events that mainstream contentious politics examines, a more detailed typology is needed. We must be mindful, as was Foucault, that, "In any case, one must try to think of struggle and its forms, objectives, means and processes in terms of a logic free of the sterilizing constraints of the dialectic [or other forms of method]" (Foucault, "Power and Strategies" 143-44). Michel de Certeau gives us just such an analytics of resistance.

Certeau breaks down resistance into two types: *tactics* and *strategies*. Tactical resistance is exercised from the "space of the other…it must play off

12   *The Present Politics of the Past*

and within a terrain imposed on it and organized by the law of a foreign power," while strategic resistance begins in "a *place* that can be delimited as its *own* and serve as a base from which the relations of an *exteriority* composed of targets or threats ... can be managed" (de Certeau, *The Practice of Everyday Life* 35, 37).

Unlike the differentiation between contained and transgressive contention (McAdam, Tarrow and Tilly), the distinction between strategic and tactical resistance does not presuppose the level of success (transgression) or failure (containment) affected by each type. Rather, it is a question for inquiry, not an *a priori* definition. Tactical resistance resembles Foucault's original presentation—resistance as the limitation of "receptivity" to power (Deleuze, *Foucault* 77). Examples of tactical resistance in the contemporary context are found throughout what Iris Marion Young (1990) terms the "politics of difference." Regimes of power/knowledge/subjectivity do not simply prohibit and deny, they also are productive of forms of subjectivity and strategic spaces where those subjectivities are given agency. Tactical resistance is the practice of taking those identities and liberties produced by the dominant form of power as tools for said power's subversion. Tactical resistance can be to take marginalized subject positions as a source of *pride* rather than *oppression*: "I am just what they say I am—a Jewboy, a colored girl, a fag, a dyke, or a hag—and proud of it" (Young, *Justice and the Politics of Difference* 166). Another aspect of tactical resistance is the utilization of liberties within the dominant power system—most prominently, consumer choice and the realm of the "private" produced by liberal government—in oppositional ways:

> In the late 1960s and 1970s the counterculture movement made the body and its adornment the site of struggles: hippies challenged "straight" society's norms of respectability, which required short, clipped hair for men and little or no facial hair, as well as tailored angular clothes. The punk movement continued in a different form this challenge to the aesthetics of professional culture. Beginning in the late 1960s food also became politicized; the "natural foods" movement, which challenged enormously the eating practices of millions of people, asked political questions about food ... Besides making demands on government for environmental regulations and on corporations to employ productive processes that do not damage the environment, the environmental movement has questioned the appropriateness of a plastic-dependent, throwaway consumer culture. (Young, *Justice and the Politics of Difference* 87)

These resistances certainly were not limited to the white, middle-class counter-cultural movements. Feminists, in their slogan "the personal is

Opening Statements   13

political," as well as the culture exhibited in the popular music and personal style of urban Blacks in America were, and continue to be, sites of struggle (Mercer 34). It is important to note that tactical resistance includes, but also goes beyond, performative value to the marginalized by introducing elements which supplement, and thus destabilize, the existing regime of power. In addition, a poststructural definition of contention treats such discursive shifts as being intimately tied to the constitution of contending identities, not merely "frames" used to motivate supporters or woo allies. Tactical resistances "provide a standpoint from which to criticize prevailing institutions and norms:" Black "brothers" and "sisters" create a sense of "solidarity absent from the calculating individualism of white professional capitalist society"; "female values of nurturing" oppose the militaristic worldview of US foreign policy; Native Americans' experiences "of a culture tied to the land" challenge liberal economic rationality (Young, *Justice and the Politics of Difference* 167). These are just a few examples from the American experience—tactical resistance is being waged in every corner of the globe from a multiplicity of subject positions.

The history of these tactical resistances (at least in liberal states), however, must be amended to include the history of their re-absorption into dominant forms of power relations. This also marks a departure from Scott, for whom the cooptation of the radical ends of resistance by the dominant power structure seems of little concern (Scott 103–06). In particular, Scott seems to ignore the possibility that material concessions made by dominant elites could represent a strategy of cooptation (Scott 187).

Resistances based upon consumer choice are especially likely to be de-politicized. This is evident in the experiences of Black Cultural Nationalists:

> Cultural Nationalists in their finery support many of the evils which have put them in the position of servitude ... they support and profit from "Being Black" ... selling earrings at 400% mark-up and buba's from dime store yardage at Saks 5th Avenue prices. (Harrison 152)

Other resistances are subsumed into the distributional games of "the politics of welfare capitalist society"—such as the Nixon administration's successful attempt to turn "Black Power" into a slogan for their state-directed community development schemes (Young, *Justice and the Politics of Difference* 89). One should never lose sight of the welfare state as a product of *liberal* government: "over and above the economic market in commodities and services" advanced liberal government requires a "second-order market of governmental goods and services" in order to solidify the reproduction of its system of power in times of market crisis (Gordon 36).

It is imperative to distinguish the *analytic* division of tactical and strategic resistance, from the *normative* claim that strategic resistance is either a more authentic or more important form of struggle. Again, such a position is contra Scott's assumption that the hidden transcript, particularly its first public expression, should be privileged over infrapolitics as a "moment of truth and a personal authentication" (Scott 208). However, Scott is correct to note that tactical resistance/infrapolitics often spawn contention of the more explicit variety (Scott 95, 200-01).

Strategic resistance is a more elusive practice than its tactical counterpart. Although Foucault (Foucault, "Two Lectures") would maintain that one could never get outside of power, it is possible to be outside the dominant *form* of power relations. Therefore strategic resistance can be identified to the extent that "one can define the ... formation of ... different strategies that are deployed in it; in other words, if one can show how they all derive from the same set of relations;" relations which are different in formation to those of the dominant forms of power (Foucault, *The Archaeology of Knowledge* 68).

It is important to note that the definition of "strategic" being utilized here is fundamentally different than that often used in conflict studies, and in particular stands opposed to the word's usage in the collective action (CA) literature. In his classic work, *The Strategy of Conflict*, Thomas Schelling illustrates the standard definition of strategy used by collective action theory: "the essence of a game of strategy is the dependence of each person's proper choice of action on what he expects the other to do" (Schelling 160). This definition comes from the formulation of game theory, which distinguishes between games of skill, games of chance, and games of strategy. What Schelling (if not all CA theorists) recognizes is that this is a severe deviation from the word's traditional military usage (Schelling 3). This is more than a semantic matter. Collective action theories assume that a strategic situation (as defined by Schelling) is the pervasive reality facing potential dissidents. Thus, the supposed importance derived by some of their number from the so called "five percent rule."

> There are, first, those with grievances who do not rebel. By far the larger category, this group represents at least ninety-five percent of aggrieved people, at least ninety-five percent of the time, in at least ninety-five percent of the places. In short, potential rebels mostly do not rebel, even when it would be in every rebel's interests to do so. This category, which critics tend to ignore, is consistent with Olson's thesis. (Lichbach 12)

Opening Statements 15

One may assume that the five percent rule generally holds, yet disagree vehemently on its meaning. Far from ignoring such a situation, one could in fact argue that its genesis lies rather in the pervasive *lack* of strategic situations (in the military sense) facing those who would resist dominant regimes of power. Particularly for those who may potentially resist modern state power, it is not at all surprising that given a tactical situation in which they are outnumbered, outgunned, and squarely on a battlefield of their opponent's choosing that they should engage in resistance a small fraction of the time. For this reason one would do well to use "strategic" in its military sense—politics being, after all, much more a war than a game.

Within dominant power relations only the privileged few (e.g., corporations, the military, scientific institutions) have their own place from which to exercise power. Three major advantages accrue to those strategic positions within the hegemonic structure. A proper place allows "a certain independence with respect to the variability of circumstances"; space is a hedge against time; a mastery of space allows for the observation and codification of objects through the "panoptic practice" of sight. Finally, a place of one's own is necessary for the production of knowledge in order to "transform the uncertainties of history into readable spaces" (de Certeau, *The Practice of Everyday Life* 36). Whereas tactics are always conducted "within the enemies field of vision," to occupy strategic space is to fight battles of one's own choosing (de Certeau, *The Practice of Everyday Life* 37). It is only then that resistance takes on the affective function of power—spontaneity (Deleuze, *Foucault* 77). I now turn to what circumstances alert us to the potentiality of the latter type of resistance.

Strategic space

What makes the formation of strategic resistance possible? To answer this question one must conceive spatio-temporally of the *strategic moment* or *strategic space*. The conditions for the exercise of strategic resistance are set by the discontinuities of existing forms of power relationships. Or, as Deleuze put it, "It is the instability of power-relations which defines a strategic or non-stratified environment" (Deleuze, *Foucault* 74).

In the analysis of collective resistance the two important factors whose formation determines whether resistance is tactical or strategic, are the power-effect and the meaning-effect. These two factors relate to Foucault's dual classification of power effects (including resistance) into visibilities and articulable elements. We can thus conceive of resistance producing "both ... description-scenes and statement-curves" (Deleuze, *Foucault* 81). The descriptions employed by a resistance group identify its adversaries, and the statements it produces constitute its interests. In the emergence of new adversaries and interests a group's subjectivity, or rather, subject-effect is also transformed.[2]

In strategic space these elements are not pre-determined by the dominant power structure. Foucault describes such strategic moments as "points of diffraction" characterized as: 1) "points of incompatibility" where identity/interests proscribed by multiple systems of power are fundamentally at odds; 2) "points of equivalence" where no set of identity/ interests have any logical priority over another, and finally, 3) "link points of systemization" in that the result of the strategic situation will be formative on a whole variety of other practices, statements, and events (Foucault, *The Archaeology of Knowledge* 65-66).

Collective resistance in either form thus is reformulated as an event of contact between the statements and subjectivities produced by the dominant set of power relations and those that challenge such formations. This accounts for why such notions do not appear in traditional analyses. In its (re)conceptualization, resistance cannot be located in "the world, the self, [or] God... three conditions that invariably obscure the event and that obstruct the successful formulation of thought" (Foucault, "Theatrum Philisophicum" 176). It has no corporeality, and thus it cannot serve as cause in empiricism. It is the collision of forces on forces, not the experience of subjects; thus it cannot be interpreted by hermeneutics. It is neither origin nor conclusion, belonging to disorder/discontinuity rather than order/ continuity; thus is cannot be a major element in traditional narrative history—it is a phantasm of "pure difference" (Foucault, "Theatrum Philisophicum" 177).

TOOLS OF INQUIRY

Now that I have outlined the theoretical and ethical basis for this project, I may identify my research question—"how has the appearance of practices of indigenous legal activism established a new problematic for liberalism?" (de Certeau, "The Laugh of Michel Foucault" 195)—and the necessary axes of analysis to answer such a question—1) "what is the historical specificity of (post)colonial settler states?"; 2) "how do liberal regimes constitute the political?"; and, 3) "how can practices within a system [of law] resist the system's rules of formation?" The project will consist of six additional chapters, dealing with both theoretical and praxeological issues.

Opening Statements   17

Strategies of interrogation

The next three chapters will focus on the development of the theoretical tools needed to interrogate the question of indigenous legal activism in liberal regimes. Chapter two will focus on the problematic nature of indigenous activism and the (post)colonial status of the white settler states for the traditional conceptions of both ethnic conflict research and postcolonial theory. Chapter three will explicate the concept of governmentality as an approach to understanding liberalism. Governmentality refers to the diagrams of power relations and discourses of knowledge that make liberal government both thinkable and possible (Foucault, "Governmentality"; Gordon; Dean, *Governmentality: Power and Rule in Modern Society*). Finally, chapter four will address the mechanism by which, I will argue, indigenous legal activism "haunts" the regime of liberal governmentality—the deconstructive logic of the *supplement* and the *trace*.[3]

Dossiers of resistance

The actual documents charting the political war of words being waged in Australia and Canada over Native Title will be contained in two dossiers. In the introduction to *I, Pierre Riviére...*, Foucault designates four key aspects of the dossier format (Foucault, *I, Pierre Rivière, Having Slaughtered My Mother, My Sister, and My Brother...: A Case of Parricide in the 19th Century* xii-xiii). First, all material evidence in a case should be published. While my dossiers will not contain all texts in their entirety, every attempt has been made to include all sections of such texts that directly involve the issues under study. In this way these dossiers will more resemble Foucault's truncated style in *Herculine Barbin* than the comprehesive *I, Pierre Rivière* (Foucault, *Herculine Barbin: Being the Recently Discovered Memoirs of a Nineteenth-Century Hermaphrodite*). Second, the documents shall not be typologized by discourse; rather they will be presented in rough chronological order to emphasize their strategic and tactical interplay. Third, I will not directly subject the texts to interpretation. This point cannot be stressed enough. Stanley Fish writes that to interpret is "the act of determining, or trying to determine, what is meant *by* an utterance or a gesture, that is of what it is intended to be the expression" (Fish 302).

Fish goes further to argue that whether one's conceptualization of meaning/intention comes from "agency, mental processes, linguistic structure, class consciousness—in short, of anything and everything" interpretation is what is being done (Fish 302). However, if one is subjecting a text to some procedure in order to see what it can be *made* to mean, then one is simply "playing with the text" (Fish 302). Indeed, I claim to be doing nothing else in these dossiers than "playing with the text(s)" for political and theoretical reasons. Thus, and this is Foucault's final aspect of the dossier, the theoretical interrogations in this study are related to the same issues and events found in the dossiers, but are not direct commentaries on them.

Although the dossier is not the only format of genealogical research, it is exemplary of Foucault's characterization of all such work as "gray, meticulous, and patiently documentary" (Foucault, "Nietzsche, Genealogy, History" 76). Dossier one will focus on the *Mabo* and *Wik* decisions, and the issue of Native Title in Australia. Dossier two will follow the divergent strategies of legal activism (the Native Title claims of the First Nations) and treaty negotiations (the Nisga'a treaty in British Columbia) following the *Delgamuukw* decision in Canada.

Beyond indigenous activism: "speaking" practice to theory

The final chapter attempts to draw out aspects of the aforementioned analysis that may have implications for the wider field of political theory with a reflection on indigenous activism's impact on theories of multiethnic democracy.[4] Issues addressed include the limitations of Western forms of constitutionalism (Tully, *Strange Multiplicity: Constitutionalism in an Age of Diversity*), tolerance versus recognition of cultural difference, and the limits of liberal governmentality (Burchell, Gordon and Miller; Dean, *Governmentality: Power and Rule in Modern Society*). Therefore, this project brings together the analysis of existing ethnopolitical practice, original historical research, and theoretical contributions to the literatures on poststructuralism, (post)coloniality, critical legal studies, and democratic theory.

It may be rightfully asked at this point: "Is all of this necessary?" If indigenous peoples have challenged liberalism, should not one simply go and talk to them about their experiences, and report their stories back to a wider audience? While not rejecting such an endeavor outright, Spivak cautions those who would practice "conscientious ethnography" to be "forewarned by its relationship to the history of the discipline of anthropology" and its frequent collaboration with structures of domination (Spivak, *A Critique of Postcolonial Reason: Toward a History of the Vanishing Present* 191). What is a white, male academic to do in the face of the seeming incompatibility of one's institutional position and the radical alterity of the indigenous subject-effect?

Opening Statements 19

> In the face of *this* question, deconstruction might propose a double gesture: Begin where you are; but, when in search of absolute justifications, remember that the margin as such is the impossible boundary marking off the wholly other, and the encounter with the wholly other, as it may be figured, has an unpredictable relationship to our ethical rules. (Spivak, *A Critique of Postcolonial Reason: Toward a History of the Vanishing Present* 173)

To begin where I am means to engage in academic debate with other academics. It also means to critically engage the dominant political tradition of the white settler states—liberal governmentality. These interrogations do not attempt to "substitute for listening"; rather, they are the necessary ethical and intellectual work to be done in order that the gesture of listening, inevitably with white man's ears, conveys a sense of openness beyond the boundary of the other (Alford ix). Those academics who would reject the need for such care either must take themselves so seriously that they assume the role of narrator and shaper of the world, or, conversely, ignore the seriousness of holding theoretical practice up to our infinite responsibility to the others we have the hubris to study in the first place.

Chapter Two

Interrogations: A Hauntology of Indigenous Peoples in World Politics

Out of what Western societies have held in contempt, combated and believed they had subjugated, there are arising political alternatives and social models which represent, perhaps, the only hope for reversing the massive acceleration and reproduction of totalitarian, homogenizing effects generated by the power structure and technology of the West.

Michel de Certeau (de Certeau, "The Politics of Silence: The Long March of the Indians" 231)

INTRODUCTION

The discursive practices surrounding Indigenous Peoples' Movements (IPMs) in liberal-democratic states are a rich, and mostly untapped, resource for political analysis, although little practical, and even less theoretical, political science literature treats the subject as a major issue.[1] IPMs continue to be a growing force in world affairs particularly in the white settler states of Australia, Canada, New Zealand, and the United States (Stavenhagen 34). In fact, Ted Robert Gurr in *Peoples versus States* (his latest book based upon the Minorities at Risk program) identifies that almost all new episodes of ethnopolitical mobilization in the 1990s are due to IPMs (Gurr 45). While one may ponder the reasons behind this mismatch of practice and theory, there is a more subtle danger in social science (mis)treatments of IPMs. The very nature of mainstream social science inquiry threatens to cover over the key aspect of IPMs—the systemic nature of the indigenous challenge to Western institutions (Gurr 2)—with the logic of a new "Orientalism."

21

NEO-ORIENTALISM: LIBERAL SOCIAL SCIENCE AND INDIGENOUS POLITICAL MOVEMENTS

Orientalism, as laid out in Edward Said's much-cited 1978 book of the same name, was the confluence of the academic study of non-Western peoples and cultures with the political project of imperialism. Such discourses "see" the colonial Other through a lens complicit with, but not identical to, a global programme of political domination.

> Therefore, Orientalism is not is not a mere political subject matter or field that is reflected passively by culture, scholarship, or institutions; ... nor is it representative and expressive of some nefarious "Western" imperial plot to hold down the "Oriental" world. It is rather a *distribution* of geopolitical awareness into aesthetic, scholarly, economic, sociological, historical, and philological texts; ... it is, above all, a discourse that is by no means in direct, corresponding relationship with political power in the raw, but rather is produced and exists in an uneven exchange with various kinds of power, shaped to a degree by the exchange with power political (as with a colonial or imperial establishment), power intellectual (as with reigning sciences like comparative linguistics or anatomy, or any of the policy sciences), power cultural (as with orthodoxies and canons of taste, texts, values), power moral (as with ideas about what "we" do and what "they" cannot do or understand "we" do). (Said 12)

What makes Said's argument so original is that he examines the role of intellectuals (who were sympathetic if not outright devoted to the "Orient" they studied) in advancing the political project of colonialism through their work, even if they opposed it politically. Similarly, one would not be surprised to find the more radical implications of ethnopolitical movements ignored in social science texts where the support and maintenance of the status quo is openly advocated.[2] What is less obvious and more troubling is to find such an attitude encoded within the discourse of social science itself. Thus, even sympathetic scholars such as Gurr, Werther, and Wilmer at times represent IPMs in such a way as to undercut the challenge that these movements pose to Western ideas and politics.

Given the assessment that only "marginal improvements" have been made in the discriminatory environment that indigenous peoples face in Western democracies, one might assume that conditions for ethnopolitical conflict were ripe (Gurr 175). However, most authors suggest that the risks of conflict escalation by IPMs are low in these states (Gurr 238). In fact, many indigenous groups are portrayed as moderately successful in achieving their goals within existing political structures.[3] The primary source of these feelings of security is a belief in the conflict management abilities of liberal regimes.

Restating the typical modernization perspective on cultural change, Martin O. Heisler contends that the type of societies present in liberal states inhibit ethnically based conflict altogether. He rests much of his case on the individualizing tendencies of open, liberal societies. Within such states ethnic politics are not expected to result in either conflict or contention, but rather in attempts at "greater integration into the larger society" (Heisler 27-28). Heisler continues along this line of thought, asserting that if group demands do emerge from ethnic groups they will take the form of autonomy rather than self-determination claims (Heisler 34). Even if more radical demands were made, Heisler finds it unlikely that those demands would meet with any kind of success, for "it is difficult to justify normatively the redrafting of fundamental social contracts on the basis of ethnic nominalism" (Heisler 45). These predictions are clearly at odds with the activities of IPMs in the 1990s, which have placed territorial self-determination/autonomy claims at the very heart of indigenous activism (Stavenhagen 34).

In a less sanguine manner, Gurr writes that "despite the imperfect application of democratic norms to ethnic identity groups" in liberal states, such groups "face few political barriers to participation and are more likely to use the tactics of protest than rebellion" (Gurr 84). Indeed, typical indigenous activism has taken the form of challenges within existing frameworks of constitutional or international law (Stavenhagen 32–34). In addition to the growing number of states with liberal regimes, international sources of liberal individual and group rights also have aided in conflict management (Gurr 277). Because democratic states are the most open to these types of international norms and incentives, these states are likely to carry through with minority protections even in cases of growing domestic opposition to such policies (Gurr 177). The conclusion Gurr draws from such evidence is clear:

> Democracy, in one of its European variants, is widely regarded as the most reliable guarantee of minority rights. It is *inherent* in the logic of democratic politics that all peoples in heterogeneous societies should have equal civil and political rights. Democratic governance also implies acceptance of peaceful means for resolving civil conflicts. [Emphasis added] (Gurr 279)

What conclusions can one to draw from this lacuna? IPMs do seem to practice protest rather than rebellion in liberal states, yet the underlying theory for why open societies reduce the salience of ethnic identity, or shift mobilization away from contentious claims, does not seem to fit. In this dissertation I will argue that mainstream social science has produced a politically salient misreading of the protest tactics of IPMs by conflating such tactics with the conclusion that these movements accept the rules of the game laid out by liberal democratic principles. This conflation is an example of how Western science engages with non-Western political traditions primarily "to the degree which they help bolster the existing and approved orthodox doctrines" (Deloria, *Red Earth, White Lies: Native Americans and the Myth of Scientific Fact* 47).

The dominant modes of social science representation serve to depoliticize IPMs even as they bring attention to them. By "depoliticize" I mean to employ the distinction drawn by Jenny Edkins between "politics" and the "political" (Edkins 1). To study the "politics" of indigenous movements is to place them within a well-demarcated field of strategic constraints and accepted tactics. To embrace their "political" nature is to problematize the "self-evident" origins of IPMs and to analyze their anti-systemic potential.

> The essential political problem for the intellectual is ... not a matter of emancipating truth from every system of power (which would be a chimera, for truth is already power) but of detaching the power of truth from the form of hegemony ... within which it operates at the present time. (Foucault quoted in Edkins 140)

Iris Marion Young makes a similar distinction between movements that seek distributional gains *within* the dominant system of power relations, and those "insurrections" that challenge the higher order logic—decision-making, the division of labor, cultural imperialism—of such systems (Young, *Justice and the Politics of Difference*). I will argue that IPMs need to be classified as the latter. Mainstream social science approaches miss the political character of IPMs because they mistake those movements' tactics for their strategies.

The major means by which IPMs are depoliticized is that their goals are represented as being *internal* to political liberalism. Wilmer depicts the interaction of IPMs and a liberalizing world society in three stages. First, the international legal doctrines of Aboriginal human rights and Aboriginal treaty rights serve as a political opportunity for mobilization, which indigenous groups can exploit (Wilmer 23). Second, IPMs can draw upon the normative support of international society as a resource for mobilization (Wilmer 93). Finally, Wilmer concludes that "Indigenous activism...can best be understood *within* the framework of a world society model because of its focus on cultural pluralism as an organizing principle of world order"

Interrogations 25

[Emphasis added] (Wilmer 199). In practice as well as theory, non-indigenous people have commonly made this assumption. Vine Deloria, Jr. writes that while American Indian activists had "learned the language of social protest, [and] mastered the complicated handshakes used by the revolutionary elect" there was utter disbelief "that the Indians were not planning on sharing the continent with their oppressed brothers once the revolution was over" (Deloria, *Behind the Trail of Broken Treaties: An Indian Declaration of Independence* 2-3). Indian activists had rather different strategic goals in mind than the "New Left" while sharing the same movement tactics. Similarly to Wilmer, Gurr argues that the political impact in "normative terms" of IPMs is grounded in the United Nations' recognition of indigenous rights (Gurr 73). From this association of IPMs and the legal recognition of indigenous rights, Gurr concludes that the implementation of more individual and groups rights should *discourage* conflict escalation by IPMs (Gurr 277). This logic only makes sense if IPMs' *tactical* reliance on legal language and international advocacy are equated with the strategic goals of these diverse movements.[4]

> These movements taking place in "politics" do not provide an account in themselves of how one social form rather than another emerges from a period of contestation and struggle. To achieve an understanding of the latter we need a "political" analysis. (Edkins 3)

Although there is no overriding *analytic* justification for this reduction of overarching strategy to existing tactics, there does exist a *political* rationale for it. Gurr concludes *Peoples versus States* with a discussion of an emerging international "regime of managed ethnic heterogeneity" (Gurr 277). This regime, according to Gurr, functions by the means of two principles—the recognition and autonomy of minority peoples within states—which are most likely to be implemented in contemporary liberal democracies (Gurr 278). Thus, IPMs can be made the objects of *problem solving* rather than the agents of *problematization* for liberal governments—the very definition of depoliticization. Whereas Gurr presents these developments in an exclusively progressive light, Wilmer makes clear that accommodation and adaptation to "noncore views and assertions" is driven by the logic of system *stability*, not transformation (Wilmer 27).

Is there a way to theorize about the strategies of IPMs without the danger that we "sublate [them] under the over-arching sign of the white Western middle-class" liberal perspective of social science (Moore-Gilbert 192-93)? I argue that a deconstructive reading of IPMs against the intertext of (post)colonialism in white settler states best avoids the aforementioned problem.[5] Such a reading emphasizes what social science leaves unsaid about its own place within the liberal political program, as much as it focuses attention on what remains unsaid about IPMs. For as Deloria has noted, "The most fatal counterattack to entrenched authority will not be directed against their facts but against their status" (Deloria, *Red Earth, White Lies: Native Americans and the Myth of Scientific Fact* 41).

THE (POST)COLONIAL POLITICS OF INDIGENOUS PEOPLES

Rewriting IPMs as deconstructive strategies within the framework of (post)colonialism allows us to hear the critical "voice" of indigenous people once more (Wilmer 194). Bart Moore-Gilbert suggests how a (post)colonial perspective is attuned to the multiple, and often marginalized, histories of indigenous-settler interactions:

> Because postcolonial histories, and their presents, are so varied, no one definition of the "postcolonial" can claim to be correct at the expense of all others, and consequently a variety of interrelated models of identity, positionality, and cultural/critical practice are both possible and necessary. (Moore-Gilbert 203)

Although it would make the (post)colonial theorist's life simple if this was as unproblematic as Moore-Gilbert suggests, (post)colonialism too can serve to homogenize and depoliticize. A prime example of this universalizing tendency is of special relevance for this analysis. Vijay Mishra and Bob Hodge write that, "The central problematic arises out of the status of the settler cultures, and their place in this unified field" (Hodge and Mishra 403). Some (post)colonial theorists have claimed that *settler populations* stand in the same relationship to colonialism as indigenous peoples within settler states do. In the introduction to *The Post-Colonial Studies Reader,* Bill Ashcroft, Gareth Griffins, and Helen Tiffin write:

> The effects of imperialism occur in many different kinds of societies including those 'settler/invader' societies in which post-colonial contestation is just as strongly and just as ambivalently engaged as it is in more obviously decolonizing states and regions. (Ashcroft, Griffins and Tiffin 3)

This not only obscures important differences between dominant and marginalized positions within settler states, but it also produces the same

Interrogations

effect as liberalism—to depoliticize IPMs. As Ella Shohat writes, "The term 'post-colonial,' in this sense, masks the white settlers' colonialist-racist policies toward indigenous peoples not only before independence but also after the official break from the imperial center, while also de-emphasizing neocolonial global positionings of First World settler-states" (Shohat 103). Indeed, Mishra and Hodge remind us not only that "an undifferentiated concept of postcolonialism overlooks ... the very radical differences in response and the unbridgeable chasms that existed between White and non-White colonies," but also that "The settler colonies provided the manpower, the support system for colonialism to flourish" (Hodge and Mishra 408, 10). Beyond the distinction between settler states and decolonizing ones, there is the issue of indigenous peoples' remaining *colonial* status within the former (McClintock 87, 89). Rather than lumping these disparate societies under a common heading, we should heed Chadwick Allen's advice that:

> An international framework that emphasizes both the rhetorical complexity of indigenous [practice] in settler nations, and, importantly, the distinct dynamics of its particular form of (post)coloniality. (Allen 60)

This allows us to extend Wilmer's reading of the indigenous "deconstruction" of Western "history and progress" to the political sphere as well (Wilmer 201).

> Then a distinctive form of the postcolonial arises, as defiant as oppositional postcolonialism but without political independence or autonomy ever a realistic option. This symbiotic postcolonial formation has many of the same features as the more exciting postcolonialism of the non-settler countries as they establish their national identity. (Hodge and Mishra 413)

Thus, (post)coloniality is not so much a delimiting of the present politics of the past, but "Rather, the question is: who is mobilizing what in the articulation of the past, deploying what identities, identifications and representations, and in the name of what political vision and goals?" (Shohat 110). In the next section I will sketch out a framework for analyzing (post)coloniality in settler states, drawing upon the "spectropolitics" of Jacques Derrida's *Specters of Marx*.

ENGAGING THE "GHOSTS" OF COLONIALISM

> This impossible 'no' to a structure, which one criticizes, yet inhabits intimately, is the deconstructive philosophical position, and the everyday here and now named 'post-coloniality' is a case of it.
> Gayatri Chakravorty Spivak (Spivak, "Marginality in the Teaching Machine" 60)

In *Specters of Marx*, Derrida shows how most readers in an attempt to grasp Marx at an ontological level ignore the spectral language of Marx's texts. Derrida's focus on spectrality allows him to align himself with "a certain spirit of Marx"—that of radical critique—without buying into the failed ontology of proletarian revolution. I will attempt to show that this theoretic tactic is useful in the analysis of (post)colonialism as well. Just as Derrida implores us to converse with Marx's ghosts, IPMs give us a concrete model of "spectropolitics" embedded in (post)coloniality. In the white settler states, (post)coloniality marks the problematique of the "present politics of the past."

Just as Derrida writes end-of-history discourses (such as that of Francis Fukuyama) as attempts to "exorcize" the ghosts of Marx, liberal reparations aimed at indigenous peoples can be written as "exorcicisms" of the ghosts of colonialism (Derrida, *Specters of Marx: The State of the Debt, the Work of Mourning, and the New International* 56-70). This attitude can be heard in Lyndon Johnson's assessment of the Indian Civil Rights Act of 1968 when he announced "a new goal for our Indian programs: ... a goal that *erases* old attitudes of paternalism" (Quoted in Wilmer 89). This exorcism of the past entailed a turning away from old concepts as well.

Two doctrines had underwritten the domination of indigenous peoples in settler states: the right of conquest and *terra nullis* or "empty land." As recently as 1987, the US State Department was arguing to the UN that "conquest renders the tribes subject to the legislative power of the United States and in substance terminates the external sovereignty of the tribe"; thus indigenous peoples had no legal standing outside of US domestic jurisdiction (Wilmer 15, 58). In Australia, aboriginal and Torres Strait Islander peoples have been marginalized under the doctrine of *terra nullis* (Wilmer 61-62). *Terra nullis* rested upon an Australian High Court ruling in *Cooper v. Stuart* (1889) that found Australia to be "settled" rather than "conquered" because the indigenous inhabitants did not count as a civilized population by Western standards (Hill 306). It was not until the *Mabo v. Queensland (No. 2)* decision was handed down by the High Court in 1992 that *terra nullis*

Interrogations

was discredited as the founding principle of Australian constitutional law (Hill 303-04).

As settler state governments have begrudgingly given up the colonial concepts of conquest and *terra nullis*, they have attempted to create a new *post*-colonial ontology within which to "solve" the indigenous "problem." This new ontology, which ostensibly breaks down the old colonial patterns of exclusion, is rhetorically grounded in the liberal discourse of rights (Wilmer 189). The most common expression of this rhetorical policy is to focus on the collective rights of indigenous peoples in the discourse of treaties and their individual human and civil rights. This language can be seen in the various reparative policies passed by settler state governments (See the examples from the United States and Australia in Wilmer 156-57). The key point is that these rights serve not only as the tactics of settler states, but their strategy as well. By instituting these reparative policies the governments involved create a new legal ontology, the purpose of which is to settle, once and for all, the issues surrounding indigenous peoples – thus "exorcizing" the ghosts of their colonial past. In the next section I will argue that IPMs stand in a very different relation to these "specters" of colonialism.

When Derrida writes of spectrality, he is making a distinction between *specters* and mere *spirits*. This distinction is threefold: 1) a specter is not simply the presence of the dead (as a spirit) but rather something which is "undead" – neither of the present/living nor of the past/dead; 2) specters are also "revenants" – returning again for the first time; 3) finally, specters have a strange phenomenological quality – being the "ungraspable visibility of the invisible, or an invisibility of a visible X" (Derrida, *Specters of Marx: The State of the Debt, the Work of Mourning, and the New International* 6-7).

Now immediately many social scientists will reject this language and these distinctions as completely irrelevant to concrete political struggles. Thus, a few examples may better help us understand the applicability of "spectropolitics" to (post)coloniality. In addition to disproportionate rates of unemployment, poverty, and incarceration, many indigenous people suffer from what Wilmer calls *deculturation* – "community anomie resulting from forced assimilation" – and posttraumatic stress disorder (PTSD) (Wilmer 193). These social problems are not simply "hold-overs" from the past, nor do they find their causes in the present. They are the current physical embodiments of the spirit of the past – the specters of colonialism. These apparitions of the past in the present unsettle the political ontology that settler states have spent centuries constructing. Being attuned to this *hauntology* of present politics, rather than their supposed *ontology*, is what allows IPMs the "strategic space" in which to create new social forms while continuing to engage liberal "politics" at the tactical level. However, this is not to say that IPMs somehow "see" the spectrality of their situation while others do not. Settler states too are aware of the insufficiency of the new liberal ontology. "This [unsettling] is what we would call hauntology. Ontology only opposes it in a movement of *exorcism*. Ontology is a conjuration" [Emphasis added] (Derrida, *Specters of Marx: The State of the Debt, the Work of Mourning, and the New International* 161).

The move to ontology thus represents a strategy of settler states that distinguishes them from the strategy of IPMs. While all parties are engaged in the (post)colonial field – what I have termed the "present politics of the past" – the strategies of IPMs are "affirmed using a different *political* mode – rather than conforming to our [Western, liberal] model in self-defense against it" (de Certeau, "The Politics of Silence: The Long March of the Indians" 230). IPMs are an expression of the kind of resistance that Derrida conceives for his "New International," movements which "proceed in a deconstructive fashion, ... without renouncing an ideal of democracy and emancipation, but rather by trying to think it and put it to work otherwise" (Derrida, *Specters of Marx: The State of the Debt, the Work of Mourning, and the New International* 90). This ability to "think and act otherwise" is tied to IPMs' acceptance, rather than rejection, of (post)coloniality.

> If *postcoloniality* can be described as a condition troubled by the consequences of a self-willed historical amnesia, then the theoretical [and political] value of *postcolonialism* inheres, in part, in its ability to elaborate the forgotten memories of this condition. (Gandhi 7-8)

The articulation of the strategies of IPMs alongside the historical series of (post)coloniality produces meaning-effects that are completely foreign to mainstream social science analysis.

> The actions the Indians take are directed less toward the construction of a common ideology [or ontology] than toward the "organization" (a word-leitmotif) of tactics and operations ... because of this, the Indian awakening has been *democratic* and *self-managing* in form. (de Certeau, "The Politics of Silence: The Long March of the Indians" 227)

The mistake made by many scholars is to assume that this indigenous "organization" reflected the ends, and not only the means of IPMs. For the existence of tactical organization has not led to IPMs adopting a typical Western-style movement organization to direct the strategies of indigenous

Interrogations 31

peoples. What could be seen as a liability for liberal social movements is actuality a strength of IPMs. As Karren Baird-Olson of the American Indian Movement has written:

> The lack of a formal structure has been an extremely valuable *strategic* force ... Just as traditional warriors went in and out of battle as they were able, so have traditional AIM people given of themselves to the goal of sovereignty. (Baird-Olson 234)

At this point it is fair to ask whether the introduction of the "erudite knowledge" of (post)structuralism is necessary. Cannot a similar argument be made from within mainstream social science? Indeed, Guntram F.A. Werther has made just such an attempt.[6]

NEO-COLONIAL IMAGINARY, PART *DUEX*: THE NEW "ORNAMENTALISM"

Werther argues that indigenous (aboriginal in his parlance) claims contain "revolutionary" notions of sovereignty, the nation, and the individual that due "immeasurable violence to the basic assumptions" of liberal democracy (Werther 89-90). He contends the lack of scholarly attention to such claims is due to IPMs' less than "sexy" techniques – "existing lobbying, administrative, electoral, and legal mechanisms" – when compared with the openly rebellious practice of other ethnopolitical movements such as the Irish Republican Army or Hamas (Werther xvii). On both of these points our arguments are nearly identical. In addition, Werther's approach mirrors aspects of my own in so far as he argues macro- (strategies) and micro-politics (tactics) cannot be collapsed, focus should be placed on indigenous claims and responses to such claims, and that currents IPMs are created through their interaction with and challenge to liberal government from within existing power structures (Werther xxv, xix, xxvii, xxix). However, Werther's mainstream framework commits him to subsume IPMs under the distinctly Western notions of early international law, even as he marks their difference from liberalism (Werther 24). This effect can be made intelligible by reference to a recent critique/update of Said's notion of Orientalism.

British Imperial historian David Cannadine's *Ornamentalism: How the British Saw Their Empire* (2001) advances the thesis that cruder articulations of colonial discourse theory have reduced Orientalism to a negative, Eurocentric stereotype of the cultural Other, and in so doing have neglected the role played by British self-projections in the colonial imaginary. He writes that one should not underestimate "the importance of seeing and understanding the British Empire as a mechanism for the export, projection and analogization of *domestic* social structures and social perceptions" [Emphasis added] (Cannadine 10). On this reading, the British were as likely to see the "natives/Negroes" in the colonies as analogues to the "dangerous classes" at home, rather than as exotic, mystical inferiors (Cannadine 6). The practice of early British imperialism (particularly in India) was animated by the visualization of local princes as mirror images of Britain's own feudal past and, therefore, attempts were often made to use these colonial elites to exercise the "indirect rule" of the Empire (Cannadine 11). Thus, "Ornamentalism" can be defined as "seeing" the other through the lens of one's own romanticized past.

By grounding his argument in traditional Western political theory, Werther complements the effect of neo-orientalist, social science readings of IPMs with a neo-ornamentalist one – which promotes the depoliticization of the very movements he claims are revolutionary. Despite his encouragement of a focus on actual indigenous claims and government responses, Werther continually lapses into the realm of pure political philosophy. Indeed, while characterizing IPMs as faithfully employing 17th and 18th century theories of international law, he reduces governmental responses to the status "of self-serving, usually unilateral, legal, and political maneuvering" (Werther 36). The reading of concrete practice as disingenuous deviation from theoretical purity is applied to indigenous claims as well. Werther asserts that concrete, indigenous legal claims provide an overly conservative impression when compared with the philosophical import he reads into the idea of such claims (Werther 83).

Using the framework of Western political philosophy results in disparaging the political practice of indigenous legal activism just as a social scientific framework deflates the meaning-effects of such practice. Neither mainstream approach to studying politics is well equipped to handle the "fine points and principles involved" in IPMs, and thus both point to "a political solution that will enable us to avoid understanding or confronting the issue altogether" (Deloria, *Red Earth, White Lies: Native Americans and the Myth of Scientific Fact* 17). The application of the nuanced formulations

Interrogations 33

of poststructural and (post)colonial theory is not merely an academic exercise, but rather a resolutely political move to highlight indigenous resistance to liberalism. Thus, beyond placing IPMs in a (post)colonial context, I further contend that a more rigorous analysis of the logic and workings of liberal regimes, and indigenous legal activism within such regimes, is necessary to produce a reading of indigenous peoples engaged in radical resistance to liberal government.

EXPLORING THE CONSTITUTIONAL THEORY OF LIBERAL-DEMOCRATIC STATES

Social scientific analyses of ethnopolitical conflict in liberal states, such as that of Gurr, are based on a thin conception of "regime" that must be operationalizable and quantifiable. Ideal political philosophy, such as that of Werther, conflates the workings of liberal government with the writing of liberal theorists (i.e. Locke). What more detailed options for the treatment of regimes are available? For such answers one can look to the field of constitutional theory. The next chapter will explore the unique perspective that poststructuralism can bring to constitutional analysis—the concept of governmentality.

Chapter Three

Governing "Free Subjects": A Genealogy of (Neo)Liberal Governmentality

INTRODUCTION

Stephen L. Elkin argues that mainstream constitutional thinking is centered around either constitutional law (as practiced in American politics), or in comparative law (as in the analysis of written constitutions and other legal documents, as was common in pre-1960s comparative politics) (Elkin 1933-34). Whereas, Elkin argues, these forms of constitutional thinking are superior to either typical positivist social science, or traditional political philosophy in adding to our understanding of regimes, all remain "empirically bereft and normatively weak" (Elkin 1934).

> Inside the thin law and parchment-obsessed thinking I have been describing is a fat constitutional theory trying to get out. And this fatter theory, if it is to be of any more use than the kind of analysis I have been considering, needs to be at once empirical and normative, must somehow bridge the theory-practice divide. Where shall we start if we wish to develop such a theory? By taking seriously the word "constitutional," and instead of thinking of it as pointing to nouns and adjectives—a constitution; a constitutional act—to think of it as a verb—to constitute. (Elkin 1935)

In order to take up Elkin's challenge, any theory of liberal regimes must understand those regimes to be *constitutive* of political subjectivities and interests, as well as the *performative* basis for their political action. What is involved in such a reconceptualization?

35

The primary shift away from comparative constitutional law is made possible by a focus on the practice of constitutional regimes.

> It is thus likely that political regimes cannot be composed of just any combination of institutions. Institutions aren't just mechanisms but patterns of behavior—and some patterns will undercut others. Moreover, these patterns of behavior, or practices, are interconnected; what we can and ought to do about one set of practices has strong implications for what happens or ought to happen elsewhere in the political-economic order (Elkin 1944).

This focus on interconnectedness allows one to question whether the indigenous rights agenda is praxeologically compatible with liberal regimes. Elkin emphasizes that regimes are not just good or bad, but good or bad in relation to "peoples with particular histories, virtues, and vices" (Elkin 1947). Thus the possibility of reading indigenous activism as a critique of liberal government *from their perspective* is opened. Elkin's conception also requires a commitment to structural holism, for the logic of a regime tends to govern the societal and economic, as well as the political, so as "we may say that there is an ethos at work which ... imparts a logic to the political whole" (Elkin 1945). Thus, a theory of liberal regimes must go beyond simply analyzing the exercise of political power, and must address all of the power relations within such a society. This includes the productive side of power, the aspects which involve creating political subjects. As Elkin writes, "the political constitution shapes the overall way of life of a people; and *indeed it makes them a people*" [Emphasis added] (Elkin 1948). Therefore, in the case of IPMs which claim an existence as a people outside of the regime under which they are subjected, one finds the first evidence that indigenous legal activism may indeed pose a challenge to liberal regimes.

In order to characterize the workings of liberal regimes, while avoiding the pitfalls identified by Elkin, a conceptualization is needed that provides a historicized definition of the practices of such a government. This consists of the set of elements that make the activity of governing "thinkable and practicable both to its practitioners and to those upon whom it is practiced" (Gordon 3). We may find just such a conception in the literature that has developed around Foucault's discussions of government—variously referred to as governmentality, government rationality, or the analytics of government.[1]

The core of this approach is the treatment of government as "*la conduite de la conduite*, or the conduct of conduct" [Emphasis in original] (Dean, *Critical and Effective Histories: Foucault's Methods and Historical*

Sociology 176). The conduct in question is both that of rulers and of the ruled, and this is an early indication of the plural character of governmentality. The analysis of governmentality is focused on both the practices and "explicit *programmes*" [Emphasis in original] of government (Foucault, "Questions of Method" 80). Thus, a more detailed definition of governmentality would be as follows:

> Government[ality] is any more or less calculated and rational activity, undertaken by a multiplicity of authorities and agencies, employing a variety of techniques and forms of knowledge, that seeks to shape conduct by working through our desires, aspirations, interests and beliefs, for definite but shifting ends and with a diverse set of relatively unpredictable consequences, effects, and outcomes. (Dean, *Governmentality: Power and Rule in Modern Society* 11)

Any study of governmentality may then consider three axes of political practice—*techne*, or the techniques of government; *episteme*, or the practices of knowledge and truth; and *ethos*, or the modes of political subjectivity (Dean, *Governmentality: Power and Rule in Modern Society* 18). Taken as a whole, the investigation of these objects and themes constitute governmentality as an independent research agenda focusing on "the contingent trajectories by which the state assumes its present and changing form" (Dean, *Critical and Effective Histories: Foucault's Methods and Historical Sociology* 181).

There are three aspects of governmentality that are of central importance to indigenous politics, and thus this study. The first is the connection of a Foucauldian "microphysics" to the study of macro-political practices, in the form of the liberal state (Dean, *Critical and Effective Histories: Foucault's Methods and Historical Sociology* 175–79). However, it is crucial to note that this analysis of state practices does not equate to a totalizing theory of the state, from which one may abstain such "as one might abstain from a indigestible meal" (Foucault quoted in Dean, *Critical and Effective Histories: Foucault's Methods and Historical Sociology* 177). A second aspect in this study will be the analysis of the *problematization* of government—in the form of indigenous legal activism. Mitchell Dean identifies such problematizations as a "key starting point in an analytics of government" (Dean, *Governmentality: Power and Rule in Modern Society* 27). The final aspect of governmentality that will animate this work is, in contrast to "value-free" social science, the author's intent to fashion these analyses as a form of criticism.

> By making explicit the forms of rationality and thought that inhere in regimes of practices, by demonstrating the fragility of the ways in which we know ourselves and are asked to know ourselves, and the tissue of connections between how we know ourselves and how we govern and are governed, an analytics of government can remove the taken-for-granted character of these practices. (Dean, *Governmentality: Power and Rule in Modern Society* 36)

Therefore, I am striving to link the indigenous problematization of liberal government practices to a problematization of how liberal social science has represented indigenous political movements.

THE DEVELOPMENT OF GOVERNMENTALITY

In order to proceed with a genealogical approach to current liberal regimes we must analyze the historical development of liberal governmentality—a set of practices that "tend towards a form of political [power] which would be a government of all and of each, and whose concerns would be at once to 'totalize' and to 'individualize'" (Gordon 3). Such a conception of liberalism also hopes to avoid the seeming contradiction of institutionalized practices that do not conform to the liberalism of political *theory*. In so doing, one need not give up the analysis of liberalism's hegemonic position in most Western societies.[2]

Sovereignty

Foucault distinguishes the modern, liberal form of government from its pre-modern predecessor "sovereignty." Like the recent work of Stephen Krasner, this study is based upon the evaluation that "the characteristics associated with sovereignty ... do not provide an accurate description" of current state practice (Krasner 237). Contra Krasner's assertion of organized hypocrisy, a governmentality approach sees this as a long-standing fact. Once, in the 15th and 16th centuries, sovereignty was the practice of both international and domestic affairs. The sovereign was concerned with his hierarchical position vis-à-vis others within and without a given territory. The only test of his rule was the fact of rule.

> However rudimentary that apparatus might be it was sufficiently credible to sustain the ruler both domestically and internationally and, if it was not, he and possibly his realm might be replaced by another. (Jackson 53)

Governing "Free Subjects"

This was the age of Machiavelli's prince; states only came into being as a result of princes securing their sovereignty. Sovereignty was a system built on an organic conception of society (including its constituent classes) and oriented towards order and self-maintenance.

> In every case, what characterizes the end of sovereignty, this common and general good, is in sum nothing other than submission to sovereignty. This means the end of sovereignty is circular: the end of sovereignty is the exercise of sovereignty. (Foucault, "Governmentality" 95)

The transformation from a sovereignty diagram to a governmental one was grounded in the development of new technologies of power and the resultant change in state capacity.

Power had only a weak capacity for "resolution," as one might say in photographic terms; it was incapable of an individualizing, exhaustive analysis of the social body. But the economic changes of the eighteenth century made it necessary to ensure the circulation of effects of power through progressively finer channels, gaining access to individuals themselves, to their bodies, their gestures and all their daily actions (Foucault, "The Eye of Power" 151-52). Thus, in relation to suppressing resistance, the early modern state used ceremonial shows of sovereign power through the military and elaborate, public punishment, while the modern state uses surveillance, non-governmental practices such as clinical medicine and psychiatry, and the discipline of the prison—a much more efficacious exercise of power. However, these technological developments were not spontaneous. Sovereignty was displaced as the central logic of power through three challenges posed to it in the period of the 17th and 18th centuries. It is to these challenges we now turn.

Pastoral Power

The diagram of sovereign power is characterized by the radical exteriority of the sovereign from the polity. Yet there is a style of government in the West, older than sovereignty, that begins from the opposite position—that the governing of individual subjects and the governance of the polity are inseparable. This is the diagram of *pastoral* power.

Foucault notes that pastoral power is tied up with a notion of the living individual and his/her needs, with the relation between the collective and the individual, with notions of obedience and duty, with knowledge and, most importantly, with ideas of salvation (Dean, *Governmentality: Power and Rule in Modern Society* 81-82).

Thus, pastoral power is that which places the problems of governing a moral community at the center of its self-reflections. This form of power relations has two independent strands within the history of western government. The first is the image of the city and the citizen, grounded in the practice of the Greek city-states and carried on through the Roman Republic. The second image is of the shepherd and the flock, brought into western civilization first by Judaism and later incorporated into Christianity. For all their antagonisms, both modes of pastoral power combine practices of statecraft with practices of soulcraft.

Medieval political theory was often concerned with the compatibility of these two forms of pastoral power—as can be noticed in the writings of St. Augustine or Thomas Aquinas. However, even as Western Christendom "vastly elaborated" on the shepherd/flock model of pastoral power, the "roles of sacredotal pastor and secular ruler never come to be unified" (Gordon 8). Thus, even in the 15th and 16th centuries (the heyday of sovereignty) not only access to political power, but the form of that power, hung in the balance between church and state. It is therefore intelligible that theorists of sovereignty, from Machiavelli to Hobbes, attempt to subordinate religious power to a mere instrument of the sovereign's will. Yet, as liberalism emerged as a distinctive art of governing in the following two hundred odd years, the two traditions of pastoral power were not only brought together, but combined with the secular institutions developed under sovereignty as well (Dean, *Governmentality: Power and Rule in Modern Society* 84).

> Our societies proved to be really demonic since they happened to combine these two games—the city-citizen game and the shepherd-flock game—in what we call the modern state. (Foucault, "Politics and Reason" 71)

Why does Foucault describe such a configuration as demonic? I argue that it is this combination of pastoral with sovereign power that provides the governmentality approach with unique tools for an analysis of modern nationalism, and that it is this "demon" to which Foucault is referring.

Two well-known texts on nationalism—Benedict Anderson's *Imagined Communities* (1991) and Eric Hobsbawm's *Nations and Nationalism since 1780* (1992)—each in their own way addresses similar themes to the Foucauldian discussion of pastoral power. Anderson argues that nationalism should be understood by aligning it with the "large cultural systems that precede it ... the two relevant cultural systems are the *religious community* and the *dynastic realm*" [Emphasis added] (Anderson 12). These "cultural systems" mirror our previous discussion of sovereignty and pastoral power.

Governing "Free Subjects" 41

Hobsbawm highlights another aspect of the relationship between the sovereign-pastoral demon and nationalism in his discussion of the two concepts of a modern nation.

> It is at the point of [the French Revolution] that two quite different concepts of the nation meet: the revolutionary-democratic and the nationalist. The equation state = nation = people applied to both, but for nationalists the creation of the political entities which would contain it derived from the prior existence of some community distinguishing itself from foreigners, while from the revolutionary-democratic point of view the central concept was the sovereign-citizen-people = state which, in relation to the remainder of the human race, constituted a 'nation'." (Hobsbawm 22)

The relationship between the two types of nationalism Hobsbawm describes and the twin forms of pastoral power is complex. On the one hand, revolutionary-democratic nationalism—with it focus on citizenship—could be linked to the city-citizen model of pastoral power, with the communalist conception of nationalism linked to the shepherd-flock model. However, the city-citizen game (at least as played by the Greeks) was one of *exclusion* grounding the notion of citizenship, while the shepherd-flock game (especially in its Christian manifestation) sought to include everyone as a single pastoral community.

In his study of nationalism and citizenship policy in France and Germany, Rogers Brubaker addresses these issues directly. Brubaker contrasts French ideas of nationhood, which "[have] been state-centered and assimilationist" with the German idea that "has been *Volk*-centered and differentialist" (Brubaker 1). He emphasizes that this distinction is "structural, not...social-psychological," making it similar to a governmental analysis of nationalism (Brubaker 5). Brubaker shows how the city-citizen game becomes open to assimilation in its modern, civic nationalist variant.

> Thus Sieyès: "What is a nation? A body of associates living under a common law and represented by the same legislature." The dominance of citizenship over nationality, of political over ethnocultural conceptions of nationhood, is perhaps best expressed in Tallien's remark of the spring of 1795: "The only foreigners in France are the bad citizens." (Brubaker 7)

This definition of the nation, where the political is constitutive, leads France and others to adopt the assimilationist techniques of the Romans, rather than the exclusionary practice of the Greek pastorate (Brubaker 8). In the German, or ethnocultural, definition of citizenship, however, "the

Volksgeist is constitutive, the state merely expressive, of nationhood" (Brubaker 9). Thus, even though its heritage has been firmly grounded in the Christian shepherd-flock model of the Holy Roman Empire, the German articulation of nationalism has been exclusionary.

Despite the cultural form that German nationalism takes, in practice it has usually been deployed as a technique of statecraft (first by Bismark, and most destructively by the Nazis) rather than an independent principle of political organization (Brubaker 10). Anderson's study—in its extensive discussion of the importance of print media, maps, the census, and museums—also points us in the direction of a focus on particular techniques of government, and their relation to government's forms. It is these issues that become paramount in the second programmatic challenge to sovereign power—the traditions of *raison d'etat* and *polizeiwissenschaft*.

Raison d'etat and the science of police

If the anti-Machiavellian treatises called for the return of pastoral concerns into princely strategies, they did not do so exclusively from a religious, conservative point of view. Many of these texts called for "something else and new, namely the art of *government*" [Emphasis added] (Foucault, "Governmentality" 90). Whereas Machiavelli calls attention to the ever-tenuous link between the Prince and a state, a new problematique emerges around state security, as opposed to the security of the Prince (Dean, *Governmentality: Power and Rule in Modern Society* 87). Thus, the art of government "poses the problem of the existence and durability, within a contested domain, of the state itself" (Dean, *Critical and Effective Histories: Foucault's Methods and Historical Sociology* 184). This new *raison d'etat*/reason of state shifts the question of governing to the terrain of rational ends and technical means.

> First, it is government by reference to reason alone. It is a rational 'art' of government—a specific, secular set of techniques conforming to rational rules. Reason of state makes reference neither to the wisdom of God nor to the strategies of the prince. (Dean, *Governmentality: Power and Rule in Modern Society* 86)

In this manner the scope of pastoral government was rearticulated in a secular form tied to the state as a political body separate from the body of the sovereign. The preeminent form that this new problematization takes is the discourse surrounding police (policy).

Governing "Free Subjects" 43

With the emergence of police in the seventeenth and eighteenth centuries we see for the first time a focus on that quintessentally modern object of government—the population.

> The notion of *police* in seventeenth and eighteenth century literature, pointing out that the term, before its current narrowing, encompasses a complete form of administration, whose object is the individual—'a live, active, productive man'—and whose intervention is 'totalitarian' in so far as it attends to every aspect of people's lives. (Dean, *Critical and Effective Histories: Foucault's Methods and Historical Sociology* 184)

This brings forth the issue of how to govern individuals as concrete bodies within the "species body" of the living population (Dean, *Critical and Effective Histories: Foucault's Methods and Historical Sociology* 184). The divergence with earlier forms of governmentality is striking. For pastoral government, selves are either a prior and subordinate object of governance compared to the city (city/citizen game), or are a coterminous object with the community itself (shepherd/flock game). Under sovereign rule, selves disappear altogether from the concerns of the prince. Government via police stands in contrast to both of the dominant forms of governmentality in medieval Europe.

> What police regulations regulate, or try to regulate, or purport to regulate, is everything which in the life of this society of three orders goes unregulated, everything which can be said, in the 'waning of the Middle Ages,' to lack order or form ... Population and individuals, where previously, in the old social structure, there had been only groups, *Stände*, orders or estates, inviolable (juridically, at least) in their eternal hierarchy. (Pasquino 111, 14)

However, the revolution of police did not consist in the new objects of population and the individual alone. It is crucial to emphasize the specific form of rationality that constitutes the *raison d'etat*.

The art of government centered on the techniques of police was legitimated and articulated in reference to a new science of police—*polizeiwissenschaft* (Dean, *Governmentality: Power and Rule in Modern Society* 90). Whereas the regimes of knowledge connected to pastoral and sovereign forms of governmentality all were elite discourses, that is to say they were concerned with the knowledge of governing (an elite activity), the science of police was an attempt at an exhaustive, total knowledge of the social body. The legacy of mixing total knowledge with total regulation continues to animate the bureaucratic approach to policy today. Pasquale Pasquino writes:

> I am thinking for example of demography and statistics, which as its derivation from the word *Staat* shows, is nothing else but the science of the state: statistics, born in Germany with Conring and Achenwall, which in England, with Petty and Davenant, came to be called "political arithmetic." (Pasquino 114)

Statistics, this new science of the state, serves not only a performative function within police government, but a constitutive one as well, as Ian Hacking reminds us:

> The bureaucracy of statistics imposes not just by creating administrative rulings but by determining classifications within which people must think of themselves and the actions which are open to them. (Hacking 194)

Indeed, the importance of statistics for the maintenance of the state has consistently been overlooked by those who seek to bring about its demise. "It is a glib but true generalization that proletarian revolutions have never occurred in any state whose assurantial technology was working properly" (Hacking 184).

The discussion of both individualization and rationalization within *raison d'etat* brings one back to the central problematique of such governmentality—maintaining the order that secures the state itself (Dean, *Governmentality: Power and Rule in Modern Society* 90). Not order for order's sake, but order for the sake of the state. In pursuing this order, police "respected few bounds, particularly of a 'private' realm, and extended to manners, morals, and the minutiae of everyday life" (Dean, *Governmentality: Power and Rule in Modern Society* 91). Yet, for all of its distance from pastoral and sovereign government, *raison d'etat* shared a traditional view of economics with prior forms of governmentality.

> 'Oeconomy' is the governance or husbandry of the household (of servants, women, children, of domestic animals, etc.) and political oeconomy is the governance of the state as household, and through it constituent households. (Dean, *Critical and Effective Histories: Foucault's Methods and Historical Sociology* 184)

The political oeconomy of police derived from Aristotle's conception of the management of the *oikos* (household) articulated two thousand years earlier. The emergence of a new problematique of economy would both spell the end of *raison d'etat* as a self-sufficient form of governmentality, and usher in the beginning of the liberal era. From this emergence forward, "the state would then signify not the site or source of power, the one great

Governing "Free Subjects"

adversary to be smashed, but rather one instrument among others, and one 'modality of government'" (Pasquino 117).

CAPITALISM AND THE CRITIQUE OF STATE REASON

While today the governing of economic relations is often seen as the prime activity of the state, this was not always so. Just as *polizeiwissenschaft* identified (for the first time) the individual and individual relations as objects of government, so too the emergence of the "economic" as a sphere of individual activity outside of the *oikos*, fundamentally altered the practice of government in the modern world. No longer would the management of the oeconomic household be practiced via the reason of state. Instead, new forms of subjectivity and knowledge would emerge to critique to total control of police.

If the regulations of police made the individual a proper object of government, and through statistics an object of state knowledge, then capitalism was to provide the positive content for the emergent space of individuality. Whereas under pastoral or sovereign governmentality the self exists politically as a function of its membership in the political community and/or its place in the social order, the individualization affected by police regulation allowed for the formation of personal "interests" that differed from one's social identification. The characterization of individuals as beings with their own interests led to the redefinition of man's nature as essentially economic—*homo economicus* (Burchell 130).

> This individual living being, the subject of particular interests, represents a new figure of social and political subjectivity, the prototype of 'economic man,' who will become the correlate and instrument of a new art of government. (Burchell 127)

This new economic man not only possesses a nature different from either the virtue/corruption of the citizen or the salvation/sin of the child of God, but this essential difference must also find its expression in a different modality of political subjectivity. When *homo economicus* wills "it is an immediately and absolutely subjective form of individual will essentially different from the juridical form of will posited in contract theories of sovereignty" (Burchell 130). No longer is the "ideal of the self-aware and self-defining citizen's (civic) virtue" the central problematique of political subjectivity—it has been displaced by the "newly emergent, essentially historical and uncertain (civil) forms of the individual's private and professionalized subjectivity and conduct" (Burchell 121). Where the state compels such a subject against his personal interests a conflict is inevitable. The emergence of economic man was thus coterminous with the emergence of a new economic knowledge, a knowledge that must be described, in quasi-Kantian terms, as a "critique of state reason" (Gordon 15).

The new political economy (which is indistinguishable from liberal political economy) emerges as both a body of knowledge appropriate to these individual economic subjects, and contra *raison d'etat*, a form of knowledge fundamentally incompatible with the singularity of the state. The Physiocrats may have been the first to express this new critique of sovereign intervention as "both futile and harmful" (Burchell 126). Thus, the new political economy demarcates nothing less than the "impossibility of an economic sovereignty" (Gordon 16). The claim to total control via police was grounded on the claim to total knowledge by *polizeiwissenschaft*. By challenging the latter, political economy undermined the former.

> The new objectivity of political economy does not consist solely in its occupation of a politically detached scientific standpoint: more profoundly, it inaugurates a new mode of objectification of governed reality, whose effect is to resituate governmental reason within a newly complicated, open and unstable politico-epistemic configuration. (Gordon 16)

This complication of the field of governance stems from the activity of individual economic subjects pursuing their own interests. Hence the prohibitions of *laissez-faire* political economy on state interference is not exclusively political or moral, but epistemic as well. Thus, Adam Smith calls for "less a state with minimal functions than one whose capacity for folly would have some ceiling" (Quoted in Gordon 17). The liberal truism that "the state that governs best, governs least" flows directly from political economy's claim that the state cannot possibly "know best." Yet, while political economy restricted the scope of state intervention, there was no concomitant reduction in the scope of government. New agents of government would emerge with liberalism.

To limit the scope of state intervention is to acknowledge a non-political realm of existence (Dean, *Governmentality: Power and Rule in Modern Society* 110). As can be seen from the analysis of political economy, a dominant way to conceive of this non-political space is via the economy. Yet, this limitation of the state's role is not itself limited to the economic; the same non-political space can be filled by "civil society, community, culture, or … population" (Dean, *Governmentality: Power and Rule in Modern*

Governing "Free Subjects" 47

Society 111). It is at this point that the "question of society" is posed to government for the first time.

> Society, as both a precondition and a final end, is what enables one to no longer ask the question: How can one govern as much as possible and at the least possible cost? Instead, the question becomes: Why must one govern? The idea of society enables a technology of government to be developed based upon the principle that it is already 'too much.' (Foucault, "The Birth of Biopolitics" 75)

Not only is society separable from the state, but conceptually prior to the state as well. This distinguishes the modern problem of government from earlier modes. For both pastoral and police forms of governmentality assume the identity of state and society (in the pastoral there is no independent state; under *raison d'etat* there is no independent society). Even the sovereign form of rule that separates the concerns of the prince from those of the people does not question the natural need to govern from above. The notion of society "which is in a complex relation of exteriority and interiority to the state"—both outside the political sphere and justifying politics itself—grounds the modern problematique of government (Foucault, "The Birth of Biopolitics" 75). Liberalism, as the dominant modality of modern government, "assumes a 'free subject,' not an individual existing in an essential space of freedom, but one whose subjection is consistent with forms of choice" (Dean, *Critical and Effective Histories: Foucault's Methods and Historical Sociology* 178). The necessity of governing through free subjects is the demarcation between liberal and illiberal forms of governmentality.[3] It is to a more detailed examination of liberal governmentality that I now shall turn.

LIBERAL GOVERNMENTALITY

> What should we understand as 'liberalism?'...I tried to analyze 'liberalism' not as a theory or an ideology—even less, certainly, as a way for 'society' to 'represent itself'—but rather, as a practice, which is to say, as a 'way of doing things' oriented toward objectives and regulating itself by means of a sustained reflection.
> Michel Foucault (Foucault, "The Birth of Biopolitics" 73-74)

What does it mean to follow Foucault in treating liberalism as a practice, a form of governmentality? As mentioned earlier, forms of governmentality may be characterized along three axes—*episteme* (knowledge), *techne* (techniques), and *ethos* (subjectivity). In addition, it is important to note the object of government that emerges from these practices. Liberalism is thus a constellation, or diagram, of relations between subjects and objects, between subjects, and between subjects and themselves.

The primary objects of liberal governmentality are the population and the market. The focus on population as object of government is something liberalism inherited from *raison d'etat*.

> Population comes to be seen through the grid of politically or administratively identified regularities in the natural phenomena and processes affecting relations between individual living beings coexisting within a general system of living beings, or 'species,' and what increasingly is seen as a kind of vital environment. At the same time, population is also objectified relatively to economic factors, or to the elements of wealth to the extent that it is possible to identify regularities in the effects of natural and artificially modifiable variables of the former on those of the latter. (Burchell 126)

This connection of population to an analogous notion of the market (that emerges from political economy) is markedly different than the oeconomic model of *polizeiwissenschaft*. The concept of the market as a "natural process constituted, in large part, by the free choices of a multitude of economic actors" (liberalism's "free subjects") finds its highest expression in Adam Smith's *The Wealth of Nations* (Hindess 213). Not only does liberal government respect these "natural" objects, for the liberal state "the finality of government resides in the pursuit of the perfection and intensification of the processes that it directs" (Foucault, "Governmentality" 95). Liberalism is thus intimately linked with the government of natural processes, indeed, the government of "life" itself—this "government of the living" is what Foucault characterizes as *biopolitics* (Foucault, "The Birth of Biopolitics" 73).

Despite its novel focus on both the population and the market as modes of life, liberal governmentality borrows many of its political means from the traditions that preceded it. In addition to inheriting the object of rationalizing the government of life from *polizeiwissenschaft*, liberalisms emerged from a complex genealogy of sovereignty, the pastoral, and the modern disciplinary sciences of man (topics covered in-depth by Foucault in *The Order of Things* [1970] and *Discipline and Punish* [1977]). Between sovereignty and the pastoral the modality of the national security state is articulated—sovereign in form, national/social in positive content. Within such states/societies, disciplinary apparatuses produce "free subjects" of docility/utility who also are citizens or members of the pastoral nation

Governing "Free Subjects" 49

(Dean, *Critical and Effective Histories: Foucault's Methods and Historical Sociology* 183). Of course, up to this point, the portrait of liberalism being drawn is characteristic of an early liberal governmentality, practiced from the eighteenth century (Foucault, "On the Government of the Living" 84-85). Since that time, liberalism has undergone two major transformations—the emergence of the welfare state, and neo-liberalism. It is to these later developments our attention will now turn.

"Society must be defended": the emergence of welfare liberalism

Welfare liberalism should not be seen as the natural outgrowth of the government of population introduced by 18th century political economy. Rather, it emerges as a programmatic response to the particular problems expressed within liberal countries in the 19th century (Donzelot 171). The revolutionary heritage endowed individuals with a duality of subjectivity. On the one hand, political power was to be vested in representative institutions supposedly constituted by a social contract, yet continuing to be expressed in the form of sovereignty. The rights and interests of *homo economicus* within civil society, however, were irreconcilable in theory and antagonistic in practice to this exercise of sovereign power, whether or not it was dressed up in representative clothes. This conflict generated the "problem of society" to which welfare liberalism proposed itself as the solution.

The Revolution of 1848 in France can be seen as the direct articulation of this conflict. As Jacques Donzelot writes:

> The founders of the Third Republic come once again to be faced with this problem, the non-resolution of which had led to the downfall of their predecessors. They seek to solve it by means of two operations which may be seen as constitutive of the welfare state: (a) The establishment of a distinction between solidarity and sovereignty. (b) The substitution of the homogenous language of statistics for the contradictory language of rights. (Donzelot 171)

Thus, the principle of solidarity—an autochthonous *totality* of heterogenous forces and subjectivities—comes to replace the social contract as the pinnacle of social organization and therefore release welfare liberalism from "this infernal circle of the metaphysics of sovereignty" (Donzelot 171). This "overwriting" of the sovereign problem of order by the social problem of solidarity reactivates elements of both pastoral and police power within the programme of liberal governmentality (Dean, *Governmentality: Power and Rule in Modern Society* 125). *Homo economicus* can be allowed free reign within civil society, while being simultaneously managed through society (Dean, *Governmentality: Power and Rule in Modern Society* 125).

The emergence of Keynesian political economy can thus be considered the epistemic articulation of welfare liberalism. In the concepts of "market failure" and "demand management" we find the double injunction for the state to manage the social objects of the market and aggregate demand, for the express purpose of the "proper" functioning of a multiplicity of economic actors within civil society.

In the programme of welfare liberalism one can see the practices of rule combined in their characteristic, modern form. While the state maintains the trappings of sovereignty, its exercise is "exported" to the international realm and the margins of society, which can also be considered outside of domestic(ated) society. Society is constituted as a pastoral totality—the nation. The ethos of liberal politics is not political at all; rather it conforms to the economic model of rational interest. The techniques of political intervention, developed under the doctrine of *raison d'etat*, are arrayed in various connections to the ultimate apparatus of liberal government—the national security state. This constellation has been dominant in practice and has dominated our conception of politics throughout most of the 20th century. However, the view of the nation state and the national economy as a coterminous and self-contained unit has recently been problematized, both from within and without (Hindess 223).

NEO-LIBERALISM AND THE EMERGENCE OF GLOBAL EMPIRE

In this final section I will address the problem of welfare liberalism from both the perspective of the discourse of *neo-liberalism* and the transformational practices that often are labeled as *globalization*. The former displaces the epistemic and subjective elements of welfare liberalism, while the latter articulates new techniques and apparatuses of government. Neo-liberalism can be seen as both direct critique of and programmatic remedy to the "excessive government" of the welfare state (Foucault, "The Birth of Biopolitics" 77).

Neo-liberalism(s): "there is no such thing as society"

After the Second World War, an assault on the constellation of welfare liberal governmentality arose in response to perceived excess in the performance of said government. Foucault notes two distinct strands of this critique. One emerges in West Germany, and is directed towards three political fronts: National Socialism, State Socialism, and Keynesian welfare liberalism (Foucault, "The Birth of Biopolitics" 78). This "Ordo-liberalism" (epitomized by Alexander von Rüstow) takes a constructivist approach to government, contriving a "vital policy that promotes the conditions of the free, entrepreneurial conduct of economically rational individuals" (Dean, *Governmentality: Power and Rule in Modern Society* 156).

The other dominant voice of neo-liberalism comes from the "Chicago School" of economics (Foucault, "The Birth of Biopolitics" 78). Unlike its German counterpart, American neo-liberalism is concerned not so much with constructing and promoting fragile markets, but introducing the "dynamism" of market mechanisms to the areas of both state and civil society grown rigid under the bureaucracy of the welfare state.

The market, at the center of all liberal visions of government, is subject to two serial displacements. Recall that for both early and welfare liberalism, the market is a quasi-natural reality whose laws must be respected by government (Dean, *Governmentality: Power and Rule in Modern Society* 157). For the Ordo-liberals, however, the market is an artificial order that must be carefully constructed and supported by the state (Foucault, "The Birth of Biopolitics" 78). However, for American neo-liberalism the market is neither a natural entity nor artifice; instead (following Hayek) it is conceived as being "a spontaneous social order governed by customary rules selected by a complex cultural learning process" (Dean, *Governmentality: Power and Rule in Modern Society* 157). The market is therefore equated with civilization itself.

As neo-liberalism challenges the "excessive government" of the welfare state, it reactivates political economy as a critique of state reason (which is why neo-liberal political economy is sometimes referred to as neo-classical, closer to the classical position of Adam Smith than the welfarism of Keynes). This critique is articulated through the epistemic tools of neo-liberal political economy.

> Among those who make use of economic models, then, the spreadsheet and the computational model has undermined the older image of the national economy as an overarching self-regulating system. (Hindess 219)

However, this critique extends farther than its classical forbearer. Whereas liberal political economy challenged sovereign intervention *in* the market, neo-liberalism challenges the state to the extent that it fails to govern *as* the market does. Thus, neo-liberalism can be described as a form of reflexive government, in the sense that it folds the notions of what is to be governed (the market) back onto the question of how to govern (Dean, *Governmentality: Power and Rule in Modern Society* 160-61). Whereas earlier forms of liberal governmentality continued to rely on the relative exteriority of sovereign power from the nation (i.e. in order to provide external defense and arbitrate social conflicts), neo-liberalism folds the state itself back into the set of governed objects—thus sovereign power recedes to the consumer and simultaneously ascends to the global system.

Neo-liberalism is not the only discourse that problematizes the practice of welfare government. The welfare state also came under siege from the left, and the emergent "counter-culture" movements of the 1960s and 1970s. Welfarism was criticized for the dependency that it engendered through paternalistic policy techniques. This "empowerment" critique dovetails with neo-liberalism to the extent that both engage in the valorization of the self-actualized subject (Dean, *Governmentality: Power and Rule in Modern Society* 155). If not conceived of beyond the framework of *individual* empowerment, this leaves such discourses subject to be easily vampirized by neo-liberal techniques, thereby "freedom ... moves away from the emancipatory aspirations of social movements towards the virtuous, disciplined and responsible autonomy of the citizenry desired by neo-[liberals]" (Dean, *Governmentality: Power and Rule in Modern Society* 155). Yet, neo-liberalism stands not just as a critique of welfare government; it also has been activated as programmatic practice in a growing number of states. Both Australia and Canada have been at the forefront of this trend.

Practices of neo-liberalism

By examining some of the recent shifts in governmental technology articulated by the Australian and Canadian states one can discern two dominant modes of neo-liberal practice. The first, what Rose and Miller have termed "government at a distance," involves the top-down reform of state apparatuses based on a market model.[4] This reform characteristically takes the form of programmes of deregulation and privatization (Bradford 204). The second consists, conversely, in a bottom-up approach centered on building the "social capital" of individual subjects (Dean, *Governmentality: Power and Rule in Modern Society* 152).

Neo-liberal "government at a distance" seeks to improve governmental performance through the disciplinary force of market mechanisms.

> Thus, in what is often seen as an "economic rationalist" or "neo-liberal" attack on the welfare state, the concern is not simply to save money but also to promote more efficient patterns of individual and organizational

Governing "Free Subjects"

> behaviour by bringing market relationships into what had once been regarded as non-market spheres of allocation. (Hindess 223)

This can be seen in the Australian Commonwealth's employment of "private corporations of training and certification" within the federal education system (Meredyth). Canada too has moved to place the criteria of market efficiency at the forefront of bureaucratic reform. Under the (neo)Liberal government of Jean Crétien, departments were subjected to the "affordability test"—they have to explain "why they, rather than the private or voluntary sectors ... should be doing what they are doing, or indeed why some things should be done at all" (Whitaker 73).

The doctrine of "social capital" formation, although located at the level of self-investment by individuals and civil society, should also be considered a neo-liberal technique of government. Thus neo-liberal government is at its apex when it works through "self-governing" individuals and communities, giving the appearance of not governing at all. In Australia neo-liberal policy has often been augmented with the support of "indigenous" community empowerment schemes:

> Often, as with the example of community crime prevention ... it is clear that governing maneuvers aim to mobilize a *particular* sense of shared interests, train participants in *specific* skills, provide information about certain *selected* "community" risks, enlist *targeted* local participation in "community" efforts, and so on. (O'Malley 159)

Through such programs neo-liberal governmentality can both advance its agenda, while reducing its formal role and resource commitment to "providing the framework for securing private returns to investment" (Bradford 213). Within Canada (as elsewhere), this has allowed neo-liberal leaders such as Crétien to both call for long-term investments in social and technological infrastructure, yet also maintain that such investment is the sole purview of civil society (Bradford 213). The discourse of "social capital" also marks the return of sovereignty within neo-liberal government—the sovereignty of the individual consumer and the local community (Dean, *Governmentality: Power and Rule in Modern Society* 169). This form of sovereignty is one that is wholly compatible with economic subjectivity, thus avoiding the problem of "society" altogether. Therefore, reflexive government reform on the one hand and the promotion of self-governing individuals/communities on the other, "both come to embody the values and orientations of the market, expressed in notions of the enterprise and the consumer" (Dean, *Governmentality: Power and Rule in Modern Society* 172). At this point our focus may shift to a different scale of neo-liberal government—an emergent global *Empire*.

Empire, or neo-liberalism goes global

The term "globalization" is often bandied about in contemporary social science accounts of the changing nature of the international system. For some it is an unstoppable force of history, making the modern state a feeble relic in the process.[5] Others have been more circumspect, seeing globalization as a challenge to states, transforming them even, yet certainly not one leading to a stateless world in the near future.[6]

Approaching globalization through the governmentality framework, Barry Hindess writes, "an important part of the impact of these developments has been on the perception of the national economy itself as an object of government" (218). Thus, the process of globalization can be identified in the ongoing mediations of national economic government—the development of neo-liberalism discussed previously. In this light "globalization" is a set of international economic pressures that lead to (or perversely are supposedly offset by) governmental restructuring according the market-inspired doctrine of competitiveness (Hindess 212). Cannot the governmentality approach be extended to analyze the practices of globalization on the world scale as well? I argue that Michael Hardt and Antonio Negri's account of an emergent *Empire* does just that. In their discussion, "Empire is emerging today as the center that supports the globalization of productive networks and casts its widely inclusive net to try and envelop all power relations within its world order" (Hardt and Negri 20). In many ways Empire can be seen as the latest chapter in the twisted story of liberal governmentality.

Hardt and Negri clearly see their argument as continuing the poststructural analysis of government; they state that "the work of Michel Foucault has prepared the terrain for such an investigation of imperial rule" (22). Empire, like government at a distance and social capital, finds its epistemological foundation in neo-liberal discourse. What characterizes Empire as a novel form of governmentality, and distinguishes it from its state-based counterparts, is the reconstitution of world political economy through the articulation of a transformed doctrine of sovereignty and police power, and a truly global network of biopolitical production—the creation of the world population as an object of government (Hardt and Negri 26).

The government of Empire has a center, but not the institutional center of the state apparatus. While a multiplicity of states remain to administer the

Governing "Free Subjects"

everyday lives of their (sub)populations, sovereignty has shifted to the system itself. The modern state had transformed sovereignty into a set of techniques for the protection and maintenance of goals outside its own genealogy—the market and population. In the move to Empire, sovereignty is restored to its previous terrain, not the government of natural processes, but the government of crisis. The new imperial sovereignty is "hailed" into existence by the call for order, peace, and equilibrium (Hardt and Negri 14). Just as Carl Schmitt argued that the decisions and will of the sovereign must be the bedrock for the very possibility of the law, without the invocation of a sovereign right to manage crisis the new global programme of neo-liberalism would be stillborn. Thus imperial sovereignty is better thought of as the government of the exception, rather than the government of the rule(s). The characteristic form for such a sovereignty to take is as the answer to a call for intervention (Hardt and Negri 18).

> Here, therefore, is born, in the name of the exceptionality of the intervention, a form of right that is really a *right of the police*. The formation of a new right is inscribed in the deployment of prevention, repression, and rhetorical force aimed at the reconstruction of social equilibrium: all this is proper to the activity of the police. We can thus recognize the initial and implicit source of imperial right in terms of police action and the capacity of the police to create and maintain order. The legitimacy of the imperial ordering supports the exercise of police power, while at the same time the activity of global police force demonstrates the real effectiveness of the imperial ordering. The juridical power to rule over the exception and the capacity to deploy police force are thus two initial coordinates that define the imperial mode of authority. (Hardt and Negri 17)

Yet where does this capacity to deploy police force reside? Surely not within international organizations like the United Nations; one could rightly argue that it is at this point where the tradition form of *state* sovereignty reenters the picture. However, what makes this exercise of state police capability different than those in earlier times is the ends to which they are employed. Whereas military intervention under imperial rule is "more often ... dictated unilaterally by the United States," such "military deployment is presented as an internationally sanctioned police action" (Hardt and Negri 37). Such actions are tied to universal values, and expressly not the national interest of the states involved in supplying Empire's military manpower.

The permanent state of crisis that calls into being police interventions "are justified by *the appeal to essential values of justice*" (Hardt and Negri 18). This justice is not the justice of a prince, not the justice of a nation-state or population—it is the justice of humanity, the cosmopolitan population. Therefore the exercise of sovereignty and police power within Empire is closely linked with the emergence of a new global pastorate. The construction of humanity, human rights, and world peace far surpass what was ever before seen as a feasible object of government. If the world population is conceived of as the object of neo-liberal government, then police actions are not the only technique of imperial intervention. Non-governmental organizations (NGOs) such as Amnesty International, Oxfam, and Médicins sans Frontières should also be analyzed as apparatuses of imperial governmentality.

> Such humanitarian NGOs are in effect (even if this runs counter to the intentions of the participants) some of the most powerful pacific weapons in the new world order—the charitable campaigns and the mendicant orders of Empire. These NGOs conduct "just wars" without arms, without violence, without borders. Like the Dominicans in the late medieval period and the Jesuits at the dawn of modernity, these groups strive to identify and defend human rights. (Hardt and Negri 36)

One should not be lured into a false sense of security by these pronouncements of humanitarian intent. Recalling Brubaker's discussion of the cosmopolitan impulses of civic nationalism in France, one should be wary of those who define their work as a *mission libératrice et civilisatrice* (Brubaker 10). The extension of citizenship rights to all peoples around the world fits hand in glove with "the sense of a priviledged mission or vocation for [the core state(s)], a concern for [global] "grandeur," and a reverance for the army as the incarnation and instrument of this grandeur" (Brubaker 12). Enemies of Empire's sacred vocation become both "banalized (reduced to an object of routine police repression) and absolutized (as the Enemy, an absolute threat to the ethical order)" (Hardt and Negri 13).

Hardt and Negri predicted that the police force most likely to be called upon to intervene against such enemies of world order would be the United States, and that, "These enemies are most often called terrorist, a crude conceptual and terminological reduction that is rooted in a police mentality" (37). These are tragically prophetic words when seen in light of the U.S.-led interventions in Afghanistan, Iraq, and global "war on terrorism."

These values of the global pastorate are constitutive of new forms of political subjectivity (Hardt and Negri 29). Just as the concept of "social capital" at the individual and civil society level sees subjectivation as a process of self-investment, so too is investment central to the constitution of subjectivity in Empire. Such an approach puts global corporations center

Governing "Free Subjects"

stage, for they serve as "the complex apparatus that selects investments and directs financial and monetary maneuvers ... [in] the new biopolitical structuring of the world" (Hardt and Negri 32). This structuring acts as not only a material function, but as a subjective one as well—or it would be better to say that corporations drive the material production of subjectivity itself.

> They produce agentic subjectivities within the biopolitical context: they produce needs, social relations, bodies, and minds—which is to say they produce producers. In the biopolitical sphere, life is made to work for production and production is made to work for life. (Hardt and Negri 32)

Of course political subjectivity is not produced in a factory; its production takes place in the seemingly immaterial materiality of language and communication. It is no surprise then that the "information economy" is so central to the constitution of Empire. Networks of communication are the "structuring structures" of imperial organization. Like the enclosed space (prison, factory, school) and the disciplinary institution (the carceral, *homo economicus*, continual training) that came before it, the information network is the dominant technique and apparatus of global neo-liberalism. The image of the computer network replacing the disciplinary apparatus was suggested by Gilles Deleuze as the coming stage in a Foucauldian analysis of contemporary government (Deleuze, "Post-Scriptum Sur Les Societes De Controle"). As Hardt and Negri write, "Communication not only expresses but also organizes the movement of globalization" (32). Therefore, through the analysis of Empire one can complete the analytics of neo-liberal government—from individual self-government and self-investment to imperial right and the pastorate of humanity.

Striking back against Empire, or the possibility of resistance

The above account of neo-liberal Empire seems to tend towards the all-encompassing, universal exercise of power. Yet, if as Foucault constantly reminds us, no power exists without engendering points of resistance, Empire should also engender such counter-power. However, as Pat O'Malley notes, the governmentality literature rarely pays sustained attention to resistance (other than as a "failure" of governmental programmes) (197).

Hardt and Negri, for their part, offer a theory of "imperial" resistance. In their writing of Empire, resistance will take the form of "new social movements" that are local articulations of a global struggle over imperial power (56).

> These struggles are at once economic, political, and cultural—and hence
> they are biopolitical struggles, struggles over the form of life. They are
> constituent struggles, creating new public spaces and new forms of
> community. (Hardt and Negri 56)

Foucault suggests that, just as governmentality moves the analysis of rule away from the language of the juridical, resistance might be though in terms of "notions derived from strategy and tactics"—the inversion of Clausewitz, politics as the conduct of war by the admixture of other means (Foucault, "Society Must Be Defended" 60). Here the analysis of Hardt and Negri takes its distance from the Foucauldian approach. They argue that:

> Faced as we are with a series of intense subversive social movements that
> attack the highest levels of imperial organization, however, it may no
> longer be useful to insist in the old distinction between strategy and
> tactics. (Hardt and Negri 58)

Instead they propose an analysis of resistance as the expression of the constituent power of "living labor." Despite their protestations to the contrary, this clearly defines resistance within the old logic of dialectical contradiction (Hardt and Negri 51-52). Such a conceptualization runs counter to the anti-foundationalism of the governmentality approach.

Therefore, this genealogy of liberal governmentality—from its differentiation from sovereign, pastoral, and police power to the emergence of Empire—has sought to respond to the deficiencies in constitutional thinking pointed out by Elkin. The governmentality framework allows one to investigate both the constitutive and performative elements of regimes of government. When combined with a shift in the level of analysis to the practices of government, such an approach may better elucidate the production of the political experience of liberalism.

Yet, forces of resistance to neo-liberal Empire clearly exist. If the counter-Empire envisioned by Hardt and Negri sacrifices the benefits of genealogy's anti-foundationalism, what account of resistance may be proffered instead? The Foucauldian language of strategic and tactical resistance can be reformulated to address the contours of imperial power. Such an approach to IPMs that takes the law of the sovereign as a "site of resistance" will be explored in the following chapter.

Chapter Four

Specters of Colonialism: Indigenous Legal Practice as Deconstructive Jurisprudence

The sense of a responsibility without limits, and so necessarily excessive, incalculable, before memory; and so the task of recalling the history, the origin and subsequent direction, thus the limits, of concepts of justice, the law and right, of values, norms, prescriptions that have been imposed and sedimented there, from then on remaining more or less readable or presupposed. As to the legacy we have received under the name of justice, and in more than one language, the task of a historical and interpretative memory is at the heart of deconstruction.

Jacques Derrida (Derrida, "Force of Law: The 'Mystical Foundation of Authority'" 19)

The successes of history belong to those who are capable of seizing these [legal] rules, to replace those who had used them, to disguise themselves so as to pervert them, invert their meaning, and redirect them against those who had initially imposed them: controlling this complex mechanism, they will make it function so as to overcome the rulers through their own rules.

Michel Foucault (Foucault, "Nietzsche, Genealogy, History" 159)

The first area of our transformative activity is the contribution of our substantive ideals to the democratic remaking of social life. The critique of objectivism and its constructive development shake the established terms of ideological controversy. They disrupt the tacit connection between the currently available set of institutional alternatives and any underlying scheme of practical or moral imperatives. They broaden the sense of collective possibility and make more controversial and precise the ideal conceptions that ordinarily serve as the starting points of normative argument.

Roberto Unger (Unger 109-10)

INTRODUCTION

In the introductory chapter it was argued that practices of resistance take two forms: tactical and strategic. Strategic resistance—practiced in the space between competing epistemes, sets of power relations, and/or subject positions—has been the focus of most of the research in contentious politics. Tactical resistance, on the other hand, is a more elusive concept. Recall the definition of tactical resistance as the practice of taking those identities and liberties produced by the dominant form of power as tools for said power's subversion. Such resistances may take the form of everyday/unobtrusive acts of defiance as described in the work of James Scott.

Of particular interest to the discussion of IPMs is Scott's category of infrapolitics (where the false language of the oppressor is utilized by the oppressed to advance their strategic interests). However, Scott's definition requires that one have prior knowledge of these true interests in order to distinguish infrapolitics from mere co-optation. Can the concept of tactical resistance make such distinctions without recourse to foundational claims? One can explore this possibility through the examination of the legal activism of IPMs.

The question of whether legal claims constitute resistance has been a contentious issue for scholars. For many, legal activism (and interest group lobbying) stands as the non-contentious counterpart to protest activity. Yet, under the current definition of contentious politics offered by McAdam, Tarrow, and Tilly, legal activism does have a place—as contained contention (McAdam, Tarrow and Tilly 2-3). As was argued previously, the category of contained contention suggests that such practices are unable to transform the context in which they are made.

This chapter will argue that legal activism conceived as tactical resistance may lead to fundamental change in the epistemic, political, and subjective structures in which such practices are articulated. Can the courtroom serve as a site of resistance, a site within the *politics* of the system where the performance of indigenous claims may open strategic space where the *political* may re-enter and disrupt the law? An investigation of the relationship between the law and indigenous peoples will serve as the hard test case for the analytics of resistance outlined above.

Such an approach to legal activism brings this line of inquiry in close proximity to the Critical Legal Studies movement (CLS) (Unger). The CLS movement has sought to "offer new insight into the struggle over power and right, within and beyond the law" in order to advance a novel form of radical and transformative politics within the legal system itself (Unger 4).

Specters of Colonialism 61

In so doing, CLS scholars have sought to chart a course outside the "blackmail" of pursuing revolution or reform (Unger 110).

> In the ruling traditions of historical and critical social theory and in the vulgar beliefs that these traditions have inspired, revolution appears as the best hope of real social change, the only clear alternative to the endless reproduction of society through reformist tinkering or its slow and obscure remaking through the accumulating of an enormous number of largely unrelated decisions and conflicts. (Unger 114)

However, if radical movements cut themselves off from "the practical or imaginative contest over institutional structure" they undergo "perversion" and become self-defeating. CLS walks this tightrope in an attempt to pioneer "types of association and action that serve as a counter-model to the dominant scheme of social life" (Unger 116).

In particular, that strand of CLS associated with Derridian deconstruction (with its focus on the indeterminacy and violence of the law, and thus the possibility of transforming the law from within) shares a poststructural heritage that makes it a likely candidate for compatibility with the genealogical ethos. Yet, it is this section of the CLS movement that has been subjected to the most intense criticism. This chapter asserts that the ethical call to justice that the deconstruction of law entails also is at the heart of answering the critiques of Derridian jurisprudence.

After summarizing the deconstructive approach to law, and answering the major criticisms of said approach, the last part of this chapter will explore how deconstructive themes take shape in the legal activism of IPMs. One may start such an investigation with the remarks of Jacques Derrida at a recent symposium in Australia, in which he draws out the connections between deconstructive justice and Aboriginal legal claims (Derrida, "A Discussion with Jacques Derrida"). Finally, a rewriting of events in indigenous legal history as the play of deconstructive "traces" and "supplements" will be explored.

DECONSTRUCTING THE LAW

Deconstruction, law, justice

Deconstructive jurisprudence undermines the objectivism and formalism of traditional liberal legal theory. The deconstruction of law has three components, or rather "movements": 1) the historical analysis of the law as the result of political struggles; 2) the critique of the indeterminacy and violence of the law; and finally, 3) the ethical imperative to open the law up to justice, despite the inevitable separation of the former from the latter. Thus (like genealogy), deconstruction involves an approach to research, an analytics, and an ethos.

Derrida's rewriting of legal theory (as first articulated in "Force of Law: the 'Mystical Foundation of Authority'") locates itself in the interplay between law, justice, and deconstruction. In the following quote, Derrida attempts to formulate this complex interrelationship:

> The structure I am describing here is a structure in which law (*droit*) is essentially deconstructible, whether because it is founded, constructed on interpretable and transformable textual strata (and that is the history of the law [*droit*], its possible and necessary transformation, sometimes its amelioration), or because its ultimate foundation is by definition unfounded. The fact that law is deconstructible is not bad news. We may even see in this a stroke of luck for politics, for all historical progress. But the paradox that I'd like to submit for discussion is the following: it is this deconstructible structure of law (*droit*), or if you prefer of justice as *droit*, that also insures the possibility of deconstruction. Justice in itself, if such a thing exists, outside or beyond law, is not deconstructible. No more than deconstruction itself, if such a thing exists. Deconstruction is justice. ... In other words, the hypothesis and propositions toward which I'm tentatively moving here call more for the subtitle: justice as the possibility of deconstruction, the structure of law (*droit*) or of the law, the foundation or the self-authorization of law (*droit*) as the possibility of the exercise of deconstruction. (Derrida, "Force of Law: The 'Mystical Foundation of Authority'" 14-15)

Now, from such a statement, it is not difficult to see how Derrida is often accused of "pretentious obscurantism" (McCormick 417). However, such a conception of law and justice has been fertile soil for the flowering of critical legal theory. In order to better understand deconstructive jurisprudence one should delve deeper into law's indeterminacy, justice's undeconstructibility, and the responsibility of judging.

Derrida points to three aporias of the law (Derrida, "Force of Law: The 'Mystical Foundation of Authority'" 23-28; Cornell 248-50; McCormick 403). The first aporia is that while judges are bound to make decisions flowing from existing law, the act of decision itself creates new law. Thus, judging both conserves and changes the law (Derrida, "Force of Law: The 'Mystical Foundation of Authority'" 23). The second aporia results from the distinction between a decision and a calculation. If legal questions could be answered by a simple calculation, there would be no need for either judge or jury. Indeed, the adversarial system employed in

Specters of Colonialism 63

many liberal states rests on the proposition that the greater part of the practice of law consists of making reasoned arguments as to which calculation is appropriate in a given case. Thus, even if the calculation itself is taken as unproblematic (a dubious assumption to be sure), the decision to calculate is indeterminate. It is this indeterminacy that legal practice is charged with overcoming. Therefore, the specter of the undecidable haunts even calculations of the law (Derrida, "Force of Law: The 'Mystical Foundation of Authority'" 24). The final aporia identified by Derrida is the "madness" of the urgency of decision. Judgments must be rendered *now*. No matter how long it takes to come to a decision, that decision is always exercised within a finite point in time. Judgment cannot wait for total knowledge or absolute proof—hence decision criteria such as "beyond a reasonable doubt." Every judicial decision must arbitrarily halt the political struggle occurring between the two sides of a case. Legal arguments only end with when a decision is rendered; therefore, decisions always must come before an issue is settled. Derrida suggests that this imperative to decide too early, to halt an ongoing struggle, is a form of madness (Derrida, "Force of Law: The 'Mystical Foundation of Authority'" 26).

Why is justice undeconstructible? To answer this question one must identify what *cannot* be justice in Derrida's account. First and foremost, deconstructive jurisprudence rejects legal positivism—law and justice cannot be one and the same. Derrida also specifically rejects justice as natural law (Derrida, "Force of Law: The 'Mystical Foundation of Authority'" 15). For if justice should take the form of a "higher" law, then that law too would be subject to the logical paradoxes that deconstruction identifies. Finally, a dualist conception (where the constitution serves as the justice of the positive law) is also inadequate, for all constitutions have contingent histories and the very act of writing a constitution involves making a performative utterance for a political subject (e.g., "We the People") that is constituted by that very document (Spivak, "Constitutions and Cultural Studies" 164). For Derrida, justice is the infinite (and thus impossible to perform) call of responsibility to a future that is forever over the horizon. Since justice has no determinate content, origin, or structure there is no place for deconstruction.

The final question that deconstructive jurisprudence begs is, "why must legal practice entail an ethical responsibility outside of the law?" The answer lies in the gap between the formal paradoxes of the law outlined above, and the practice of law in spite of such undecidability. As Drucilla Cornell writes, "Deconstruction challenges the possibility that the lawyer or the

64 *The Present Politics of the Past*

judge can be identified with the mere instrument for the replication of the system. The judge and the lawyer 'act' when they remember precedent" (Cornell 234). The responsibility for such action cannot be placed back on the system; the legal system is not self-present, as it relies on the supplement of legal practice. Thus the act of judicial decision affects the relationship of a juridical subject with itself. Though the deconstruction of law is intellectually rich, politically salient, and ethically disturbing to liberal legal practice and theory (or possibly because of such factors), it has been the target of virulent critique. It is to the content of such attacks the following section turns.

Against the deconstruction of the law

Deconstruction in general and the deconstruction of the law in particular, have been highly controversial within the academy. This section will recount some of the recent, recurring, and relevant critiques of Derridian approaches to law. Since a complete review of such critiques would fill a book by itself, the focus here will be on three of the most damaging attacks on the deconstructive project: 1) deconstruction is decisionist, and therefore aligns itself with Nazi thinkers like Heidegger and Carl Schmitt; 2) the law that deconstruction takes as its target is without history; and finally, 3) deconstruction itself is ahistorical, and thus unable to understand its own historical contingency.

Some have gone so far as to paint deconstruction as a danger to the project of the Enlightenment, a danger reminiscent of the ideology of Nazi Germany (McCormick 396). This association with fascism comes from the (supposed) similarities between Derrida's jurisprudence and the work of Nazi thinkers. This similarity rests on the assessment of deconstructive legal theory as decisionist. Since the three aporias identified by Derrida deny the possibility that legal decisions can conform to existing law, then those decisions must be pure acts of will untempered by reason. The critique of such theories is that they lack any meaningful criteria to distinguish between legitimate and illegitimate applications of the force of law (McCormick 404). It is at this point in many arguments where the specter of fascism reappears—how can deconstructive jurisprudence reject Nazi law as illegitimate? While at worst this critique identifies the underlying authoritarian implications of deconstruction, at best its proponents argue that Derridian legal theory is no more than "salon radicalism," unable to protect against fascism despite its leftist intentions (McCormick 417). Others have focused on deconstruction's weaknesses with a slightly less polemical tone.

Specters of Colonialism   *65*

Deconstructive legal theory also has been criticized for it lack of engagement with socio-legal studies aimed at specifying the historical contingency of the law (Norrie 85-86). Whereas Derrida writes in "Force of Law" of two styles of deconstruction, one formal-logical and one historical-genealogical, he practices only the former (quoted in Norrie 94). Thus the law that deconstruction approaches is not the law of any given time of place, but rather the (rather) empty idea of the law as an ahistorical formal system. By ignoring the historical sociology of the law, Derridian jurisprudence amounts to little more than an intellectual parlor trick, unable to provide a case-specific critique of existing institutional forms. At the root of this critique is the argument that for deconstruction to become useful to the critical study of law, it must address itself anew to the "issues of social and political power, structure and history, a 'post-poststructuralist' sociology of law" (Norrie 108). This general line of critique, deconstruction's lack of historical imagination, has been extended to Derridian legal theory itself.

Systems theorists in particular have chided Derridians for their lack of historical self-awareness; deconstruction cannot account for its own emergence (Teubner 768). The argument is that while deconstructive jurisprudence sees itself as opening up the legal system to destabilization and critique, it fails to entertain the possibility that a historical event or process could be overdetermining both law's self-deconstruction and the emergence of deconstruction itself (Teubner 771). The likely first mover behind both events, according to systems theory, is globalization (Teubner 770). This has a number of side-effects: 1) deconstruction has "fallen in love" with its object (the form of law) and thus contains little impetus to make the "liberating move beyond" the law (Teubner 772); 2) the ethical imperative of Derridian jurisprudence amounts to little more than advocating negotiation and compromise (Teubner 776); and finally, 3) because of points one and two, deconstruction lacks any means to guide critical praxis in the 21st century (Teubner 773).

All of these challenges need to be taken seriously. However, they need not be fatal to a poststructural account of law. The following section will focus on the resources available to deconstruction in Derrida's more recent writings, the refinements to deconstructing the law made by CLS scholars since "Force of Law," and the manner in which other poststructural approaches (especially genealogy) can buttress deconstruction. All of these arguments hinge on tools internal to Derrida's call to justice that can effectively answer the aforementioned critiques of deconstructive jurisprudence.

Deconstruction answers the call

The most striking charge leveled at Derrida's approach to law is that it is to be classed with decisionistic theories that were used to buttress Nazi ideology. At worst this critique implies that deconstruction is an enemy to progressive politics, and at best provides no clear means for differentiating such politics from fascism. This characterization certainly runs counter to Derrida's pronouncements of his political agenda, where he describes himself as a "progressist" (Derrida, "A Discussion with Jacques Derrida" 31). Political theorist John McCormick has argued that "Force of Law" can be read as Derrida's reply to just such charges (McCormick 395). Indeed, McCormick suggests that deconstructive jurisprudence is profoundly *less* decisionistic than most of Western political theory (McCormick 397). At the heart of this assertion is the distinction that Derrida draws between mythic and mystical violence, and the relation of each to sovereignty.

Derrida contends that mainstream jurisprudence (especially in its liberal variant) sets its goal on the differentiation of the force of law from arbitrary state violence. His argument goes further along this same line of thinking in describing a repeated instance of arbitrary violence that most theory seems to ignore—the violent act of founding a system of law. Derrida calls this type of violence mythic, and contrasts it with mystical violence, those deconstructive acts which undermine structures of power but cannot be said to structure or order things themselves (Derrida, "Force of Law: The 'Mystical Foundation of Authority'" 52). He uses the example of the general strike, which, while doing violence to the economic and political system, does not found a new system of power relations. While acknowledging that no programme of politics has ever been carried out purely in such a manner, the possibility of purging politics of mythic violence brings to light the extent to which traditional jurisprudence must, in the last instance, rationalize a founding instance of arbitrary violence. He forces the question of "what might *further* render this law less arbitrary and less violent?" upon us (McCormick 405). If previous legal theory had been concerned with limiting and legitimizing sovereign violence, can we conceive of law without recourse to sovereign violence at all (Derrida, *On Cosmopolitanism and Forgiveness* 59)?

> Derrida's essay points to the fact that we must act with certain violence today but never rules out the possibility that we may do without [sovereign] violence altogether tomorrow. This is something quite different from the "decisionism" ... On the contrary, part of it is the practice of enlightenment. (McCormick 416)

Specters of Colonialism 67

The enlightenment of which McCormick writes is certainly not the rational limitation of arbitrary violence characteristic of liberal legal theory, but instead the continual questioning of any such limit as enlightened enough. In this way Derrida's recent work on law may be the realization of Foucault's notion of the counter-modern ethos from his "What is Enlightenment?" (McCormick fn. 12). The interplay of Derridian deconstruction and Foucauldian genealogy also may help answer the charges that deconstruction approaches an ahistorical idea of law.

Critics contend that deconstructive jurisprudence is far removed from a socio-historical account of legal struggles. Derrida's three aporias of law are formal elements of law as such, not substantive elements of any particular, historical legal structure. Indeed, if the deconstructive project was no more than the abstract critique of the founding violence of the law, this would be a compelling critique (Norrie 86). However, if (as Derrida often states in "Forces of Law") deconstruction in such a formal style must be combined with "critiques of judicial ideology" and the "desedimentation of the superstructure of law" then the critique is misdirected (Derrida, "Force of Law: The 'Mystical Foundation of Authority'"). The fact that Derrida does not take up such an analysis in "Force of Law" itself is more likely due to its introductory character and lecture/essay format than a theoretical "marginalization of the social and political character of the law" (Norrie 85).

It is with the aforementioned critique in mind that this dissertation has placed a deconstructive account of indigenous legal activism within the broader framework of a genealogical account of liberal governmentality in white settler states. Genealogy treats any system of law as also a regime of knowledge/power/subjectivity (Leonard 140). Therefore, the seemingly abstract rule(s) of law subject to deconstruction are the results of historical, political struggles (Leonard 142). Derrida, too, emphasizes this historicity in his recent discussions of international law:

> Even if words like "crime against humanity" now circulate in everyday language, that event itself was *produced* and authorized by an international community on a date and according to a figure determined by its history. (Derrida, *On Cosmopolitanism and Forgiveness* 29)

Deconstructive jurisprudence, when combined with a genealogy of law, calls for both the historical study of particular laws and the formal critique of law's violence. While such a hybrid theory of law is neither purely Derridian nor Foucauldian, it remains distinctively poststructuralist, and thus a challenge to traditional jurisprudence.

The final critique of Derrida's legal theory is that it lacks historical consciousness of itself. This critique is most strongly leveled by practitioners of Niklas Luhman's version of systems theory. Those influenced by deconstruction, particularly CLS theorist Drucilla Cornell, have launched a counterattack on systems theory, chiding its advocates for both ignoring Derrida's frequent pronouncements that any strategy of deconstruction is deconstructible (Derrida, "A Discussion with Jacques Derrida" 10) and that even aporias have history (Derrida, *On Cosmopolitanism and Forgiveness* 53), and that their own theory is a degenerative development in jurisprudence in that it once again rationalizes the founding violence of the law by describing it as an *autopoetic* system (Cornell 237, 46). A systems-theoretic approach to law can be said to be more "in love with its object" to a much greater extent than deconstruction because of its divergent account of temporality.

With its focus on the recursive self-authorization of law, systems theory must treat justice as the horizon of said legal system. Justice can only be the future present state of the present system, in accordance with its self-identified principles of operation (Cornell 240). Such a restriction in comparison with the aporetic definition of justice in deconstruction is by definition more conservative and tied to its object of study than a Derridian approach (Cornell 233). This conservatism has serious implications for the ability of systems theory to provide a "critical praxis for the 21st century." Only with the deconstruction of the traditional modality of time can CLS "find a beyond to its own metaphysical presuppositions" rather than being tied to a reformist project of reconciling legal practice with the ideals of the existing regime of law (Cornell 250).

While (as Derrida points out) such legal arguments can only end by the arbitrary imposition of a judgment, perhaps the better question is not one of demonstrative theory but practical applicability. What does deconstructive jurisprudence have to add to the study of indigenous legal activism? The rest of this chapter will provide a (re)writing of indigenous peoples and the law as deconstructive practice in order to answer that question.

IPMs AND THE DECONSTRUCTION OF THE LIBERAL ONTOLOGY OF RIGHTS

In his remarks at a symposium in Australia, Derrida addressed the High Court's decision in *Wik* (and by inference *Mabo*): "of course in that case there was a partial reparation, a partial act of justice, but ... it was phrased

Specters of Colonialism   69

and produced in the name of the colonizer, it was still an injustice" (Derrida, "A Discussion with Jacques Derrida" 9). In making that claim, Derrida highlighted the distinction between reconciliation, which must always be conditional, and the unconditional element of forgiveness called for by an equally unconditional justice (Derrida, "A Discussion with Jacques Derrida" 12). The language of reconciliation will then always be the language of law (and politics) rather than that of justice (Derrida, *On Cosmopolitanism and Forgiveness* 31). Derrida contends that the current shift in settler state policy to seek reconciliation with, and offer recompense to indigenous peoples neither removes the responsibility of current generations for the offenses of colonialism, nor acknowledges the impossibility of justice within colonial power relations (Derrida, "A Discussion with Jacques Derrida" 35, 12). This is reflected in indigenous criticism of the "practical reconciliation" program of the Howard government in Australia, as "more than a backwards step" towards justice (Behrendt 32). Therefore, an investigation of indigenous politics within (post)colonial states may begin with a deconstruction of acts of reconciliation towards the Other, but in the language of the (liberal) self (Derrida, "A Discussion with Jacques Derrida" 15).

The strategy of settler states to institute reparative policies in regards to "their" indigenous populations can be read as the creation of a binary opposition with "indigenous rights" privileged over "colonial conquest"—therefore, the situation is a prime candidate for deconstruction. A deconstructive analysis of the new liberal ontology of indigenous rights is composed of two interrelated theoretical moves: 1) an unsettling of the privileged term of the binary opposition—indigenous rights—by showing how the self-sufficiency of its presence is undercut by the traces of the marginalized term—colonial conquest—in its formation; 2) next, by showing that indigenous definitions of those same rights follow the logic of the supplement rather than ontology. Thus, both steps of deconstruction—reversal and displacement—are evident in the hauntological politics of IPMs. However, this deconstruction will not be merely a theoretical exercise. Rather, it is performed by the practical resistance of IPMs. In this section I will draw events and series from IPMs in Aotearoa/New Zealand, Australia, Canada, and the United States for examples of this process.

The trace of colonialism in liberal ontology

Derrida uses the concept of "trace" to illustrate the precariousness of claims to ontological self-sufficiency. Whereas ontology is presented as complete in its present form, traces of the past (and future) are necessary for this expression. For example, an arrow in flight is assumed to be, in its present

70 The Present Politics of the Past

ontological state, in motion. However, at any given moment an arrow can only be defined as in motion by reference made to the past and future position of the arrow—these references are the traces of which Derrida writes (Edkins 67). This observation is not unique to deconstruction; it also serves as the basis for Heisenberg's "uncertainty principle" and much of post-Newtonian physics. Events from Aotearoa/New Zealand, Canada, and the United States illustrate how the liberal discourse of treaty rights and sovereignty bear the trace of the colonial past.

One of the best examples of how liberal treaty rights contain the trace of the colonial past is found in the proclamation of the "Indians of all Tribes" from 1969. This group represented urban Red Power activists (mostly from UC Berkeley and other Bay Area colleges) who occupied the island of Alcatraz from 1969-1971. Their statement of purpose, as relayed to both the US government and the media, shows that they believed themselves justified in their occupation by the terms of the Fort Laramie Treaty, but also employs a mocking of the language and nature of most treaties concluded with the US government.

> To the Great White Father and All His People:
> We, the native Americans, re-claim the land known as Alcatraz Island in the name of all American Indians by right of discovery ...
> We will purchase said Alcatraz Island for twenty-four dollars ($24) in glass beads and red cloth, a precedent set by the white man's purchase of a similar island [Manhattan] about 300 years ago ...
> We will give to the inhabitants of this island a portion of that land for their own, to be held in trust by the American Indian Government—for as long as the sun shall rise and the rivers go down to the sea—to be administered by the Bureau of Caucasian Affairs (BCA) [...].
> (quoted in Josephy, Johnson and Nagel 60-61)

This double standard of pursuing treaty grievances while reflecting on the colonial nature of the treaties themselves is also evident in much of American Indian literature. In Chadwick Allen's treatment of the 1993 poetry collection, *First Indian on the Moon*, by Sherman Alexie, reveals a similar split attitude towards treaties, "[Alexie] represents treaties as broken, false, 'tragic.' Yet ... treaty discourse remains the only possibility for respectful relations between Indians and whites" (Allen 73-74).[1]

This skepticism is not limited to indigenous peoples in the United States. Howard Adams (a member of the Metis people in Canada) describes treaties as "contracts of continuing oppression" and warns that, "When Indians hold the treaties as sacred testaments, the process of colonization is indeed complete" (Adams). In Aotearoa/New Zealand, government celebrations of

Specters of Colonialism 71

the Treaty of Waitangi (1840) as the national holiday of "Waitangi Day" have served as "the focus of radical Maori protest" since 1971, while Maori IPMs have concurrently been seeking the ratification of the treaty (Walker 246). The case of the Maori leads to another example of liberal ontology bearing the trace of colonialism—the "sovereignty" of indigenous "nations."

The topic of indigenous sovereign nations is another example of an important concept of liberal ontology that is haunted with the traces of colonialism. Allen Hanson started a heated controversy when he argued that the Maori nation was a creation of the 19th century "King movement" rather than a pre-colonial identity.[2] There is little doubt that the concepts of sovereignty and the nation originated in the West. However, what may be less clear is that the expansion of sovereignty to non-Western peoples often was part and parcel of imperial expansion. The Maori people did not exist in any meaningful way as a collectivity until their declaration of independence in 1835 (a move suggested and largely directed by the British Resident, James Busby) (Brownlie 7, fn. 9). The British *needed* the Maori to be a sovereign people in order to legitimize via consent the entry of New Zealand into the British Empire. This is made clear in the Crown's instructions to Lieutenant-General Hobson, who was to conclude the Treaty of Waitangi with the Maori chiefs in 1840:

> We acknowledge New Zealand as a sovereign and independent state, so far at least as it is possible to make that acknowledgement in favour of a people composed of numerous, dispersed and petty tribes, who possess few political relations to each other and are incompetent to act, or even to deliberate in concert. (quoted in McHugh 32)

What is so striking about this document is that it shows the Crown's full awareness that the Maori had little or no capacity to act as a single, sovereign people. Yet the desire to validate British hegemony in Aotearoa/ New Zealand with the "free and intelligent" consent of *someone* acting in the name of the Maori people was important enough to justify whatever means were necessary to create such a person or persons. This process is found in the American context as well. American Indian "tribes" are considered by many commentators as either "historical constructions arising out of European-aboriginal contact" or "white creations used by Indians to survive" (Nagel xii; Fried; Deloria and Lytle).

The need of settler society to identify Western-style leaders and organizations in IPMs is also present in recent times. Robert A. Runstrom writes of the white media's attempts to locate "spokesmen" for the Indian activists on Alcatraz Island, and the similarity of this search with the construction of "chiefs" and "tribes" during colonization (Runstrom 198). Whereas the liberal ontology of treaty rights and sovereignty bear the trace of colonialism, IPMs approach rights in a hauntological manner—by the logic of the supplement.

SUPPLEMENTARITY IN INDIGENOUS HAUNTOLOGY

Ontology begins with the *always already* assumption of its own completeness. As has been explored in the previous section, (post)coloniality haunts the completeness of the liberal ontology of indigenous rights. IPMs speak to these specters by addressing rights according to the logic of the supplement. Derrida writes of the supplement as:

> An inessential extra, added to something complete in itself, but ... added in order to complete, to compensate for a lack in what was supposed to be complete in itself. (quoted in Edkins 70)

The most familiar example of this logic is the famous phrase, "the King is Dead, long live the King!" The King (the father) was considered complete, yet his death leads to the proclamation of the King's (the son's) life.The concept of "the King" was complete in the father, but needed the addition of the son to define the immortality of the monarchy. It is important to note also that the supplement of the son for the father affects both the *replacement* of one life for another and the *displacement* of the concept from a mortal to immortal plane. The logic of supplementarity can be seen at work in two areas of prime concern to IPMs—land rights and the definition of indigenous peoples.

Wilmer identifies land rights as the number one issue of priority for IPMs (Wilmer 131). In describing the roots of IPMs in Latin America, Michel de Certeau emphasizes that it is the indigenous ties to the soil which serve as the foundation of a politics that is neither co-opted by nor simply a reversal of Western politics (de Certeau, "The Politics of Silence: The Long March of the Indians" 229). This deconstructive stance is fashioned by the supplemental nature of indigenous claims to land. In his analysis of Witi Ihimaera's story, "The Greenstone Patu," Chadwick Allen distinguishes between Pakeha understandings of property value as *ownership* with Maori understanding of property as *responsibility* (Allen 67). Ronald Paul Hill spent time among the Aboriginal people of the "Kimberly" in Australia in order to better understand their views of native title. He too finds that

Specters of Colonialism   73

indigenous use of "land rights" cannot be contained within liberal ontology. "Aborigines view land as a religious phenomenon, and believe that the relationship between themselves and the land originated with the Dreaming" (Hill 308-9). Thus the loss of land has a different meaning for Aboriginal people, "if they take your *land* away from you ... [you can't] practice those things [which constitute Aboriginal culture] and you just gotta disintegrate" (Hill 316). Vine Deloria, Jr. expresses a similar connection between American Indians and the land:

> The movement set its roots in its desire to reclaim a sacred place for the tribal community which existed partially in time and space and partially in the determinations of unknown Indians who preserved a dignity that was timeless [...]. (Deloria, *Behind the Trail of Broken Treaties: An Indian Declaration of Independence* 251)

It is no wonder that mining, logging, and pastoral interests in areas claimed by right of Native Title are threatened by the indigenous definition of land rights. The history of the 19th century in settler states shows the impact of supplementing one concept of land right for another. The expropriation of indigenous lands during colonialism was advanced rather than retarded by the extension of liberal land rights to indigenous people.

> The net result [of the 1867 establishment of the Native Land Court in New Zealand] was a wholesale dispossession of a people of their patrimony. By 1960, only four million of the original sixty-six million acres of Maori land remained. (Walker 272)

Even institutions of settler state government have acknowledged these effects:

> "critical damage" was done by the 1865 and 1867 Native Land Acts and a 1869 Order of the Native Land Court: "vesting the whole of the land then in communal ownership in thirteen members only of the [Orakei] tribe as legal and beneficial owners ..." This necessarily destroyed the mana or authority of the tribe in and over the land. (quoted from a 1987 Report of the Waitangi Tribunal in Sorrenson 172)

Wilmer shows how similar policies in the US focused on finding "competent" Indians who would use property "consistent with the capitalist rather than traditional economic system" (Wilmer 195). This dispossession of land was not necessarily the intention of liberals who instituted the new ontology of land rights; rather as Deloria suggests, the logic of the supplement was at work "behind the naïve ideas of Eastern liberals"

(Deloria, *Behind the Trail of Broken Treaties: An Indian Declaration of Independence* 6). This discussion of the transformation of land rights in the 19th century underscores the radical results that would occur should IPMs succeed in supplementing the now dominant liberal ontology with native rights once again.

IPMs' orientation to the defining of "indigenous people(s)" also follows the logic of the supplement. Interesting debate of this question goes on at the international level, surrounding the UN working group on indigenous populations. In 1982 the group agreed on a working definition of "indigenous peoples" that focused on those "who today live more in conformity with their particular ... customs and traditions than with the institutions of the country of which they now form a part" (reprinted as Appendix C Wilmer 216). Significantly, though, the definition extends to those "descendents of [such] groups ... [who] are, even if only formally, placed under a State structure which incorporates national, social and cultural characteristics alien to theirs." The expansiveness of this definition is notable. However, a recent executive summary of the working group's activities (produced by the Australian Aboriginal and Torres Strait Islander Council) shows that State governments have been much more interested in the definition (in order to limit it) than organizations of IPMs have been.

One key point of IPMs, however, has been to keep language which refers to "indigenous peoples" rather than "indigenous populations" to support claims to self-determination as "peoples" under international law (Wilmer 202-3). Should such a reduction of "peoples" to "populations" occur, then once more the process of supplementing particularly liberal conceptions for those of indigenous groups themselves would produce the predictable depoliticization.

The practice of identifying indigenous people within individual states is quite a different matter. Paradoxically, in the United States, a government focus on the individual (liberal) rights to claim indigenous status has led to a reliance on hereditary and cultural standards, rather than self-definition, to determine indigeneity (Nagel 234-48). Nagel points out that the US government's criteria for identifying Indians are stricter by orders of magnitude than the criteria to identify other minorities, such as African Americans (Nagel 71). In this political setting there are strong incentives for even indigenous groups to limit self-identification. For example, the Association of American Indian and Alaskan Native Professors' "Statement of Ethnic Fraud" relies on "documentation of enrollment in a state or federally recognized nation/tribe" even though such tribal enrollment often involves rules that exclude those who live off the reservation, and children

Specters of Colonialism

of unmarried tribal women (Josephy, Johnson and Nagel 277-8). The logic behind such actions is not difficult to understand. Given a limited set of resources allocated by settler states for indigenous entitlement programs, distributional advantage is served by limiting the number of those qualifying for such benefits.

A similar problem has come up in the context of the right to market "indigenous" goods. As a global market for the crafts and artwork of the world's native peoples has developed, so too has the incentive to draw authoritative boundaries around those who may legitimately produce and sell such items. What is most striking about both of the preceding examples is how the incentives of a market economy work in a distinctly antagonistic and *depolitical* manner against the *political* incentive for indigenous groups to see their numbers swell.

However, IPM activists often resist these ontological definitions of indigeneity. Indeed, only increased self-identification can account for the dramatic growth of the American Indian community in the United States—and the consciousness-raising efforts of the Red Power movements are often credited with stimulating these conversions to indigenous subjectivity. For such reasons, some within IPMs have begun to call for a "citizenship model" to supplement existing state-led identification in the membership policies of indigenous governments; this model would allow for naturalization as well as membership based on ancestry and residence (Jaimes 280). The Haida people in Alaska, and the Oglala Lakota on the Pine Ridge Reservation in South Dakota have pioneered such an approach. M. Annette Jaimes expresses the frustration of many indigenous people over the state imposition of standards for "indigeneity" when she writes:

> Federal policymakers have increasingly imposed "Indian identification standards" of their own design. Typically centering upon a notion of "blood quantum"—not especially different in conception from the eugenics code once adopted by Nazi Germany ... has increasingly wrought havoc with the American Indian sense of nationhood (and often the individuals sense of self) over the past century. (Jaimes 280)

The battle over the use of ontological versus hauntological definitions of "indigenous peoples" is another key example of the way in which IPMs may diverge from liberal settler governments (and certain of their own number).

CONCLUSIONS

In the preceding discussion of treaty rights, native sovereignty, land rights, and indigenous (self)-definition I have illustrated the deconstructive processes by which indigenous peoples' movements have practiced resistance to the ontology of settler state governments. There are clear distinctions to be made between the selective use of rights discourse by IPMs, and the hauntology of movement strategies. The opportunity that led to the emergence of these deconstructive forms of social resistance can be traced back to the condition of (post)coloniality. The spectral quality of this "present politics of the past" provides a unique environment where traditional models of revolution (such as the Marxist model) are not necessary to advance a radical critique of the current liberal hegemony in power relations. IPMs provide a rich set of examples and challenges for the practice of theorizing cultural recognition and democracy. Mainstream social scientific representations of these movements cannot and do not highlight the distinctiveness of IPMs, and thus serve to depoliticize the message they carry. This effacement of the critical "voice" of indigenous peoples serves to aid the political program of global liberalism, and ignores the "political alternatives and social models which represent, perhaps, the only hope" of a world in which we speak to the specters of colonialism without repeating the mistakes of the past (de Certeau, "The Politics of Silence: The Long March of the Indians").

Chapter Five

Dossiers Introduction

The following two chapters will be historical dossiers—"that is to say, a case, an affair, an event that provided the intersection of discourses that differed in origin, form, organization, and function" (Foucault, *I, Pierre Riviére, Having Slaughtered My Mother, My Sister, and My Brother...: A Case of Parricide in the 19th Century* x)—of indigenous legal activism in the white settler states of Australia and Canada. The reason for adopting such an approach is to:

> Draw a map, so to speak of those combats, to reconstruct these confrontations and battles, to rediscover the interaction of those discourses as weapons of attack and defense in the relations of power and knowledge [and subjectivity]. (Foucault, *I, Pierre Riviére, Having Slaughtered My Mother, My Sister, and My Brother...: A Case of Parricide in the 19th Century* xi)

Dossiers attempt to present a wide range of documentary evidence, without a scheme of classification, without subjecting the documents to direct interpretation, and with a selection of accompanying theoretical essays. Why adopt such a research strategy? In the following pages this question will be answered in reference to the relation between the dossier form and genealogy, dossiers and the subject matter under study, and finally, some specific objections to the dossier format will be addressed.

DOSSIERS AND THE GENEALOGICAL ETHOS

Foucault maintained that, "Genealogy is gray, meticulous, and patiently *documentary*. It operates on a fields of tangled and confused parchments, on documents that have been scratched over and recopied many times" [Emphasis added] (Foucault, "Nietzsche, Genealogy, History" 139). The approach of genealogy is most often associated with its identification of the discursive as a level of analysis, separated from any assumption of the speaking subject "beneath" discourse (Foucault, *The Archaeology of Knowledge* 27-28). What holds at the level of discourse is highlighted at the point of the document itself.

> The document, then, is no longer for history an inert material through which it tries to reconstitute what men have done or said, the events of which only the trace remains; history is now trying to define within the documentary material itself unities, totalities, series, relations. (Foucault, *The Archaeology of Knowledge*)

The dossier is a direct expression of this focus on the document. This reorientation of the historian's treatment of the dossier is closely linked to the critical-political impetus of genealogical research. As Richard Harvey Brown and Beth Davis-Brown write, "The awareness of the importance of documents ... as social political constructions also betokens our ability to criticize ourselves and, thereby, to avoid self-destructive illusions" (Brown and Davis-Brown 30–31). Despite this close conceptual overlap between genealogy and documentary research, many of Foucault's "followers" (especially in America) have not approached their work in this manner.

Particularly in the realm of (post)Imperial history, Foucauldians have been accused of having "little stomach for rooting about in archives" (Winks 659). This project seeks to correct this inexplicable imbalance between the programme and practice of genealogy. After all, "What genealogy attempts to do is to realign our political thought, so that it will catch up with our political reality" (May 112). This is not possible if genealogists are not willing to leave the ivory tower behind and get the hands dusty with primary research. The politics of archival work are exactly the micropolitical site of power that Foucault directed our attention (Brown and Davis-Brown 25). In particular, genealogy should seek out the emergence of new debates within and between historical documents. These emergences mark the sites of struggle and the reversal of forces (Foucault, "Nietzsche, Genealogy, History" 148–49). In addition to these connections between the dossier form and genealogy, the substantive content of this project also leads one into the archive.

Dossiers Introduction

DOSSIERS AND INDIGENOUS LEGAL ACTIVISM

One of the arguments made herein is that the present legal claims of indigenous groups in settler states may profitably be framed in terms of their (post)colonial context. Thus, these analyses can be seen as belonging to the continuing history of the British Empire. A.G. Hopkins suggests that two of the most fertile directions for post-Imperial history are the critical examination of Western political institutions and the emerging mechanisms of globalism (Hopkins 650). Indeed, this is exactly what is being attempted here, with reference to the interrogation of liberal governmentality and its emerging *"Empire-*al" context. Hopkins also notes that one of the largest shortcoming of current scholarship is the lost focus on constitutional history (Hopkins 651). These dossiers begin with what can defensively be called the most important constitutional shifts in recent Australian and Canadian history—the *Mabo* and *Delgamuukw* decisions, respectively. But more than anything else, the documents presented in the following chapters need to be removed from the assumed neutrality of liberal historiography in order to make the case that indigenous claims challenge the terms of liberalism itself (Guha 6). The dossier format does just that.

The documents presented here mark the event of "the ruling culture [coming] increasingly under attack from a historic opposition invested with such ideals, values, and ways of interpreting the world as constitute a challenge to liberalism" (Guha 13). The status of these documents as events rests not so much on some action or intention that they represent, but rather the manner in which indigenous claims differentially articulate the terms of liberal discourse—sovereignty, nation, and property.

> An event, consequently, is not a decision, a treaty, a reign, or a battle, but the reversal of a relationship of forces, the usurpation of power, *the appropriation of a vocabulary turned against those who had once used it.* [Emphasis added] (Foucault, "Nietzsche, Genealogy, History" 154)

Such a *political* performance of the elements given by the dominant regime of *politics* opens the possibility of carving out a "concrete space of transformation" (May 120). Therefore, the presentation of documentary material in the form of dossiers serves many of the specific goals of the argument being offered. However, not surprisingly, the dossiers also raise many questions of method as well.

OBJECTIONS

The first potential objection to these dossiers may be the selection criteria for inclusion of documents. Both of the following chapters begin with the landmark high court cases that established the principle of Native Title in each country. Subsequent materials were selected for their relevance to the debates over indigenous land claims that emerged from these decisions. Multiple positions (indigenous, government, and both supportive and oppositional forces within settler societies) and diverse discursive realms (legal, governmental, press statements, opinion-editorials, media coverage) were included to provide a wide frame of view. However, one may still argue that since all material has not been included, the selection criteria can still be accused of generating only supportive evidence. There are two ways of answering this charge. This first is that such "source-mining is not an unqualified historical vice" (Hexter 241). This project has attempted to avoid the pernicious combination of both mining sources for supportive data, and proffering a systemic, causal historical argument—being a "lumper" (Hexter 242). Rather, the very goal of this argument is to "point out divergences, perceive differences, to draw distinctions" between this account and the treatment of indigenous claims by liberal social science, theory, and historiography—to be a "splitter" (Hexter 242). One may press harder for assurances against "selection bias" and "invalid inference"—yet, none will be forthcoming.

> To such people, with their quite legitimate impatience, to all the counter-examples which, as I am very well aware, they could supply, I will reply: of course, I not only admit that my analysis is limited, I want it so; I have made it so ... The relations that I have described are valid in order to define a particular configuration: they are not signs to describe the face of a cultural totality. It is the friends of the *Weltanschauung* who will be disappointed; I insist that the description that I have undertaken is quite different than theirs. What for them is a lacuna, an omission, an error, is for me, a deliberate, methodological exclusion. (Foucault, *The Archaeology of Knowledge* 158-59)

This research is not an explanation, nor an interpretation, but rather an argument, as that made in a courtroom—to ignore this difference is to have missed the point from the beginning. But why not subject these documents to direct interpretation? It is to that question one now may turn.

If the documents presented in the dossiers are important, why not interpret their meaning for both indigenous politics and liberalism? Again, it is a question of treating the discursive domain of statements as an object it itself, rather than as a mark of some originary meaning-generating

Dossiers Introduction 81

consciousness. Thus Foucault suggests the replacement of "the analysis of [statements'] coexistence, their succession, their mutual functioning, their reciprocal determination, and their independent or correlative transformation" for interpretation (recall here the distinction drawn in chapter one between interpretation and "playing with the text") (Foucault, *The Archaeology of Knowledge* 29). Rather than a standard hermeneutic interpretation of historical statements, genealogy offers a history of interpretations embodied in statements. By placing the documents in these dossiers on the "stage of historical process" one may divorce them from both their "organic" link to a speaking subject and their "context" within traditional modes of historical and textual interpretation (Foucault, "Nietzsche, Genealogy, History" 152). When all is said and done, for the genealogist, "knowledge is not *made* for understanding; it is *made* for cutting" [Emphasis added] (Foucault, "Nietzsche, Genealogy, History" 154).

DOSSIERS AND CRITIQUE

Whereas these dossiers contain numerous documents produced by indigenous peoples, some may object that the "voice" of such people is absent. This, of course, relies on the distinction between a subject that makes statements and the subject-effect of statements that the genealogist must reject. Why reject such a common sense position? Precisely because this is the "common sense" of most academics, it must be "made inoperative" in a critical analysis, "For no criticism can be fully activated unless it is distanced from its agency" (Guha 7). Obviously, one cannot sidestep every convention of thought without being left totally mute. Therefore a *total* genealogy is impossible. Genealogy is always a partial project, both in the sense of being limited and interested.

> It must be recalled that, in order for genealogy to function, not all knowledge can be suspect at the same time. This does not mean that genealogy is immune to critique; the categories that genealogy holds constant in any of its analyses can always be put up for investigation by another history in an attempt to show that it was not power but something else that was at work. What is does mean, though, is that criticism is always situated; one does not criticize something except in the name of something else to which one gives one's assent. (May 112-13)

Thus genealogy stands as an "affirmation of knowledge as perspective" (Foucault, "Nietzsche, Genealogy, History" 156). These dossiers, like those of a prosecutor, are meant from the outset to convict—someone else must stand as the defender of liberalism against indigenous claims. To take up such an adversarial role in both academic and political disputes is something that all scholars engage in, yet few are open about. The ethos of genealogy produces the openness of (to paraphrase Foucault) a "happy inquisitor." This is nothing less than a refusal of our taught obligation toward "objective" scholarship. As Michael Clifford writes of genealogy's crimes against neutrality, "there is freedom in this refusal, in this transgression—for those who have the stomach for it" (Clifford 134-35). It is only for others without such a stomach that the dossier will be a hard pill to swallow.

Chapter Six

Native Title in Australia

MABO AND OTHERS v. QUEENSLAND (No. 2) (3 June 1992) 175 CLR 1 F.C. 92/014

JUDGE 1

MASON C.J. AND McHUGH J. We agree with the reasons for judgment of Brennan J. and with the declaration which he proposes.

2. In the result, six members of the Court (Dawson J. dissenting) are in agreement that the common law of this country recognizes a form of native title which, in the cases where it has not been extinguished, reflects the entitlement of the indigenous inhabitants, in accordance with their laws or customs, to their traditional lands and that, subject to the effect of some particular Crown leases, the land entitlement of the Murray Islanders in accordance with their laws or customs is preserved, as native title, under the law of Queensland. The main difference between those members of the Court who constitute the majority is that, subject to the operation of the Racial Discrimination Act 1975 (Cth), neither of us nor Brennan J. agrees with the conclusion to be drawn from the judgments of Deane, Toohey and Gaudron JJ. that, at least in the absence of clear and unambiguous statutory provision to the contrary, extinguishment of native title by the Crown by inconsistent grant is wrongful and gives rise to a claim for compensatory damages. We note that the judgment of Dawson J. supports the conclusion of Brennan J. and ourselves on that aspect of the case since his Honour considers that native title, where it exists, is a form of permissive occupancy at the will of the Crown.

3. We are authorized to say that the other members of the Court agree with what is said in the preceding paragraph about the outcome of the case.

4. The formal order to be made by the Court accords with the declaration proposed by Brennan J. but is cast in a form which will not give rise to any

83

84 *The Present Politics of the Past*

possible implication affecting the status of land which is not the subject of the declaration in par.2 of the formal order.

JUDGE 2

BRENNAN J. The Murray Islands lie in the Torres Strait, at about 10 degrees S. Latitude and 144 degrees E. Longitude. They are the easternmost of the Eastern Islands of the Strait. Their total land area is of the order of 9 square kilometres. The biggest is Mer (known also as Murray Island), oval in shape about 2.79 kms long and about 1.65 kms across. A channel about 900 m. wide separates Mer from the other two islands, Dauar and Waier, which lie closely adjacent to each other to the south of Mer. The Islands are surrounded for the most part by fringing reefs. The people who were in occupation of these Islands before first European contact and who have continued to occupy those Islands to the present day are known as the Meriam people. Although outsiders, relatively few in number, have lived on the Murray Islands from time to time and worked as missionaries, government officials, or fishermen, there has not been a permanent immigrant population. Anthropological records and research show that the present inhabitants of the Islands are descended from the people described in early European reports. The component of foreign ancestry among the present population is small compared with most communities living in the Torres Strait. The Meriam people of today retain a strong sense of affiliation with their forbears and with the society and culture of earlier times. They have a strong sense of identity with their Islands. The plaintiffs are members of the Meriam people. In this case, the legal rights of the members of the Meriam people to the land of the Murray Islands are in question.

Early contact with Europeans
2. The Meriam people were in occupation of the Islands for generations before the first European contact. They are a Melanesian people (perhaps an integration of differing groups) who probably came to the Murray Islands from Papua New Guinea. Their numbers have fluctuated, probably no more than 1000, no less than 400.
3. Some of the features of life in the Murray Islands at the time of first European contact, at the end of the 18th century, are described by Moynihan J. in his findings in the present case:

"Communal life based on group membership seems to have been the predominant feature of life. Many of the activities of daily life were social activities which took place in the context of group activities of a

Native Title in Australia

ceremonial or ritualistic nature. Behaviour was regulated in the interest of the community by social pressures....

The people lived in groups of huts strung along the foreshore or strand immediately behind the sandy beach. They still do although there has been a contraction of the villages and the huts are increasingly houses. The cultivated garden land was and is in the higher central portion of the island. There seems however in recent times a trend for cultivation to be in more close proximity with habitation.

The groups of houses were and are organised in named villages. It is far from obvious to the uninitiated, but is patent to an islander, that one is moving from one village to another. The area occupied by an individual village is, even having regard to the confined area on a fairly small island which is in any event available for 'village land', quite small.

Garden land is identified by reference to a named locality coupled with the name of relevant individuals if further differentiation is necessary.

The Islands are not surveyed and boundaries are in terms of known land marks such as specific trees or mounds of rocks.

Gardening was of the most profound importance to the inhabitants of Murray Island at and prior to European contact. Its importance seems to have transcended that of fishing...

Gardening was important not only from the point of view of subsistence but to provide produce for consumption or exchange during the various rituals associated with different aspects of community life. Marriage and adoption involved the provision or exchange of considerable quantity of produce. Surplus produce was also required for the rituals associated with the various cults at least to sustain those who engaged in them and in connection with the various activities associated with death.

Prestige depended on gardening prowess both in terms of the production of a sufficient surplus for the social purposes such as those to which I have referred and to be manifest in the show gardens and the cultivation of yams to a huge size. Considerable ritual was associated with gardening and gardening techniques were passed on and preserved by these rituals. Boys in particular worked with their fathers and by observations and imitations reinforced by the rituals and other aspects of the social fabric gardening practices were passed on."

Later, his Honour said:

"It seems that before European contact social cohesion was sought by the combined operation of a number of factors. Children were inculcated from a very early age with knowledge of their relationships in terms of social groupings and what was expected of them by a constant pattern of example, imitation and repetition with reinforcing behaviour. It was part of their environment - the way in which they lived. [...] Initiation and other group activities reinforced these patterns. A sense of shame was the outcome of a failure to observe.

It could be reinforced by group pressures leading to retribution.

Ultimately force might be resorted to by those who had access to the

86 *The Present Politics of the Past*

means of exerting it. Sorcery, magic and taboo were obviously important cohesive factors and a source of sanction."
The findings show that Meriam society was regulated more by custom than by law.

4. Contacts with Europeans were initially few and sporadic. There were occasional visits by passing ships in the early 19th century. In 1834, two young British castaways were rescued and they stayed on Mer until a ship called there 2 years later. The ship's captain, Captain Lewis, recorded that the natives "acknowledge no chief each family being distinct and independent of each other. Quarrels frequently take place which, after a fight are generally followed by a speedy reconciliation." The London Missionary Society came to the Murray Islands in about 1871 and moved its Torres Strait headquarters to Mer in 1877. It was a significant influence in keeping the peace among the Meriam people and in modifying some of their customs. It appears that, prior to the arrival of the London Missionary Society, elaborate funeral ceremonies and the collection and preservation of human heads were features of life in the Murray Islands.

5. Although the Murray Islands, prior to their annexation to Queensland in 1879, were not part of her Majesty's dominions, Imperial and Colonial authorities were concerned for the maintenance of order in, and the protection of the indigenous inhabitants of, those Islands and other islands in the Western Pacific. "Blackbirding" was being practised and in the 1860s the Murray Islands were raided, women seized and some of the Meriam people murdered. The Pacific Islanders Protection Acts of 1872 and 1875 (Imp) (1) 35 and 36 Vict c 19 (P9/579); 38 and 39 Vict c 51. were enacted to stamp out blackbirding (2) See O'Connell and Riordan, *Opinions on Imperial Constitutional Law*, (1971), pp 100-103 and to confer on a High Commissioner's Court jurisdiction over British subjects in the islands of the Western Pacific. However, the 1875 Act expressly disavowed "any claim or title whatsoever to dominion or sovereignty over any such islands or places" and any intention "to derogate from the rights of the tribes or people inhabiting such islands or places, or of chiefs or rulers thereof, to such sovereignty or dominion."

[...]

21. In 1894, some doubts had arisen in the Colonial Office as to the legality of the annexation of the islands included in the 1879 Letters Patent to Queensland. Queensland had been separated from New South Wales and erected into a Colony pursuant to The New South Wales Constitution Act, 1855 (Imp) (4) 18 and 19 Vict c 54 by Letters Patent of 6 June 1859 and an Order in Council of the same day. The boundaries of the new colony were

Native Title in Australia 87

fixed, the Colony was granted a constitution with representative institutions and the laws of New South Wales became the laws of Queensland on separation. The doubts which arose in the Colonial Office related to the legality of incorporating new territory into a colony with representative institutions once the boundaries of the colony were fixed by or under Imperial legislation. To settle these doubts, the Colonial Boundaries Act 1895 (Imp) (5) 58 and 59 Vict c 34 was enacted. As this Court held in Wacando, if the Queensland Coast Islands Act of 1879 did not suffice to effect the incorporation of the Murray Islands into Queensland (either by its own force or by satisfying a condition bringing the Letters Patent of 1879 into operation), the requisite Imperial legislative authority could be found in the Colonial Boundaries Act.

[...]

23. It may be assumed that on 1 August 1879 the Meriam people knew nothing of the events in Westminster and in Brisbane that effected the annexation of the Murray Islands and their incorporation into Queensland and that, had the Meriam people been told of the Proclamation made in Brisbane on 21 July 1879, they would not have appreciated its significance. The legal consequences of these events are in issue in this case. Oversimplified, the chief question in this case is whether these transactions had the effect on 1 August 1879 of vesting in the Crown absolute ownership of, legal possession of and exclusive power to confer title to, all land in the Murray Islands. The defendant submits that that was the legal consequence of the Letters Patent and of the events which brought them into effect. If that submission be right, the Queen took the land occupied by Meriam people on 1 August 1879 without their knowing of the expropriation; they were no longer entitled without the consent of the Crown to continue to occupy the land they had occupied for centuries past.

24. The defendant's submission is founded on propositions that were stated in cases arising from the acquisition of other colonial territory by the Imperial Crown. Although there are differences which might be said to distinguish the Murray Islands and the Meriam people of 1879 from other colonial territories and their indigenous inhabitants when those territories respectively became British colonies, the propositions on which the defendant seeks to rely have been expressed to apply universally to all colonial territories "settled" by British subjects. Assuming that the Murray Islands were acquired as a "settled" colony (for sovereignty was not acquired by the Crown either by conquest or by cession), the validity of the propositions in the defendant's chain of argument cannot be determined by reference to circumstances unique to the Murray Islands; they are advanced

88   *The Present Politics of the Past*

as general propositions of law applicable to all settled colonies. Nor can the circumstances which might be thought to differentiate the Murray Islands from other parts of Australia be invoked as an acceptable ground for distinguishing the entitlement of the Meriam people from the entitlement of other indigenous inhabitants to the use and enjoyment of their traditional lands. As we shall see, such a ground of distinction discriminates on the basis of race or ethnic origin for it denies the capacity of some categories of indigenous inhabitants to have any rights or interests in land. It will be necessary to consider presently the racial or ethnic basis of the law stated in earlier cases relating to the entitlement of indigenous people to land in settled colonies.

25. On analysis, the defendant's argument is that, when the territory of a settled colony became part of the Crown's dominions, the law of England so far as applicable to colonial conditions became the law of the colony and, by that law, the Crown acquired the absolute beneficial ownership of all land in the territory so that the colony became the Crown's demesne and no right or interest in any land in the territory could thereafter be possessed by any other person unless granted by the Crown. Perhaps the clearest statement of these propositions is to be found in *Attorney-General v. Brown* (6) (1847) 1Legge 312, at p 316, when the Supreme Court of New South Wales rejected a challenge to the Crown's title to and possession of the land in the Colony.

Stephen C.J. stated the law to be -

"that the waste lands of this Colony are, and ever have been, from the time of its first settlement in 1788, in the Crown; that they are, and ever have been, from that date (in point of legal intendment), without office found, in the Sovereign's possession; and that, as his or her property, they have been and may now be effectually granted to subjects of the Crown."

The reasons for this conclusion were stated (7): ibid., at pp 317-318

"The territory of New South Wales, and eventually the whole of the vast island of which it forms a part, have been taken possession of by British subjects in the name of the Sovereign. They belong, therefore, to the British Crown. [...] The fact of the settlement of New South Wales in that manner, and that it forms a portion of the Queen's Dominions, and is subject to and governed by British laws, may be learned from public colonial records, and from Acts of Parliament. New South Wales is termed in the statute 54 GEO III, c.15, and in the 59 GEO III, c.122, His Majesty's Colony; not the colony of the people, not even the colony of the empire. It was maintained that this supposed property in the Crown was a fiction. Doubtless, in one sense, it was so. The right of the people of England to their property, does not in fact depend on any royal grant, and the principle that all lands are holden mediately or immediately of

Native Title in Australia

the Crown flows from the adoption of the feudal system merely (Co Lit 1, and ibid.191, a, Mr. Butler's note 6; Bac Ab Prerog B.; Vin Ab same title K.A. 19). That principle, however, is universal in the law of England, and we can see no reason why it shall be said not to be equally in operation here. The Sovereign, by that law is (as it is termed) universal occupant. All property is supposed to have been, originally, in him. Though this be generally a fiction, it is one "adopted by the Constitution to answer the ends of government, for the good of the people." (Bac Ab ubi supra, marginal note.) But, in a newly-discovered country, settled by British subjects, the occupancy of the Crown with respect to the waste lands of that country, is no fiction. If, in one sense, those lands be the patrimony of the nation, the Sovereign is the representative, and the executive authority of the nation, the 'moral personality' (as Vattel calls him, *Law of Nations*, book 1, chap 4), by whom the nation acts, and in whom for such purposes its power resides. Here is a property, depending for its support on no feudal notions or principle. But if the feudal system of tenures be, as we take it to be, part of the universal law of the parent state, on what shall it be said not to be law, in New South Wales? At the moment of its settlement the colonists brought the common law of England with them."

So conceiving the common law, his Honour understood a statutory reference to "the waste lands of the Crown" to mean "all the waste and unoccupied lands of the colony; for, at any rate, there is no other proprietor of such lands." (8) ibid., at p 319.

26. This judgment has formidable support. It was described as "notable" by Windeyer J. (9) In *Wade v. New South Wales Rutile Mining Co. Pty. Ltd.* (1969) 121 CLR 177, at p 194 who followed its doctrine in *Randwick Corporation v. Rutledge* (10) (1959) 102 CLR 54, at p 71:

"On the first settlement of New South Wales (then comprising the whole of eastern Australia), all the land in the colony became in law vested in the Crown. The early Governors had express powers under their commissions to make grants of land. The principles of English real property law, with socage tenure as the basis, were introduced into the colony from the beginning - all lands of the territory lying in the grant of the Crown, and until granted forming a royal demesne. The colonial Act, 6 Wm IV No. 16 (1836), recited in its preamble that the Governors by their commissions under the Great Seal had authority 'to grant and dispose of the waste lands' - the purpose of the Act being simply to validate grants which had been made in the names of the Governors instead of in the name of the Sovereign. And when in 1847 a bold argument, which then had a political flavour, challenged the right of the Crown, that was to say of the Home Government, to dispose of land in the colony, it was as a legal proposition firmly and finally disposed of by Sir Alfred Stephen C.J.: *The Attorney-General v. Brown* (11) (1847) 1 Legge, at pp 317-320."

90   *The Present Politics of the Past*

27. The doctrine of exclusive Crown ownership of all land in the Australian colonies was again affirmed by Stephen J. in *New South Wales v. The Commonwealth* ("the Seas and Submerged Lands Case") (12) (1975) 135 CLR 337, at pp 438-439:

> "That originally the waste lands in the colonies were owned by the British Crown is not in doubt. Such ownership may perhaps be regarded as springing from a prerogative right, proprietary in nature, such as is described by Dr. Evatt in his unpublished work on the subject [...] the prerogatives of the Crown were a part of the common law which the settlers brought with them on settlement (*R. v. Kidman*, per Griffith C.J. (13) (1915) 20 CLR 425, at pp 435-436); 'the prerogative of the Queen, when it has not been expressly limited by local law or statute, is as extensive in Her Majesty's colonial possessions as in Great Britain' (per Lord Watson speaking for their Lordships in *Liquidators of Maritime Bank of Canada v. Receiver-General* (New Brunswick) (14) (1892) AC 437, at p 441); cited by Isaacs J. in *The Commonwealth v. New South Wales* (15) (1923) 33 CLR 1, at p 37. On the other hand that ownership may be described as a consequence of the feudal principle which, on first settlement in Australia, was 'extended to the lands oversea', so that all colonial land belonged 'to the Crown until the Crown chose to grant it' (per Isaacs J. in Williams' Case (16) *Williams v. Attorney-General for New South Wales* (1913) 16 CLR 404, at p 439). In either event the consequence is the same, the lands of Australia became the property of the King of England (*Attorney-General v. Brown* (17) (1847) 1 Legge, at pp 317-320)."

Dawson J., following this line of authority in *Mabo v. Queensland* (18) (1988) 166 CLR 186, at p 236, said that "colonial lands which remained unalienated were owned by the British Crown."

28. The proposition that, when the Crown assumed sovereignty over an Australian colony, it became the universal and absolute beneficial owner of all the land therein, invites critical examination. If the conclusion at which Stephen C.J. arrived in *Attorney-General v. Brown* be right, the interests of indigenous inhabitants in colonial land were extinguished so soon as British subjects settled in a colony, though the indigenous inhabitants had neither ceded their lands to the Crown nor suffered them to be taken as the spoils of conquest. According to the cases, the common law itself took from indigenous inhabitants any right to occupy their traditional land, exposed them to deprivation of the religious, cultural and economic sustenance which the land provides, vested the land effectively in the control of the Imperial authorities without any right to compensation and made the indigenous inhabitants intruders in their own homes and mendicants for a place to live. Judged by any civilized standard, such a law is unjust and its claim to be part of the common law to be applied in contemporary Australia

Native Title in Australia

must be questioned. This Court must now determine whether, by the common law of this country, the rights and interests of the Meriam people of today are to be determined on the footing that their ancestors lost their traditional rights and interests in the land of the Murray Islands on 1 August 1879.

29. In discharging its duty to declare the common law of Australia, this Court is not free to adopt rules that accord with contemporary notions of justice and human rights if their adoption would fracture the skeleton of principle which gives the body of our law its shape and internal consistency. Australian law is not only the historical successor of, but is an organic development from, the law of England. Although our law is the prisoner of its history, it is not now bound by decisions of courts in the hierarchy of an Empire then concerned with the development of its colonies. It is not immaterial to the resolution of the present problem that, since the Australia Act 1986 (Cth) came into operation, the law of this country is entirely free of Imperial control. The law which governs Australia is Australian law. The Privy Council itself held that the common law of this country might legitimately develop independently of English precedent (19) See *Australian Consolidated Press Ltd. v. Uren* (1967) 117 CLR 221, at pp 238, 241; (1969) AC 590, at pp 641, 644. Increasingly since 1968 (20) See the Privy Council (Limitation of Appeals) Act 1968 (Cth) and see the Privy Council (Appeals from the High Court) Act 1975 (Cth), the common law of Australia has been substantially in the hands of this Court. Here rests the ultimate responsibility of declaring the law of the nation. Although this Court is free to depart from English precedent which was earlier followed as stating the common law of this country (21) *Cook v. Cook* (1986) 162 CLR 376, at pp 390, 394; *Viro v. The Queen* (1978) 141 CLR 88, at pp 93, 120-121, 132, 135, 150-151, 166, 174, it cannot do so where the departure would fracture what I have called the skeleton of principle. The Court is even more reluctant to depart from earlier decisions of its own (22) *Jones v. The Commonwealth* (1987) 61 ALJR 348, at p 349; 71 ALR 497, at pp 498-499; *John v. Federal Commissioner of Taxation* (1989) 166 CLR 417, at pp 438-439, 451-452; *McKinney v. The Queen* (1991) 171 CLR 468, at pp 481-482. The peace and order of Australian society is built on the legal system. It can be modified to bring it into conformity with contemporary notions of justice and human rights, but it cannot be destroyed. It is not possible, *a priori,* to distinguish between cases that express a skeletal principle and those which do not, but no case can command unquestioning adherence if the rule it expresses seriously offends the values of justice and human rights (especially equality before the law) which are aspirations of

92 *The Present Politics of the Past*

the contemporary Australian legal system. If a postulated rule of the common law expressed in earlier cases seriously offends those contemporary values, the question arises whether the rule should be maintained and applied. Whenever such a question arises, it is necessary to assess whether the particular rule is an essential doctrine of our legal system and whether, if the rule were to be overturned, the disturbance to be apprehended would be disproportionate to the benefit flowing from the overturning.

30. In the present case, the defendant's chain of argument contains several links, each of which must be separately considered although, as we shall see, a common theme or thread runs through them. Some of these links are unchallenged. We start with the proposition that the Imperial Crown acquired sovereignty over the Murray Islands on 1 August 1879 and that the laws of Queensland (including the common law) became the law of the Murray Islands on that day - or, if it be necessary to rely on the Colonial Boundaries Act 1895, is deemed to have become the law of the Murray Islands on that day. Next, by the common law, the Crown acquired a radical or ultimate title to the Murray Islands. The plaintiffs accept these propositions but challenge the final link in the chain, namely, that the Crown also acquired absolute beneficial ownership of the land in the Murray Islands when the Crown acquired sovereignty over them.

31. As the passages cited from the judgments in *Attorney-General v. Brown* and the Seas and Submerged Lands Case show, the proposition that, by the common law, the Sovereign acquired absolute beneficial ownership of all land in the Murray Islands rests on a number of bases. In the first place, it is said that the Crown is absolute owner because "there is no other proprietor." This basis denies that the indigenous inhabitants possessed a proprietary interest. The negative basis is then buttressed by three positive bases to show why it is necessary to attribute absolute beneficial ownership to the Crown. One basis is that, when English law was brought to Australia with and by British colonists, the common law to be applied in the colonies included the feudal doctrine of tenure. Just as the Crown acquired or is deemed to have acquired universal ownership of all land in England, so the Crown became the owner of all land in the Australian colonies. We may call this the feudal basis.

Another basis is that all land in a colony is "the patrimony of the nation" and, on this basis, the Crown acquired ownership of the patrimony on behalf of the nation. A third basis is the prerogative basis mentioned by Stephen J. in the Seas and Submerged Lands Case. In order to determine whether, on any or all of these bases, the Crown acquired beneficial ownership of the land in the Murray Islands when the Crown acquired

Native Title in Australia 93

sovereignty over them, we must first review the legal theories relating to the acquisition of sovereignty and the introduction of the common law.

The acquisition of sovereignty
   "The acquisition of territory by a sovereign state for the first time is an act of state which cannot be challenged, controlled or interfered with by the courts of that state."
This principle, stated by Gibbs J. in the Seas and Submerged Lands Case (23) *New South Wales v. The Commonwealth* (1975) 135 CLR, at p 388, precludes any contest between the executive and the judicial branches of government as to whether a territory is or is not within the Crown's Dominions. The Murray Islands were annexed by an exercise of the prerogative evidenced by the Letters Patent; a mode of acquisition recognized by the common law as a valid means of acquiring sovereignty over foreign territory. The recognition is accorded simply on the footing that such a prerogative act is an act of State the validity of which is not justiciable in the municipal courts (24) *Sobhuza II. v. Miller* (1926) AC 518, at p 525; The Fagernes (1927) P 311; *Re.g., v. Kent Justices; Ex parte Lye* (1967) 2 QB 153, at pp 176-177, 181-182; *Ffrost v. Stevenson* (1937) 58 CLR 528, at pp 565-566; *A Raptis and Son v. South Australia* (1977) 138 CLR 346, at p 360; cf. *Bonser v. La Macchia* (1969) 122 CLR 177, at pp 193, 217, where the meaning of a constitutional term was in issue. In *Post Office v. Estuary Radio Ltd.*, Diplock L.J. said (25) (1968) 2 QB 740, at p 753:
"It still lies within the prerogative power of the Crown to extend its sovereignty and jurisdiction to areas of land or sea over which it has not previously claimed or exercised sovereignty or jurisdiction. For such extension the authority of Parliament is not required."
This proposition was approved by Gibbs J. in the Seas and Submerged Lands Case and, in Wacando, Gibbs C.J. and Mason J. accepted that an annexation of territory by exercise of the prerogative is an act of State (26) (1981) 148 CLR, per Gibbs C.J. at p 11; per Mason J. at p 21. See also *Coe v. The Commonwealth* (1979) 53 ALJR 403, per Jacobs J. at p 410.
32. Although the question whether a territory has been acquired by the Crown is not justiciable before municipal courts, those courts have jurisdiction to determine the consequences of an acquisition under municipal law.
Accordingly, the municipal courts must determine the body of law which is in force in the new territory. By the common law, the law in force in a newly-acquired territory depends on the manner of its acquisition by the Crown. Although the manner in which a sovereign state might acquire new territory is a matter for international law, the common law has had to march

94   *The Present Politics of the Past*

in step with international law in order to provide the body of law to apply in a territory newly acquired by the Crown.

33. International law recognized conquest, cession, and occupation of territory that was terra nullius as three of the effective ways of acquiring sovereignty. No other way is presently relevant (27) See E. Evatt, "The Acquisition of Territory in Australia and New Zealand" in (1968) *Grotian Society Papers,* p 16, who mentions only cession and occupation as relevant to the Australasian colonies. The great voyages of European discovery opened to European nations the prospect of occupying new and valuable territories that were already inhabited. As among themselves, the European nations parceled out the territories newly discovered to the sovereigns of the respective discoverers (28) *Worcester v. Georgia* (1832) 6 Pet 515, at pp 543-544 (31 US 350, at p 369), provided the discovery was confirmed by occupation and provided the indigenous inhabitants were not organized in a society that was united permanently for political action (29) Lindley, *The Acquisition and Government of Backward Territory in International Law,* (1926), Chs III and IV.

To these territories the European colonial nations applied the doctrines relating to acquisition of territory that was terra nullius. They recognized the sovereignty of the respective European nations over the territory of "backward peoples" and, by State practice, permitted the acquisition of sovereignty of such territory by occupation rather than by conquest (30) See Lindley, ibid., p 47. Various justifications for the acquisition of sovereignty over the territory of "backward peoples" were advanced. The benefits of Christianity and European civilization had been seen as a sufficient justification from mediaeval times (31) See Williams, *The American Indian in Western Legal Thought,* (1990), pp 78ff; and *Johnson v. McIntosh* (1823) 8 Wheat 543, at p 573 (21 US 240, at p 253). Another justification for the application of the theory of terra nullius to inhabited territory – a justification first advanced by Vattel at the end of the 18th century – was that new territories could be claimed by occupation if the land were uncultivated, for Europeans had a right to bring lands into production if they were left uncultivated by the indigenous inhabitants (32) Vattel, *The Law of Nations* (1797), Bk I, pp 100-101. See Castles, *An Australian Legal History,* (1982), pp 16-17. It may be doubted whether, even if these justifications were accepted, the facts would have sufficed to permit acquisition of the Murray Islands as though the Islands were terra nullius. The Meriam people were, as Moynihan J. found, devoted gardeners. In 1879, having accepted the influence of the London Missionary Society, they were living peacefully in a land-based society under some sort of governance

Native Title in Australia 95

by the Mamoose and the London Missionary Society. However that may be, it is not for this Court to canvass the validity of the Crown's acquisition of sovereignty over the Islands which, in any event, was consolidated by uninterrupted control of the Islands by Queensland authorities (33) 10 Encyclopaedia of Public International Law, (1987), p 500; cf. J. Crawford, "The Criteria for Statehood in International Law," (1977) 48 *The British Year Book of International Law* 93, at p 116.

34. The enlarging of the concept of terra nullius by international law to justify the acquisition of inhabited territory by occupation on behalf of the acquiring sovereign raised some difficulties in the expounding of the common law doctrines as to the law to be applied when inhabited territories were acquired by occupation (or "settlement," to use the term of the common law).

Although Blackstone commended the practice of "sending colonies (of settlers) to find out new habitations," he wrote (34) *Commentaries on the Laws of England*, 17th ed. (1830), Bk II, ch 1, p 7-

"so long as it was confined to the stocking and cultivation of desert uninhabited countries, it kept strictly within the limits of the law of nature. But how far the seising on countries already peopled, and driving out or massacring the innocent and defenceless natives, merely because they differed from their invaders in language, in religion, in customs, in government, or in colour; how far such a conduct was consonant to nature, to reason, or to christianity, deserved well to be considered by those, who have rendered their names immortal by thus civilizing mankind."

As we shall see, Blackstone's misgivings found a resonance in international law after two centuries (35) *Advisory Opinion on Western Sahara* (1975) 1 ICJR 12. But he was unable to declare any rule by which the laws of England became the laws of a territory which was not a "desert uninhabited" country when the Crown acquired sovereignty over that territory by discovery and occupation as terra nullius. As the British acquisition of sovereignty over the Colony of New South Wales was regarded as dependent upon the settlement of territory that was terra nullius consequent on discovery (36) See E. Evatt, op cit, at p 25; *Cooper v. Stuart* (1889) 14 App Cas 286, and as the law of New South Wales is the source of the law applicable to the Murray Islands, we must next examine the basis on which the common law was received as the law of the Colony of New South Wales.

Reception of the common law

35. The means by which the municipal laws of England, including the common law, became the law of a country that had been outside the King's dominions were stated by Blackstone (37) *Commentaries*, Bk I, ch.4, pp

106-108; accord: *Forbes v. Cochrane* (1824) 2 B and C 448, at p 463 (107 ER 450, at p 456) as follows:

"Plantations or colonies, in distant countries, are either such where the lands are claimed by right of occupancy only, by finding them desert and uncultivated, and peopling them from the mother-country; or where, when already cultivated, they have been either gained by conquest, or ceded to us by treaties. And both these rights are founded upon the law of nature, or at least upon that of nations. But there is a difference between these two species of colonies, with respect to the laws by which they are bound. For it hath been held, that if an uninhabited country be discovered and planted by English subjects, all the English laws then in being, which are the birthright of every subject, are immediately there in force. But this must be understood with very many and very great restrictions.

Such colonists carry with them only so much of the English law, as is applicable to their own situation and the condition of an infant colony;[...] What shall be admitted and what rejected, at what times, and under what restrictions, must, in case of dispute, be decided in the first instance by their own provincial judicature, subject to the revision and control of the king in council: the whole of their constitution being also liable to be new-modelled and reformed by the general superintending power of the legislature in the mother-country. But in conquered or ceded countries, that have already laws of their own, the king may indeed alter and change those laws; but, till he does actually change them, the ancient laws of the country remain, unless such as are against the law of God, as in the case of an infidel country. Our American plantations are principally of this latter sort, being obtained in the last century either by right of conquest and driving out the natives (with what natural justice I shall not at present inquire) or by treaties. And therefore the common law of England, as such, has no allowance or authority there; they being no part of the mother-country, but distinct (though dependent) dominions. They are subject, however, to the control of the parliament."

According to Blackstone, English law would become the law of a country outside England either upon first settlement by English colonists of a "desert uninhabited" country or by the exercise of the Sovereign's legislative power over a conquered or ceded country. Blackstone did not contemplate other ways by which sovereignty might be acquired. In the case of a conquered country, the general rule was that the laws of the country continued after the conquest until those laws were altered by the conqueror (38) *Blankard v. Galdy* (1693) Holt KB 341 (90 ER 1089); *Campbell v. Hall* (1774) Lofft 655, at p 741 (98 ER 848, at pp 895-896); *Beaumont v. Barrett* (1836) 1 Moo PC 59 (12 ER 733). The Crown had a prerogative power to make new laws for a conquered country although that power was subject to laws

Native Title in Australia

enacted by the Imperial Parliament (39) *Campbell v. Hall*, (1774) Lofft, at pp 741, 742 (98 ER, at pp 895, 896).

The same rule applied to ceded colonies, though the prerogative may have been limited by the treaty of cession (40) See the discussion in Roberts-Wray, *Commonwealth and Colonial Law*, (1966), pp 214ff; *Sammut v. Strickland* (1938) AC 678; *Blankard v. Galdy* (1693) 2 Salk 411 (91 ER 356); *Buchanan v. The Commonwealth* (1913) 16 CLR 315, at p 334. When "desert uninhabited countries" were colonized by English settlers, however, they brought with them "so much of the English law as (was) applicable to their own situation and the condition of an infant colony" (41) *Commentaries*, Bk I, ch 4, p 107; State *Government Insurance Commission v. Trigwell* (1979) 142 CLR 617, at pp 625, 634. English colonists were, in the eye of the common law, entitled to live under the common law of England which Blackstone described as their "birthright" (42) *Commentaries*, Bk I, ch 4, p 107. And see *Sabally* and *N'Jie v. H.M. Attorney-General* (1965) 1 QB 273, at p 294. That law was not amenable to alteration by exercise of the prerogative (43) *Sammut v. Strickland* (1938) AC, at p 701. The tender concern of the common law of England for British settlers in foreign parts led to the recognition that such settlers should be regarded as living under the law of England if the local law was unsuitable for Christian Europeans (44) *Ruding v. Smith* (1821) 2 Hag.Con.371 (161 ER 774); *Freeman v. Fairlie* (1828) 1 Moo Ind App 306, at pp 323-325, aff p 341 (18 ER 117, at pp 127-128, 137); cf. *Campbell v. Hall* (1774) Lofft, at p 741 (98 ER, at pp 895,896). See also *Yeap Cheah Neo v. Ong Cheng Neo* (1875) 6 LR 381, at p 393; cf. *Re.g., v. Willans* (1858) 3 Kyshe 16, at pp 20-25; and see *Re Loh Toh Met* (1961) 27 MLJ 234, at pp 237-243; *Khoo Hooi Leong v. Khoo Chong Yeok* (1930) AC 346, at p 355. This rule was applied even to English residents in Eastern countries which were not under British sovereignty (45) The "Indian Chief" (1801) 3 C Rob 12, at pp 28-29 (165 ER 367, at pp 373-374).

36. When British colonists went out to other inhabited parts of the world, including New South Wales, and settled there under the protection of the forces of the Crown, so that the Crown acquired sovereignty recognized by the European family of nations under the enlarged notion of terra nullis, it was necessary for the common law to prescribe a doctrine relating to the law to be applied in such colonies, for sovereignty imports supreme internal legal authority (46) See A. James, *Sovereign Statehood*, (1986), pp 3ff., 203-209. The view was taken that, when sovereignty of a territory could be acquired under the enlarged notion of terra nullius, for the purposes of the municipal law that territory (though inhabited) could be treated as a "desert

uninhabited" country. The hypothesis being that there was no local law already in existence in the territory (47) *Lyons (Mayor of) v. East India Co.* (1836) 1 Moo PC 175, at pp 272-273 (12 ER 782, at p 818); *Cooper v. Stuart* (1889) 14 App Cas; *The Lauderdale Peerage* (1885) 10 App Cas 692, at pp 744-745; *Kielley v. Carson* (1842) 4 Moo PC 63, at pp 84-85 (13 ER 225, at p 233), the law of England became the law of the territory (and not merely the personal law of the colonists). Colonies of this kind were called "settled colonies." Ex hypothesi, the indigenous inhabitants of a settled colony had no recognized sovereign, else the territory could have been acquired only by conquest or cession. The indigenous people of a settled colony were thus taken to be without laws, without a sovereign and primitive in their social organization. In *Advocate-General of Bengal v. Ranee Surnomoye Dossee* (48) (1863) 2 Moo N S 22, at p 59 (15 ER 811, at p 824); 9 Moo Ind App 391, at p 428 (19 ER 786, at p 800) Lord Kingsdown used the term "barbarous" to describe the native state of a settled colony:

"Where Englishmen establish themselves in an uninhabited or
barbarous country, they carry with them not only the laws, but
the sovereignty of their own State; and those who live amongst
them and become members of their community become also
partakers of, and subject to the same laws."

In *Campbell v. Hall* Lord Mansfield suggested that Jamaica should be regarded as a settled colony because the English colonists arrived after the Spaniards had left (49) His Lordship may have wrongly appreciated the history of Jamaica: see Roberts-Wray, op cit, pp 46-47, 851-852, the negro inhabitants presumably being of no significance (50) See (1774) Lofft, at p 745 (98 ER, at p 898). In *Cooper v. Stuart* Lord Watson proffered the absence of "settled inhabitants" and "settled law" as a criterion for determining whether inhabited territory had been acquired by "settlement" under English law (51) (1889) 14 App Cas, at p 291:

"The extent to which English law is introduced into a British Colony,
and the manner of its introduction, must necessarily vary according to
circumstances. There is a great difference between the case of a Colony
acquired by conquest or cession, in which there is an established system
of law, and that of a Colony which consisted of a tract of territory
practically unoccupied, without settled inhabitants or settled law, at the
time when it was peacefully annexed to the British dominions. The
Colony of New South Wales belongs to the latter class. In the case of
such a Colony the Crown may by ordinance, and the Imperial
Parliament, or its own legislature when it comes to possess one, may by
statute declare what parts of the common and statute law of England
shall have effect within its limits. But, when that is not done, the law of
England must (subject to well-established exceptions) become from the

Native Title in Australia   99

outset the law of the Colony, and be administered by its tribunals. In so far as it is reasonably applicable to the circumstances of the Colony, the law of England must prevail, until it is abrogated or modified, either by ordinance or statute."

As the settlement of an inhabited territory is equated with settlement of an uninhabited territory in ascertaining the law of the territory on colonization, the common law which the English settlers brought with them to New South Wales could not have been altered or amended by the prerogative - only by the Imperial Parliament or by the local legislature (52) Holdsworth, *A History of English Law*, 3rd ed., vol.ix, (1944), p 84; *Sammut v. Strickland* (1938) AC, at p 701; *Kielley v. Carson* (1843) 4 Moo PC, at pp 84-85 (13 ER, at p 233); *Falkland Islands Co. v. The Queen* (1863) 2 Moo PC (NS) 266, at p 273 (15 ER 902, at p 905); *Sabally and N'Jie v. H.M. Attorney-General* (1965) 1 QB, at p 294. (This principle raises some doubts about the validity of the exercise of legislative power by the Governor of New South Wales before a Legislative Council was established in 1823, but we need not pause to consider that question (53) See the discussion by Windeyer, *Lectures on Legal History*, 2nd ed. (1949), pp 332-333; H.V. Evatt, "The Legal Foundations of New South Wales," (1938) 11 *Australian Law Journal* 409, at pp 417-422; and Enid Campbell, "Prerogative Rule in New South Wales, 1788-1823," (1964) 50 *Royal Australian Historical Society* 161) In a settled colony in inhabited territory, the law of England was not merely the personal law of the English colonists; it became the law of the land, protecting and binding colonists and indigenous inhabitants alike and equally. Thus the theory which underpins the application of English law to the Colony of New South Wales is that English settlers brought with them the law of England and that, as the indigenous inhabitants were regarded as barbarous or unsettled and without a settled law, the law of England including the common law became the law of the Colony (so far as it was locally applicable) as though New South Wales were "an uninhabited country... discovered and planted by English subjects" (54) See per Lord Watson in *Cooper v. Stuart* (1889) 14 App Cas, at p 291; and cf. Roberts-Wray, op cit, p 540. The common law thus became the common law of all subjects within the Colony who were equally entitled to the law's protection as subjects of the Crown (55) As the subjects of a conquered territory (*Calvin's Case* (1608) 7 Co Rep 1a, at p 6a (77 ER 377, at p 384)); *Campbell v. Hall* (1774) Lofft, at p 741 (98 ER, at p 895) and of a ceded territory (*Donegani v. Donegani* (1835) 3 Knapp 63, at p 85 (12 ER 571, at p 580)) became British subjects (*Lyons (Mayor of) v. East India Co.* (1836) 1 Moo PC, at pp 286-287 (12 ER, at p 823); 1 Moo Ind App 175, at pp 286-187 (18 ER 66, at pp 108-109)), a fortiori the subjects of a settled territory must have acquired that status. And see *Re.g., v. Wedge* (1976) 1 NSWLR 581, at p 585. Its introduction to New South Wales was confirmed by s.24 of the Australian Courts Act 1828 (Imp) (56) 9 GEO IV c.83. As the laws of New South Wales became the laws of Queensland on separation of the two Colonies in 1859 (57) Letters Patent of 6 June 1859: see p 11 above and, by the terms of the Queensland Coast Islands Act 1879 and the Governor's Proclamation, the Murray Islands on annexation became subject to the laws in force in Queensland, the common law became the basic law of the Murray Islands. Thus the Meriam people in 1879, like Australian Aborigines in earlier times, became British subjects owing allegiance to the Imperial Sovereign entitled to such rights and privileges and subject to such liabilities as the common law and applicable statutes provided. And this is so irrespective of the fact that, in 1879, the Meriam people were settled on their land, the gardens were being tilled, the Mamoose and the London Missionary Society were keeping the peace and a form of justice was being administered.

The basis of the theory of universal and absolute Crown ownership
37. It is one thing for our contemporary law to accept that the laws of England, so far as applicable, became the laws of New South Wales and of the other Australian colonies. It is another thing for our contemporary law to accept that, when the common law of England became the common law of the several colonies, the theory which was advanced to support the introduction of the common law of England accords with our present knowledge and appreciation of the facts. When it was sought to apply Lord Watson's assumption in *Cooper v. Stuart* that the colony of New South Wales was "without settled inhabitants or settled law" to Aboriginal society in the Northern Territory, the assumption proved false. In *Milirrpum v. Nabalco Pty. Ltd.* Blackburn J. said (58) (1971) 17 FLR 141, at p 267:
"The evidence shows a subtle and elaborate system highly adapted to the country in which the people led their lives, which provided a stable order of society and was remarkably free from the vagaries of personal whim or influence. If ever a system could be called 'a government of laws, and not of men', it is that shown in the evidence before me."
Faced with a contradiction between the authority of the Privy Council and the evidence, his Honour held that the class to which a colony belonged was a question of law, not of fact (59) ibid., at p 244; McNeil, *Common Law Aboriginal Title*, (1989), p 292, fn.207; Lester, *The Territorial Rights of the Inuit of the Canadian Northwest Territories: A Legal Argument*, (unpublished doctoral thesis (1981)), pp 100-107, 155-157:
"Whether or not the Australian aboriginals living in any part of New South Wales had in 1788 a system of law which was beyond the powers

Native Title in Australia

of the settlers at that time to perceive or comprehend, it is beyond the
power of this Court to decide otherwise than that New South Wales
came into the category of a settled or occupied colony."

38. The facts as we know them today do not fit the "absence of law" or
"barbarian" theory underpinning the colonial reception of the common law
of England. That being so, there is no warrant for applying in these times
rules of the English common law which were the product of that theory. It
would be a curious doctrine to propound today that, when the benefit of the
common law was first extended to Her Majesty's indigenous subjects in the
Antipodes, its first fruits were to strip them of their right to occupy their
ancestral lands. Yet the supposedly barbarian nature of indigenous people
provided the common law of England with the justification for denying
them their traditional rights and interests in land, as Lord Sumner speaking
for the Privy Council said in *In re Southern Rhodesia* (60) (1919) AC 211,
at pp 233-234:

"The estimation of the rights of aboriginal tribes is always inherently
difficult. Some tribes are so low in the scale of social organization that
their usages and conceptions of rights and duties are not to be reconciled
with the institutions or the legal ideas of civilized society. Such a gulf
cannot be bridged. It would be idle to impute to such people some
shadow of the rights known to our law and then to transmute it into the
substance of transferable rights of property as we know them."

39. As the indigenous inhabitants of a settled colony were regarded as "low
in the scale of social organization," they and their occupancy of colonial
land were ignored in considering the title to land in a settled colony.
Ignoring those rights and interests, the Crown's sovereignty over a territory
which had been acquired under the enlarged notion of terra nullius was
equated with Crown ownership of the lands therein, because, as Stephen
C.J. said, there was "no other proprietor of such lands." Thus, a Select Committee on Aborigines reported in 1837 to the House of Commons that the
state of Australian Aborigines was "barbarous" and "so entirely destitute
[...] of the rudest forms of civil polity, that their claims, whether as sovereigns or proprietors of the soil, have been utterly disregarded" (61) Cited by
Lindley, op cit, at p 41. The theory that the indigenous inhabitants of a "settled" colony had no proprietary interest in the land thus depended on a discriminatory denigration of indigenous inhabitants, their social organization
and customs. As the basis of the theory is false in fact and unacceptable in
our society, there is a choice of legal principle to be made in the present case.
This Court can either apply the existing authorities and proceed to inquire
whether the Meriam people are higher "in the scale of social organization"
than the Australian Aborigines whose claims were "utterly disregarded" by

102   *The Present Politics of the Past*

the existing authorities or the Court can overrule the existing authorities, discarding the distinction between inhabited colonies that were terra nullius and those which were not.

40. The theory of terra nullius has been critically examined in recent times by the International Court of Justice in its *Advisory Opinion on Western Sahara* (62) (1975) ICJR, at p 39. There the majority judgment read:

"'Occupation' being legally an original means of peaceably acquiring sovereignty over territory otherwise than by cession or succession, it was a cardinal condition of a valid 'occupation' that the territory should be terra nullius - a territory belonging to no-one - at the time of the act alleged to constitute the 'occupation' (cf. *Legal Status of Eastern Greenland*, P.C.I.J., Series A/B, No.53, pp 44 f. and 63 f.). In the view of the Court, therefore, a determination that Western Sahara was a 'terra nullius' at the time of colonization by Spain would be possible only if it were established that at that time the territory belonged to no-one in the sense that it was then open to acquisition through the legal process of 'occupation'. 80. Whatever differences of opinion there may have been among jurists, the State practice of the relevant period indicates that territories inhabited by tribes or peoples having a social and political organization were not regarded as terrae nullius. It shows that in the case of such territories the acquisition of sovereignty was not generally considered as effected unilaterally through 'occupation' of terra nullius by original title but through agreements concluded with local rulers. On occasion, it is true, the word 'occupation' was used in a non-technical sense denoting simply acquisition of sovereignty; but that did not signify that the acquisition of sovereignty through such agreements with authorities of the country was regarded as an 'occupation' of a "terra nullius" in the proper sense of these terms. On the contrary, such agreements with local rulers, whether or not considered as an actual 'cession' of the territory, were regarded as derivative roots of title, and not original titles obtained by occupation of terrae nullius."

Judge Ammoun, Vice-President of the Court, delivered a separate opinion in which he commended as penetrating the views expressed on behalf of the Republic of Zaire which he restated as follows (63) ibid., at pp 85-86:

"Mr. Bayona-Ba-Meya, goes on to dismiss the materialistic concept of terra nullius, which led to this dismemberment of Africa following the Berlin Conference of 1885. Mr. Bayona-Ba-Meya substitutes for this a spiritual notion: the ancestral tie between the land, or 'mother nature', and the man who was born therefrom, remains attached thereto, and must one day return thither to be united with his ancestors. This link is the basis of the ownership of the soil, or better, of sovereignty. This amounts to a denial of the very concept of terra nullius in the sense of a land which is capable of being appropriated by someone who is not born therefrom. It is a condemnation of the modern concept, as defined by Pasquale Fiore, which regards as terrae nullius territories inhabited by populations whose civilization, in the sense of the public law of Europe,

Native Title in Australia

103

is backward, and whose political organization is not conceived
according to Western norms.

One might go still further in analysing the statement of the
representative of Zaire so as to say that he would exclude from the
concept of terra nullius any inhabited territory. His view thus agrees
with that of Vattel, who defined terra nullius as a land empty of
inhabitants."

He concluded (64) ibid., at p 86 that "the concept of terra nullius, employed at all periods, to the brink of the twentieth century, to justify conquest and colonization, stands condemned." The court was unanimously of the opinion that Western Sahara at the time of colonization by Spain in 1884 was not a territory belonging to no-one (terra nullius).

41. If the international law notion that inhabited land may be classified as terra nullius no longer commands general support, the doctrines of the common law which depend on the notion that native peoples may be "so low in the scale of social organization" that it is "idle to impute to such people some shadow of the rights known to our law" (65) *In re Southern Rhodesia* (1919) AC, at pp 233-234 can hardly be retained. If it were permissible in past centuries to keep the common law in step with international law, it is imperative in today's world that the common law should neither be nor be seen to be frozen in an age of racial discrimination.

42. The fiction by which the rights and interests of indigenous inhabitants in land were treated as non-existent was justified by a policy which has no place in the contemporary law of this country. The policy appears explicitly in the judgment of the Privy Council in *In re Southern Rhodesia* in rejecting an argument (66) ibid., at p 232 that the native people "were the owners of the unalienated lands long before either the Company or the Crown became concerned with them and from time immemorial[...]and that the unalienated lands belonged to them still." Their Lordships replied (67) ibid., at p 234-

"the maintenance of their rights was fatally inconsistent with white
settlement of the country, and yet white settlement was the object of the
whole forward movement, pioneered by the Company and controlled by
the Crown, and that object was successfully accomplished, with the
result that the aboriginal system gave place to another prescribed by the
Order in Council."

Whatever the justification advanced in earlier days for refusing to recognize the rights and interests in land of the indigenous inhabitants of settled colonies, an unjust and discriminatory doctrine of that kind can no longer be accepted. The expectations of the international community accord in this respect with the contemporary values of the Australian people. The opening up of international remedies to individuals pursuant to Australia's accession to the Optional Protocol to the International Covenant on Civil and Political

Rights (68) See Communication 78/1980 in *Selected Decisions of the Human Rights Committee under the Optional Protocol*, vol.2, p 23 brings to bear on the common law the powerful influence of the Covenant and the international standards it imports. The common law does not necessarily conform with international law, but international law is a legitimate and important influence on the development of the common law, especially when international law declares the existence of universal human rights. A common law doctrine founded on unjust discrimination in the enjoyment of civil and political rights demands reconsideration. It is contrary both to international standards and to the fundamental values of our common law to entrench a discriminatory rule which, because of the supposed position on the scale of social organization of the indigenous inhabitants of a settled colony, denies them a right to occupy their traditional lands. It was such a rule which evoked from Deane J. (69) *Gerhardy v. Brown* (1985) 159 CLR 70, at p 149 the criticism that -

"the common law of this land has still not reached the stage of retreat from injustice which the law of Illinois and Virginia had reached in 1823 when Marshall C.J., in *Johnson v. McIntosh* (70) (1823) 8 wheat, at p 574 (21 US, at p 253), accepted that, subject to the assertion of ultimate dominion (including the power to convey title by grant) by the State, the 'original inhabitants' should be recognized as having 'a legal as well as just claim' to retain the occupancy of their traditional lands."

43. However, recognition by our common law of the rights and interests in land of the indigenous inhabitants of a settled colony would be precluded if the recognition were to fracture a skeletal principle of our legal system.

The proposition that the Crown became the beneficial owner of all colonial land on first settlement has been supported by more than a disregard of indigenous rights and interests. It is necessary to consider these other reasons for past disregard of indigenous rights and interests and then to return to a consideration of the question whether and in what way our contemporary common law recognizes such rights and interests in land.

Crown title to colonies and Crown ownership of colonial land distinguished...
44. In the trilogy of cases cited earlier in this judgment (71) Supra, pp 12-15: *Attorney-General v. Brown; Randwick Corporation v. Rutledge*; the Seas and Submerged Lands Case, it was said that colonial land became a royal demesne - that is, that the Crown became the absolute beneficial owner in possession of all colonial land - on first settlement, the event which conferred sovereignty on the Imperial Crown. Curiously, in *Williams v. Attorney-General for New South Wales* (72) (1913) 16 CLR 404, at p 439, Isaacs J. said it was unquestionable that -

Native Title in Australia

"when Governor Phillip received his first Commission from King
George III. on 12th October 1786, the whole of the lands of Australia
were already in law the property of the King of England."

With respect to Isaacs J., that proposition is wholly unsupported.

Roberts-Wray comments (73) *Commonwealth and Colonial Law* op cit, p
631 that the proposition is "startling and, indeed, incredible." We need not
be concerned with the date on which sovereignty over the Australian
colonies was acquired by the Crown but we are concerned with the
proposition that on, and by reason of, the acquisition of sovereignty, the
Crown acquired all colonial land as a royal demesne.

45. There is a distinction between the Crown's title to a colony and the
Crown's ownership of land in the colony, as Roberts-Wray points out (74)
ibid., p 625:

"If a country is part of Her Majesty's dominions, the sovereignty vested in
her is of two kinds. The first is the power of government. The second is title
to the country...

This ownership of the country is radically different from ownership of the
land: the former can belong only to a sovereign, the latter to anyone. Title
to land is not, per se, relevant to the constitutional status of a country; land
may have become vested in the Queen, equally in a Protectorate or in a
Colony, by conveyance or under statute...

The distinction between these two conceptions has, however, become
blurred by the doctrine that the acquisition of sovereignty over a
Colony, whether by settlement, cession or conquest, or even of
jurisdiction in territory which remains outside the British dominions,
imports Crown rights in, or in relation to, the land itself."

Similarly, Sir John Salmond distinguished the acquisition of territory from
the Crown's acquisition of property (75) *Jurisprudence*, 7th ed. (1924),
appendix "The Territory of the State," p 554:

"The first conception pertains to the domain of public law, the second
to that of private law. Territory is the subject-matter of the right of
sovereignty or imperium while property is the subject-matter of the right
of ownership or dominium. These two rights may or may not co-exist in
the Crown in respect of the same area. Land may be held by the Crown
as territory but not as property, or as property but not as territory, or in
both rights at the same time. As property, though not as territory, land
may be held by one state within the dominions of another."

Professor O'Connell in his work *International Law* (76) 2nd ed. (1970), at
p 378, cited by Hall J. in *Calder v. Attorney-General of British Columbia*
(1973) SCR.313, at pp 404-405; (1973) 34 DLR (3d) 145, at p 210 points
to the distinction between acquisition of territory by act of State and the
abolition of acquired rights:

"This doctrine (of act of State), which was affirmed in several cases
arising out of the acquisition of territory in Africa and India, has been

106   *The Present Politics of the Past*

misinterpreted to the effect that the substantive rights themselves have
not survived the change."
The acquisition of territory is chiefly the province of international law; the
acquisition of property is chiefly the province of the common law. The
distinction between the Crown's title to territory and the Crown's
ownership of land within a territory is made as well by the common law as
by international law. A.W.B. Simpson (77) *A History of the Land Law*, 2nd
ed. (1986) distinguishes the land law rule in England that all land is held of
the Crown from the notion that all land is owned by the Crown. Speaking
of the mediaeval conception of materialism, he comments (78) ibid., p 47:
"This attitude of mind also encouraged the rejection of any theory
which would say that the lord 'owned' the land, and that the rights of
tenants in the land were iura in re aliena. Such a theory would have led
inevitably to saying that the King, who was ultimately lord of all land,
was the 'owner' of all land.
The lawyers never adopted the premise that the King owned all the land;
such a dogma is of very modern appearance. It was sufficient for them
to note that the King was lord, ultimately, of all the tenants in the realm,
and that as lord he had many rights common to other lords (e.g., rights
to escheats) and some peculiar to his position as supreme lord (e.g.,
rights to forfeitures)."
The general rule of the common law was that ownership could not be
acquired by occupying land that was already occupied by another. As Blackstone pointed out (79) *Commentaries*, Bk.II, ch.1, p 8:
"Occupancy is the thing by which the title was in fact originally gained;
every man seizing such spots of ground as he found most agreeable to
his own convenience, provided he found them unoccupied by any one
else."
46. It was only by fastening on the notion that a settled colony was terra
nullius that it was possible to predicate of the Crown the acquisition of ownership of land in a colony already occupied by indigenous inhabitants. It was
only on the hypothesis that there was nobody in occupation that it could be
said that the Crown was the owner because there was no other. If that hypothesis be rejected, the notion that sovereignty carried ownership in its
wake must be rejected too. Though the rejection of the notion of terra nullius clears away the fictional impediment to the recognition of indigenous
rights and interests in colonial land, it would be impossible for the common
law to recognize such rights and interests if the basic doctrines of the
common law are inconsistent with their recognition.
[...]
53. If it be necessary to categorize an interest in land as proprietary in order
that it survive a change in sovereignty, the interest possessed by a
community that is in exclusive possession of land falls into that category.

Whether or not land is owned by individual members of a community, a community which asserts and asserts effectively that none but its members has any right to occupy or use the land has an interest in the land that must be proprietary in nature: there is no other proprietor. It would be wrong, in my opinion, to point to the inalienability of land by that community and, by importing definitions of "property" which require alienability under the municipal laws of our society(101) See, for example, *National Provincial Bank Ltd. v. Ainsworth* (1965) AC 1175, at pp 1247-1248, to deny that the indigenous people owned their land. The ownership of land within a territory in the exclusive occupation of a people must be vested in that people: land is susceptible of ownership, and there are no other owners. True it is that land in exclusive possession of an indigenous people is not, in any private law sense, alienable property for the laws and customs of an indigenous people do not generally contemplate the alienation of the people's traditional land. But the common law has asserted that, if the Crown should acquire sovereignty over that land, the new sovereign may extinguish the indigenous people's interest in the land and create proprietary rights in its place and it would be curious if, in place of interests that were classified as non-proprietary, proprietary rights could be created. Where a proprietary title capable of recognition by the common law is found to have been possessed by a community in occupation of a territory, there is no reason why that title should not be recognized as a burden on the Crown's radical title when the Crown acquires sovereignty over that territory. The fact that individual members of the community, like the individual plaintiff Aborigines in *Milirrpum*(102) (1971) 17 FLR, at p 272, enjoy only usufructuary rights that are not proprietary in nature is no impediment to the recognition of a proprietary community title. Indeed, it is not possible to admit traditional usufructuary rights without admitting a traditional proprietary community title. There may be difficulties of proof of boundaries or of membership of the community or of representatives of the community which was in exclusive possession, but those difficulties afford no reason for denying the existence of a proprietary community title capable of recognition by the common law. That being so, there is no impediment to the recognition of individual non-proprietary rights that are derived from the community's laws and customs and are dependent on the community title. A fortiori, there can be no impediment to the recognition of individual proprietary rights.

54. Once it is accepted that indigenous inhabitants in occupation of a territory when sovereignty is acquired by the Crown are capable of enjoying - whether in community, as a group or as individuals - proprietary interests

108 *The Present Politics of the Past*

in land, the rights and interests in the land which they had theretofore enjoyed under the customs of their community are seen to be a burden on the radical title which the Crown acquires. The notion that feudal principle dictates that the land in a settled colony be taken to be a royal demesne upon the Crown's acquisition of sovereignty is mistaken. However, that was not the only basis advanced to establish the proposition of absolute Crown ownership and the alternative bases must next be considered.

The "patrimony of the nation" basis of the proposition of absolute Crown ownership
55. In *Williams v. Attorney-General for New South Wales* (103) (1913) 16 CLR, at pp 449-450 and in *The Commonwealth v. Tasmania*. The Tasmanian Dam Case (104) (1983) 158 CLR 1, at pp 208-212, there are references to the importance of the revenue derived from exercise of the power of sale of colonial land. The funds derived from sales of colonial land were applied to defray the cost of carrying on colonial government and to subsidize emigration to the Australian Colonies. Further, the power to reserve and dedicate land for public purposes was important to the government and development of the Colonies as it remains important to the government and development of the Commonwealth and the States and Territories. Therefore it is right to describe the powers which the Crown - at first the Imperial Crown and later the Crown in right of the respective Colonies - exercised with respect to colonial lands as powers conferred for the benefit of the nation as a whole (105) *Re.g., v. Symonds* (1847) NZPCC 387, at p 395, but it does not follow that those were proprietary as distinct from political powers. Nor does it follow that a combination of radical title to land and a power of sale or dedication of that land was not a valuable asset of the Colonies. It can be acknowledged that the nation obtained its patrimony by sales and dedications of land which dispossessed its indigenous citizens and that, to the extent that the patrimony has been realized, the rights and interests of the indigenous citizens in land have been extinguished. But that is not to say that the patrimony was realized by sales and dedications of land owned absolutely by the Crown. What the Crown acquired was a radical title to land and a sovereign political power over land, the sum of which is not tantamount to absolute ownership of land. Until recent times, the political power to dispose of land in disregard of native title was exercised so as to expand the radical title of the Crown to absolute ownership but, where that has not occurred, there is no reason to deny the law's protection to the descendants of indigenous citizens who can establish their entitlement to rights and interests which survived the Crown's acquisition of sovereignty. Those are

Native Title in Australia

rights and interests which may now claim the protection of s.10(1) of the Racial Discrimination Act 1975 (Cth) which "clothes the holders of traditional native title who are of the native ethnic group with the same immunity from legislative interference with their enjoyment of their human right to own and inherit property as it clothes other persons in the community": *Mabo v. Queensland*(106) (1988) 166 CLR, at p 219.

The Royal Prerogative basis of the proposition of absolute Crown ownership

56. Mr Justice Evatt described ownership of vacant lands in a new colony as one of the proprietary prerogatives(107) See *The Attorney-General for New South Wales v. Butterworth and Co.* (Australia) Ltd. (1938) 38 SR (NSW) 195, at pp 246-247. But, as that author's lately published work on *The Royal Prerogative* shows (108) (1987), at pp 102-103, there was no judicial consensus as to whether title to ownership of the vacant lands in the Australian Colonies was vested in the King as representing the supreme executive power of the British Empire or in the Crown in right of the respective Colonies. The management and control of the waste lands of the Crown were passed by Imperial legislation to the respective Colonial Governments as a transfer of political power or governmental function not as a matter of title(109) *Williams v. Attorney-General for New South Wales* (1913) 16 CLR, at pp 453, 456. The suggestion that, after the passing of these powers to colonial governments the Crown commenced to hold Crown lands "in right of the colony"(110) Per Stephen J. in the Seas and Submerged Lands Case (1975) 135 CLR, at p 439; and note per O'Connor J. in *The State of South Australia v. The State of Victoria* (1911) 12 CLR 667, at pp 710-711 and held those lands in absolute ownership, involves the notion that ownership resided in the Executive Government whose legislature was vested with power to enact laws governing the management and control of colonial waste lands. But the Imperial Parliament retained the sovereign - that is, the ultimate - legislative power over colonial affairs, at least until the adoption of the Statute of Westminster (111) *Madzimbamuto v. Lardner-Burke* (1969) 1 AC 645, at p 722 and it is hardly to be supposed that absolute ownership of colonial land was vested in colonial governments while the ultimate legislative power over that land was retained by the Imperial Parliament. However, if the Crown's title is merely a radical title - no more than a postulate to support the exercise of sovereign power within the familiar feudal framework of the common law - the problem of the vesting of the absolute beneficial ownership of colonial land does not arise: absolute and beneficial Crown ownership can be acquired, if at all, by an exercise of the appropriate sovereign power.

110   *The Present Politics of the Past*

57. As none of the grounds advanced for attributing to the Crown an universal and absolute ownership of colonial land is acceptable, we must now turn to consider a further obstacle advanced against the survival of the rights and interests of indigenous inhabitants on the Crown's acquisition of sovereignty.

The need for recognition by the Crown of native title
58. The defendant contests the view that the common law recognizes the possession of rights and interests in land by indigenous inhabitants of British colonies and submits that, by the common law governing colonization, pre-existing customary rights and interests in land are abolished upon colonization of inhabited territory, unless expressly recognized by the new sovereign. There is a formidable body of authority, mostly cases relating to Indian colonies created by cession, to support this submission(112) *Secretary of State for India v. Bai Rajbai* (1915) LR 42 Ind App 229, at pp 237, 238-239; *Vajesingji Joravarsingji v. Secretary of State for India* (1924) LR 51 Ind App 357, at pp 360, 361; *Secretary of State for India v. Sardar Rustam Khan* (1941) AC 356, at pp 370-372. Thus Lord Dunedin's judgment in *Vajesingji Joravarsingji v. Secretary of State for India* contains the following oft-cited passage(113) (1924) LR 51 Ind App, at p 360:

"But a summary of the matter is this: when a territory is acquired by a sovereign state for the first time that is an act of state. It matters not how the acquisition has been brought about. It may be by conquest, it may be by cession following on treaty, it may be by occupation of territory hitherto unoccupied by a recognized ruler. In all cases the result is the same. Any inhabitant of the territory can make good in the municipal Courts established by the new sovereign only such rights as that sovereign has, through his officers, recognized. Such rights as he had under the rule of predecessors avail him nothing. Nay more, even if in a treaty of cession it is stipulated that certain inhabitants should enjoy certain rights, that does not give a title to those inhabitants to enforce these stipulations in the municipal Courts."

59. The proposition that pre-existing rights and interests in land must be established, if at all, under the new legal system introduced on an acquisition of sovereignty is axiomatic, and the proposition that treaties do not create rights enforceable in municipal courts is well established (114) *Cook v. Sprigg* (1899) AC 572, at pp 578-579; *Winfat Ltd. v. Attorney-General* (1985) AC 733, at p 746. However, the relevant question is whether the rights and interests in land derived from the old regime survive the acquisition of sovereignty or do they achieve recognition only upon an express act of recognition by the new sovereign? Lord Dunedin's view in *Vajesingji Joravarsingji*(115) (1924) LR 51 Ind App, at p 361 was that

Native Title in Australia

recognition by the sovereign of rights and interests possessed under the old regime was a condition of their recognition by the common law:

"The moment that cession is admitted the appellants necessarily become petitioners and have the onus cast on them of showing the acts of acknowledgment, which give them the right they wish to be declared."

Presumably, until the relevant "acts of acknowledgment" occur, the Crown would be the absolute owner of private property but, when those acts occur, the rights and interests acknowledged would revest in their erstwhile possessor. One might think that the consequence of such a rule would be to create or compound chaos. Of course, if the Crown were to confiscate private property as an act of State(116) As in *Secretary of State in Council of India v. Kamachee Boye Sahaba* (1859) 7 Moo Ind App 476 (19 ER 388); but cf. *Attorney-General v. Nissan* (1970) AC 179, at p 227, and *Burmah Oil Co. Ltd. v. Lord Advocate* (1965) AC 75 in acquiring sovereignty of a territory or if the Crown were to extinguish private property pursuant to a law having effect in the territory(117) As in *Winfat Ltd. v. Attorney-General* (1985) AC 733, thereafter no recognition of the rights and interests which had existed under the old regime would be possible. In either of those events, however, the loss of the rights or interests possessed under the old regime is attributable to the action of the Crown, not to an absence of an act of recognition of those rights or interests. Those cases apart, Lord Dunedin's view that the rights and interests in land possessed by the inhabitants of a territory when the Crown acquires sovereignty are lost unless the Crown acts to acknowledge those rights is not in accord with the weight of authority. For example, Lord Sumner in *In re Southern Rhodesia*(118) (1919) AC, at p 233 understood the true rule as to the survival of private proprietary rights on conquest to be that -

"it is to be presumed, in the absence of express confiscation or of subsequent exproprietary legislation, that the conqueror has respected them and forborne to diminish or modify them."

This view accords with the old authorities of The Case of Tanistry and Witrong and Blany(119) Supra, pp 37-38, earlier mentioned. Again, Lord Dunedin's view does not accord with the rule stated by Viscount Haldane in *Amodu Tijani*(120) (1921) 2 AC, at p 407:

"A mere change in sovereignty is not to be presumed as meant to disturb rights of private owners; and the general terms of a cession are prima facie to be construed accordingly."

His Lordship does not limit the generality of the first sentence to acquisitions by cession; rather, he appears to be construing the terms of a cession in the light of the general principle by which private proprietary rights survive a change in sovereignty by whatever means. Despite his judgment in *Vajesingji*

Joravarsingji, Viscount Dunedin subsequently accepted (121) In *Sakariyawo Oshodi v. Moriamo Dakolo* (1930) AC 667, at p 668 that the decision in *Amodu Tijani* laid down that the cession of Lagos in 1861 "did not affect the character of the private native rights." As Viscount Haldane's statement of the rule was limited neither to the construction of a treaty of cession nor to the cession of Lagos, must it not be taken as the general rule of the common law? Again Lord Denning, speaking for the Privy Council in *Adeyinka Oyekan v. Musendiku Adele*(122) (1957) 1 WLR 876, at p 880; (1957) 2 All ER 785, at p 788, said:

"In inquiring [...] what rights are recognized, there is one guiding principle. It is this: The courts will assume that the British Crown intends that the rights of property of the inhabitants are to be fully respected. Whilst, therefore, the British Crown, as Sovereign, can make laws enabling it compulsorily to acquire land for public purposes, it will see that proper compensation is awarded to every one of the inhabitants who has by native law an interest in it: and the courts will declare the inhabitants entitled to compensation according to their interests, even though those interests are of a kind unknown to English law."

We are not concerned here with compensation for expropriation but we are concerned with the survival of private rights and interests in land and their liability to be extinguished by action of the Crown. The rule in *Amodu Tijani* was followed by the Privy Council in *Sobhuza II. v. Miller* (123) (1926) AC, at p 525 where the title of an indigenous community, which their Lordships thought to be generally usufructuary in character, was held to survive as "a mere qualification of a burden on the radical or final title of whoever is sovereign," capable of being extinguished "by the action of a paramount power which assumes possession or the entire control of land."

60. In *Calder v. Attorney-General of British Columbia* (124) (1973) SCR, at p 416; contra per Judson J. at pp 328-330; (1973) 34 DLR (3d), at p 218; contra per Judson J. at pp 156, 157 Hall J. rejected as "wholly wrong" "the proposition that after conquest or discovery the native peoples have no rights at all except those subsequently granted or recognized by the conqueror or discoverer."

61. The preferable rule, supported by the authorities cited, is that a mere change in sovereignty does not extinguish native title to land. (The term "native title" conveniently describes the interests and rights of indigenous inhabitants in land, whether communal, group or individual, possessed under the traditional laws acknowledged by and the traditional customs observed by the indigenous inhabitants.) The preferable rule equates the indigenous inhabitants of a settled colony with the inhabitants of a conquered colony in respect of their rights and interests in land and recognizes in the indigenous

Native Title in Australia 113

inhabitants of a settled colony the rights and interests recognized by the Privy Council in *In re Southern Rhodesia* as surviving to the benefit of the residents of a conquered colony.

62. If native title survives the Crown's acquisition of sovereignty as, in my view, it does, it is unnecessary to examine the alternative arguments advanced to support the rights and interests of the Meriam people to their traditional land. One argument raised the presumption of a Crown grant arising from the Meriam people's possession of the Murray Islands from a time before annexation; another was the existence of a title arising after annexation in accordance with a supposed local legal custom under the common law whereby the Meriam people were said to be entitled to possess the Murray Islands. There are substantial difficulties in the way of accepting either of these arguments, but it is unnecessary to pursue them. It is sufficient to state that, in my opinion, the common law of Australia rejects the notion that, when the Crown acquired sovereignty over territory which is now part of Australia it thereby acquired the absolute beneficial ownership of the land therein, and accepts that the antecedent rights and interests in land possessed by the indigenous inhabitants of the territory survived the change in sovereignty.

Those antecedent rights and interests thus constitute a burden on the radical title of the Crown.

63. It must be acknowledged that, to state the common law in this way involves the overruling of cases which have held the contrary. To maintain the authority of those cases would destroy the equality of all Australian citizens before the law. The common law of this country would perpetuate injustice if it were to continue to embrace the enlarged notion of terra nullius and to persist in characterizing the indigenous inhabitants of the Australian colonies as people too low in the scale of social organization to be acknowledged as possessing rights and interests in land. Moreover, to reject the theory that the Crown acquired absolute beneficial ownership of land is to bring the law into conformity with Australian history. The dispossession of the indigenous inhabitants of Australia was not worked by a transfer of beneficial ownership when sovereignty was acquired by the Crown, but by the recurrent exercise of a paramount power to exclude the indigenous inhabitants from their traditional lands as colonial settlement expanded and land was granted to the colonists. Dispossession is attributable not to a failure of native title to survive the acquisition of sovereignty, but to its subsequent extinction by a paramount power. Before examining the power to extinguish native title, it is necessary to say something about the nature

114   *The Present Politics of the Past*

and incidents of the native title which, surviving the Crown's acquisition of
sovereignty, burdens the Crown's radical title.

The nature and incidents of native title
64. Native title has its origin in and is given its content by the traditional
laws acknowledged by and the traditional customs observed by the
indigenous inhabitants of a territory. The nature and incidents of native title
must be ascertained as a matter of fact by reference to those laws and
customs. The ascertainment may present a problem of considerable
difficulty, as Moynihan J. perceived in the present case. It is a problem that
did not arise in the case of a settled colony so long as the fictions were
maintained that customary rights could not be reconciled "with the
institutions or the legal ideas of civilized society"(125) *In re Southern
Rhodesia* (1919) AC, at p 233, that there was no law before the arrival of
the British colonists in a settled colony and that there was no sovereign
law-maker in the territory of a settled colony before sovereignty was
acquired by the Crown. These fictions denied the possibility of a native title
recognized by our laws. But once it is acknowledged that an inhabited
territory which became a settled colony was no more a legal desert than it
was "desert uninhabited" in fact, it is necessary to ascertain by evidence the
nature and incidents of native title.

Though these are matters of fact, some general propositions about native
title can be stated without reference to evidence.
65. First, unless there are pre-existing laws of a territory over which the
Crown acquires sovereignty which provide for the alienation of interests in
land to strangers, the rights and interests which constitute a native title can
be possessed only by the indigenous inhabitants and their descendants.
Native title, though recognized by the common law, is not an institution of
the common law and is not alienable by the common law. Its alienability is
dependent on the laws from which it is derived. If alienation of a right or
interest in land is a mere matter of the custom observed by the indigenous
inhabitants, not provided for by law enforced by a sovereign power, there is
no machinery which can enforce the rights of the alienee. The common law
cannot enforce as a proprietary interest the rights of a putative alienee whose
title is not created either under a law which was enforceable against the
putative alienor at the time of the alienation and thereafter until the change
of sovereignty or under the common law. And, subject to an important qualification, the only title dependent on custom which the common law will recognize is one which is consistent with the common law. Thus, in The Case

Native Title in Australia   115

of Tanistry, the Irish custom of tanistry was held to be void because it was founded in violence and because the vesting of title under the custom was uncertain (126) (1608) Davis (80 ER); 4th ed. Dublin (1762) English translation, at pp 94-99. The inconsistency that the court perceived between the custom of tanistry known to the Brehon law of Ireland and the common law precluded the recognition of the custom by the common law. At that stage in its development, the common law was too rigid to admit recognition of a native title based on other laws or customs, but that rigidity has been relaxed, at least since the decision of the Privy Council in *Amodu Tijani*. The general principle that the common law will recognize a customary title only if it be consistent with the common law is subject to an exception in favour of traditional native title.

66. Of course, since European settlement of Australia, many clans or groups of indigenous people have been physically separated from their traditional land and have lost their connexion with it. But that is not the universal position. It is clearly not the position of the Meriam people. Where a clan or group has continued to acknowledge the laws and (so far as practicable) to observe the customs based on the traditions of that clan or group, whereby their traditional connexion with the land has been substantially maintained, the traditional community title of that clan or group can be said to remain in existence. The common law can, by reference to the traditional laws and customs of an indigenous people, identify and protect the native rights and interests to which they give rise. However, when the tide of history has washed away any real acknowledgment of traditional law and any real observance of traditional customs, the foundation of native title has disappeared. A native title which has ceased with the abandoning of laws and customs based on tradition cannot be revived for contemporary recognition. Australian law can protect the interests of members of an indigenous clan or group, whether communally or individually, only in conformity with the traditional laws and customs of the people to whom the clan or group belongs and only where members of the clan or group acknowledge those laws and observe those customs (so far as it is practicable to do so). Once traditional native title expires, the Crown's radical title expands to a full beneficial title, for then there is no other proprietor than the Crown.

67. It follows that a right or interest possessed as a native title cannot be acquired from an indigenous people by one who, not being a member of the indigenous people, does not acknowledge their laws and observe their customs; nor can such a right or interest be acquired by a clan, group or member of the indigenous people unless the acquisition is consistent with the

laws and customs of that people. Such a right or interest can be acquired outside those laws and customs only by the Crown (127). This result has been reached in other jurisdictions, though for different reasons: see *Re.g., v. Symonds* (1847) NZPCC, at p 390; *Johnson v. McIntosh* (1823) 8 wheat, at p 586 (21 US, at p 259); *St. Catherine's Milling and Lumber Co. v. The Queen* (1887) 13 SCR 577, at p 599. Once the Crown acquires sovereignty and the common law becomes the law of the territory, the Crown's sovereignty over all land in the territory carries the capacity to accept a surrender of native title. The native title may be surrendered on purchase or surrendered voluntarily, whereupon the Crown's radical title is expanded to absolute ownership, a plenum dominium, for there is then no other owner(128) *St. Catherine's Milling and Lumber Co. v. The Queen* (1888) 14 App Cas, at p 55. If native title were surrendered to the Crown in expectation of a grant of a tenure to the indigenous title holders, there may be a fiduciary duty on the Crown to exercise its discretionary power to grant a tenure in land so as to satisfy the expectation (129) See *Guerin v. The Queen* (1984) 13 DLR (4th) 321, at pp 334, 339, 342-343, 356-357, 360-361, but it is unnecessary to consider the existence or extent of such a fiduciary duty in this case. Here, the fact is that strangers were not allowed to settle on the Murray Islands and, even after annexation in 1879, strangers who were living on the Islands were deported. The Meriam people asserted an exclusive right to occupy the Murray Islands and, as a community, held a proprietary interest in the Islands. They have maintained their identity as a people and they observe customs which are traditionally based. There was a possible alienation of some kind of interest in 2 acres to the London Missionary Society prior to annexation but it is unnecessary to consider whether that land was alienated by Meriam law or whether the alienation was sanctioned by custom alone. As we shall see, native title to that land was lost to the Meriam people in any event on the grant of a lease by the Crown in 1882 or by its subsequent renewal.

68. Second, native title, being recognized by the common law (though not as a common law tenure), may be protected by such legal or equitable remedies as are appropriate to the particular rights and interests established by the evidence, whether proprietary or personal and usufructuary in nature and whether possessed by a community, a group or an individual. The incidents of a particular native title relating to inheritance, the transmission or acquisition of rights and interests on death or marriage, the transfer of rights and interests in land and the grouping of persons to possess rights and interests in land are matters to be determined by the laws and customs of the indigenous inhabitants, provided those laws and customs are not so

Native Title in Australia

repugnant to natural justice, equity and good conscience that judicial sanctions under the new regime must be withheld: *Idewu Inasa v. Oshodi* (130) (1934) AC 99, at p 105. Of course in time the laws and customs of any people will change and the rights and interests of the members of the people among themselves will change too. But so long as the people remain as an identifiable community, the members of whom are identified by one another as members of that community living under its laws and customs, the communal native title survives to be enjoyed by the members according to the rights and interests to which they are respectively entitled under the traditionally based laws and customs, as currently acknowledged and observed. Here, the Meriam people have maintained their own identity and their own customs. The Murray Islands clearly remain their home country. Their land disputes have been dealt with over the years by the Island Court in accordance with the customs of the Meriam people.

69. Third, where an indigenous people (including a clan or group), as a community, are in possession or are entitled to possession of land under a proprietary native title, their possession may be protected or their entitlement to possession may be enforced by a representative action brought on behalf of the people or by a sub-group or individual who sues to protect or enforce rights or interests which are dependent on the communal native title. Those rights and interests are, so to speak, carved out of the communal native title. A sub-group or individual asserting a native title dependent on a communal native title has a sufficient interest to sue to enforce or protect the communal title (131) *Australian Conservation Foundation v. The Commonwealth* (1980) 146 CLR 493, at pp 530-531, 537-539, 547-548; *Onus v. Alcoa of Australia Ltd.* (1981) 149 CLR 27, at pp 35-36, 41-42, 46, 51, 62, 74-75. A communal native title ensures for the benefit of the community as a whole and for the sub-groups and individuals within it who have particular rights and interests in the community's lands.

70. The recognition of the rights and interests of a sub-group or individual dependent on a communal native title is not precluded by an absence of a communal law to determine a point in contest between rival claimants. By custom, such a point may have to be settled by community consensus or in some other manner prescribed by custom. A court may have to act on evidence which lacks specificity in determining a question of that kind. That is statutorily recognized in the case of the Murray Islands. The jurisdiction conferred on the Island Court by s.41(2)(b) of the Community Services (Torres Strait) Act 1984-1990 (Q.) includes a jurisdiction which must be exercised in accordance with the customs of the Meriam people. The Act provides -

118   *The Present Politics of the Past*

"An Island Court has jurisdiction to hear and determine -

...

    (b) disputes concerning any matter that -
      (i) is a matter accepted by the community resident in
      its area as a matter rightly governed by the usages
      and customs of that community; and
      (ii) is not a breach of the by-laws applicable within
      its area or of a law of the Commonwealth or the State
      or a matter arising under a law of the Commonwealth
      or the State; and shall exercise[...]that jurisdiction
      referred to in provision (b) in accordance with the
      usages and customs of the community within its
      area."

71. Whatever be the precision of Meriam laws and customs with respect to land, there is abundant evidence that land was traditionally occupied by individuals or family groups and that contemporary rights and interests are capable of being established with sufficient precision to attract declaratory or other relief. Although the findings made by Moynihan J. do not permit a confident conclusion that, in 1879, there were parcels of land in the Murray Islands owned allodially by individuals or groups, the absence of such a finding is not critical to the final resolution of this case. If the doctrine of *Attorney-General v. Brown* were applied to the Murray Islands, allodial ownership would have been no bar to the Crown's acquisition of universal and absolute ownership of the land and the extinguishing of all native titles. But, by applying the rule that the communal proprietary interests of the indigenous inhabitants survive the Crown's acquisition of sovereignty, it is possible to determine, according to the laws and customs of the Meriam people, contests among members of the Meriam people relating to rights and interests in particular parcels of land.

72. The native titles claimed by the Meriam people - communally, by group or individually - avoid the Scylla of the 1879 annexation of the Murray Islands to Queensland, but we must now consider whether they avoid the Charybdis of subsequent extinction.

The extinguishing of native title

73. Sovereignty carries the power to create and to extinguish private rights and interests in land within the Sovereign's territory (132) *Joint Tribal Council of the Passamaquoddy Tribe v. Morton* (1975) 528 Fed 2d 370, at p 376 n.6. It follows that, on a change of sovereignty, rights and interests in land that may have been indefeasible under the old regime become liable to

Native Title in Australia

extinction by exercise of the new sovereign power. The sovereign power may or may not be exercised with solicitude for the welfare of indigenous inhabitants but, in the case of common law countries, the courts cannot review the merits, as distinct from the legality, of the exercise of sovereign power(133) *United States v. Santa Fe Pacific Railroad Company* (1941) 314 US 339, at p 347; *Tee-Hit-Ton Indians v. United States* (1954) 348 US 272, at pp 281-285. However, under the constitutional law of this country, the legality (and hence the validity) of an exercise of a sovereign power depends on the authority vested in the organ of government purporting to exercise it: municipal constitutional law determines the scope of authority to exercise a sovereign power over matters governed by municipal law, including rights and interests in land.

74. In Queensland, the Crown's power to grant an interest in land is, by force of ss.30 and 40 of the Constitution Act of 1867 (Q.), an exclusively statutory power and the validity of a particular grant depends upon conformity with the relevant statute(134) *Cudgen Rutile (No.2) Ltd. v. Chalk* (1975) AC 520, at pp 533-534. When validly made, a grant of an interest in land binds the Crown and the Sovereign's successors (135) Halsbury, op cit, 4th ed., vol.8, par.1047. The courts cannot refuse to give effect to a Crown grant "except perhaps in a proceeding by scire facias or otherwise, on the prosecution of the Crown itself"(136) *Wi Parata v. Bishop of Wellington* (1877) 3 NZ(Jur) NS 72, at p 77. Therefore an interest validly granted by the Crown, or a right or interest dependent on an interest validly granted by the Crown cannot be extinguished by the Crown without statutory authority. As the Crown is not competent to derogate from a grant once made (137), a statute which confers a power on the Crown will be presumed (so far as consistent with the purpose for which the power is conferred) to stop short of authorizing any impairment of an interest in land granted by the Crown or dependent on a Crown grant. But, as native title is not granted by the Crown, there is no comparable presumption affecting the conferring of any executive power on the Crown the exercise of which is apt to extinguish native title.

75. However, the exercise of a power to extinguish native title must reveal a clear and plain intention to do so, whether the action be taken by the Legislature or by the Executive. This requirement, which flows from the seriousness of the consequences to indigenous inhabitants of extinguishing their traditional rights and interests in land, has been repeatedly emphasized by courts dealing with the extinguishing of the native title of Indian bands in North America. It is unnecessary for our purposes to consider the several juristic foundations - proclamation, policy, treaty or occupation - on which

native title has been rested in Canada and the United States but reference to the leading cases in each jurisdiction reveals that, whatever the juristic foundation assigned by those courts might be, native title is not extinguished unless there be a clear and plain intention to do so (138) *Calder v. Attorney-General of British Columbia* (1973) SCR, at p 404; (1973) 34 DLR (3d), at p 210; *Hamlet of Baker Lake v. Minister of Indian Affairs* (1979) 107 DLR (3d) 513, at p 552; *Re.g., v. Sparrow* (1990) 1 SCR.1075, at p 1094; (1990) 70 DLR (4th) 385, at p 401; *United States v. Santa Fe Pacific Railroad Co.* (1941) 314 US, at pp 353, 354; *Lipan Apache Tribe v. United States* (1967) 180 Ct Cl 487, at p 492. That approach has been followed in New Zealand (139) *Te Weehi v. Regional Fisheries Officer* (1986) 1 NZLR 680, at pp 691-692. It is patently the right rule.

76. A clear and plain intention to extinguish native title is not revealed by a law which merely regulates the enjoyment of native title (140) *Re.g., v. Sparrow* (1990) 1 SCR, at p 1097; (1990) 70 DLR (4th), at p 400 or which creates a regime of control that is consistent with the continued enjoyment of native title (141) *United States v. Santa Fe Pacific Railroad Co.* (1941) 314 US, at pp 353-354. A fortiori, a law which reserves or authorizes the reservation of land from sale for the purpose of permitting indigenous inhabitants and their descendants to enjoy their native title works no extinguishment.

77. The Crown did not purport to extinguish native title to the Murray Islands when they were annexed in 1879. In 1882, in purported exercise of powers conferred by the Crown Lands Alienation Act of 1876 (Q.), the Murray Islands were reserved from sale. The 1882 instrument of reservation has not been traced, and it is arguable that the 1876 Act did not apply to land in the Murray Islands for the Murray Islands were not part of Queensland when that Act was passed. That Act was repealed by the Crown Lands Act 1884 (Q.), which took its place. In 1912, a proclamation was made pursuant to s.180 of the Land Act 1910 which "permanently reserved and set apart" the Murray Islands "for use of the Aboriginal Inhabitants of the State." Section 180(1) of the Land Act 1910 empowered the Governor in Council to reserve any Crown land from sale or lease "which, in the opinion of the Governor in Council, is or may be required for public purposes." "Public purposes" included "Aboriginal reserves"(142) s.4. "Crown land" was defined by s.4 of the Land Act 1910 as follows:

"All land in Queensland, except land which is, for the time being -
  (a) Lawfully granted or contracted to be granted in fee-
      simple by the Crown; or
  (b) Reserved for or dedicated to public purposes; or

Native Title in Australia

121

(c) Subject to any lease or license lawfully granted by the
  Crown: Provided that land held under an occupation
  license shall be deemed to be Crown land."

If the Murray Islands had been effectively "reserved for public purposes" by the 1882 reservation, they would not have been "Crown land" by reason of par. (b) of the definition but, in that event, they would have fallen within s.180(3) which provided:

"All land heretofore reserved or set apart for any public purpose,
and the fee-simple whereof has not been granted by the Crown, shall
hereafter be deemed to be a reserve for public purposes under this Act,
and deemed to have been so reserved under this section."

Section 181 of the Land Act 1910 empowered the Governor in Council "without issuing any deed of grant, (to) place any land reserved, either temporarily or permanently, for any public purpose under the control of trustees; and may declare the style or title of such trustees and the trusts of the land." In 1939, the Governor in Council placed the Murray Islands reserve under the control of trustees but did not declare "the trusts of the land." By s.4(15) of The Land Act of 1962 (Q.) the reservation of the Murray Islands and the appointment of trustees of the reserve continue in force notwithstanding the repeal of the Land Act 1910 and are deemed to have been made under the analogous provisions of the Land Act 1962. Sections 334(1) and (3) and 335 are provisions analogous respectively to ss.180(1) and (3) and 181 of the Land Act 1910. The definition of "Crown land" in s.5 of the Land Act 1962 corresponds with the definition in the Land Act 1910.

78. No doubt the term "Crown land" was defined in these Acts in the belief, which has been current since *Attorney-General v. Brown*, that the absolute ownership of all land in Queensland is vested in the Crown until it is alienated by Crown grant. Nevertheless, the denotation of the term "Crown land" in the Land Act 1910 and the Land Act 1962 is the same whether the common law attributes to the Crown the radical title or absolute ownership. A difficulty of construction arises, however, in connection with the provisions relating to the removal of intruders from Crown land or land reserved for public purposes. Section 91 of the Crown Lands Alienation Act, for example, makes it an offence for a person to be found in occupation of any such land "unless lawfully claiming under a subsisting lease or licence." If this provision were construed as having denied to the Meriam people any right to remain in occupation of their land, there would have been an indication that their native title was extinguished. The Solicitor-General for Queensland conceded that, if s.91 applied - and he did not contend that it did – the Meriam people could lawfully have been driven into the sea at any

time after annexation and that they have been illegally allowed to remain on the Murray Islands ever since. Such a conclusion would make nonsense of the law. As Hall J. said of a similar proposition in *Calder v. Attorney-General of British Columbia* (143) (1973) SCR, at p 414; (1973) 34 DLR (3d), at p 217: "The idea is self-destructive." To construe s.91 or similar provisions as applying to the Meriam people in occupation of the Murray Islands would be truly barbarian. Such provisions should be construed as being directed to those who were or are in occupation under colour of a Crown grant or without any colour of right; they are not directed to indigenous inhabitants who were or are in occupation of land by right of their unextinguished native title.

79. Native title was not extinguished by the creation of reserves nor by the mere appointment of "trustees" to control a reserve where no grant of title was made. To reserve land from sale is to protect native title from being extinguished by alienation under a power of sale. To appoint trustees to control a reserve does not confer on the trustees a power to interfere with the rights and interests in land possessed by indigenous inhabitants under a native title. Nor is native title impaired by a declaration that land is reserved not merely for use by the indigenous inhabitants of the land but "for use of Aboriginal Inhabitants of the State" generally(144) Assuming that that term relates to all indigenous inhabitants of the State whether having any connection with the particular reserve or not: see *Corporation of the Director of Aboriginal and Islanders Advancement v. Peinkinna* (1978) 52 ALJR 286. If the creation of a reserve of land for Aboriginal Inhabitants of the State who have no other rights or interest in that land confers a right to use that land, the right of user is necessarily subordinate to the right of user consisting in legal rights and interests conferred by native title. Of course, a native title which confers a mere usufruct may leave room for other persons to use the land either contemporaneously or from time to time.

80. In this case, the Solicitor-General did not contend that if, contrary to his submissions, native title became, after annexation and without an act of recognition by the Crown, a legally recognized interest in the Murray Islands, the Crown had extinguished that title. He drew attention to the fact that the Meriam people had been left in peaceful occupation of the Murray Islands. For his part, counsel for the plaintiffs submitted that the State of Queensland had no power to extinguish native title. That argument proceeded on the footing that sovereignty is an attribute possessed only by an internationally recognized sovereign and that the Commonwealth answers that description but the States of the Commonwealth do not(145) Seas and Submerged Lands Case (1975) 135 CLR, at p 373. Although that

Native Title in Australia

123

proposition is significant in determining title to the territorial sea, seabed and airspace and continental shelf and incline, it has no relevance to the power to extinguish native title to land which is not a matter of international concern (146) ibid., at pp 373, 467. The sovereign powers which might be exercised over the waste lands of the Crown within Queensland were vested in the Colony of Queensland subject to the ultimate legislative power of the Imperial Parliament so long as that Parliament retained that power and, after Federation, subject to the Constitution of the Commonwealth of Australia. The power to reserve and dedicate land to a public purpose and the power to grant interests in land are conferred by statute on the Governor in Council of Queensland and an exercise of these powers is, subject to the Racial Discrimination Act, apt to extinguish native title. The Queensland Parliament retains, subject to the Constitution and to restrictions imposed by valid laws of the Commonwealth (147) *Mabo v. Queensland* (1988) 166 CLR 186, a legislative power to extinguish native title. This being so, it is necessary to consider the effect which the granting of leases over parts of the Murray Islands has had on native title before the Racial Discrimination Act came into force.

81. A Crown grant which vests in the grantee an interest in land which is inconsistent with the continued right to enjoy a native title in respect of the same land necessarily extinguishes the native title. The extinguishing of native title does not depend on the actual intention of the Governor in Council (who may not have adverted to the rights and interests of the indigenous inhabitants or their descendants), but on the effect which the grant has on the right to enjoy the native title. If a lease be granted, the lessee acquires possession and the Crown acquires the reversion expectant on the expiry of the term. The Crown's title is thus expanded from the mere radical title and, on the expiry of the term, becomes a plenum dominium.

Where the Crown grants land in trust or reserves and dedicates land for a public purpose, the question whether the Crown has revealed a clear and plain intention to extinguish native title will sometimes be a question of fact, sometimes a question of law and sometimes a mixed question of fact and law. Thus, if a reservation is made for a public purpose other than for the benefit of the indigenous inhabitants, a right to continued enjoyment of native title may be consistent with the specified purpose – at least for a time – and native title will not be extinguished. But if the land is used and occupied for the public purpose and the manner of occupation is inconsistent with the continued enjoyment of native title, native title will be extinguished. A reservation of land for future use as a school, a courthouse or a public office will not by itself extinguish native title: construction of the building,

124   *The Present Politics of the Past*

however, would be inconsistent with the continued enjoyment of native title which would thereby be extinguished. But where the Crown has not granted interests in land or reserved and dedicated land inconsistently with the right to continued enjoyment of native title by the indigenous inhabitants, native title survives and is legally enforceable.

82. As the Governments of the Australian Colonies and, latterly, the Governments of the Commonwealth, States and Territories have alienated or appropriated to their own purposes most of the land in this country during the last 200 years, the Australian Aboriginal peoples have been substantially dispossessed of their traditional lands. They were dispossessed by the Crown's exercise of its sovereign powers to grant land to whom it chose and to appropriate to itself the beneficial ownership of parcels of land for the Crown's purposes. Aboriginal rights and interests were not stripped away by operation of the common law on first settlement by British colonists, but by the exercise of a sovereign authority over land exercised recurrently by Governments. To treat the dispossession of the Australian Aborigines as the working out of the Crown's acquisition of ownership of all land on first settlement is contrary to history. Aborigines were dispossessed of their land parcel by parcel, to make way for expanding colonial settlement. Their dispossession underwrote the development of the nation. But, if this be the consequence in law of colonial settlement, is there any occasion now to overturn the cases which held the Crown to have become the absolute beneficial owner of land when British colonists first settled here? Does it make any difference whether native title failed to survive British colonization or was subsequently extinguished by government action? In this case, the difference is critical: except for certain transactions next to be mentioned, nothing has been done to extinguish native title in the Murray Islands. There, the Crown has alienated only part of the land and has not acquired for itself the beneficial ownership of any substantial area. And there may be other areas of Australia where native title has not been extinguished and where an Aboriginal people, maintaining their identity and their customs, are entitled to enjoy their native title. Even if there be no such areas, it is appropriate to identify the events which resulted in the dispossession of the indigenous inhabitants of Australia, in order to dispel the misconception that it is the common law rather than the action of governments which made many of the indigenous people of this country trespassers on their own land.

83. After this lengthy examination of the problem, it is desirable to state in summary form what I hold to be the common law of Australia with reference to land titles:

Native Title in Australia

1. The Crown's acquisition of sovereignty over the several parts of Australia cannot be challenged in an Australian municipal court.

2. On acquisition of sovereignty over a particular part of Australia, the Crown acquired a radical title to the land in that part.

3. Native title to land survived the Crown's acquisition of sovereignty and radical title. The rights and privileges conferred by native title were unaffected by the Crown's acquisition of radical title but the acquisition of sovereignty exposed native title to extinguishment by a valid exercise of sovereign power inconsistent with the continued right to enjoy native title.

4. Where the Crown has validly alienated land by granting an interest that is wholly or partially inconsistent with a continuing right to enjoy native title, native title is extinguished to the extent of the inconsistency. Thus native title has been extinguished by grants of estates of freehold or of leases but not necessarily by the grant of lesser interests (e.g., authorities to prospect for minerals).

5. Where the Crown has validly and effectively appropriated land to itself and the appropriation is wholly or partially inconsistent with a continuing right to enjoy native title, native title is extinguished to the extent of the inconsistency. Thus native title has been extinguished to parcels of the waste lands of the Crown that have been validly appropriated for use (whether by dedication, setting aside, reservation or other valid means) and used for roads, railways, post offices and other permanent public works which preclude the continuing concurrent enjoyment of native title. Native title continues where the waste lands of the Crown have not been so appropriated or used or where the appropriation and use is consistent with the continuing concurrent enjoyment of native title over the land (e.g., land set aside as a national park).

6. Native title to particular land (whether classified by the common law as proprietary, usufructuary or otherwise), its incidents and the persons entitled thereto are ascertained according to the laws and customs of the indigenous people who, by those laws and customs, have a connection with the land. It is immaterial that the laws and customs have undergone some change since the Crown acquired sovereignty provided the general nature of the connection between the indigenous people and the land remains. Membership of the indigenous people depends on biological descent from the indigenous people and on mutual recognition of a particular person's membership by that person and by the elders or other persons enjoying traditional authority among those people.

7. Native title to an area of land which a clan or group is entitled to enjoy under the laws and customs of an indigenous people is extinguished if the

clan or group, by ceasing to acknowledge those laws, and (so far as practicable) observe those customs, loses its connection with the land or on the death of the last of the members of the group or clan.

8. Native title over any parcel of land can be surrendered to the Crown voluntarily by all those clans or groups who, by the traditional laws and customs of the indigenous people, have a relevant connection with the land but the rights and privileges conferred by native title are otherwise inalienable to persons who are not members of the indigenous people to whom alienation is permitted by the traditional laws and customs.

9. If native title to any parcel of the waste lands of the Crown is extinguished, the Crown becomes the absolute beneficial owner.

84. These propositions leave for resolution by the general law the question of the validity of any purported exercise by the Crown of the power to alienate or to appropriate to itself waste lands of the Crown. In Queensland, these powers are and at all material times have been exercisable by the Executive Government subject, in the case of the power of alienation, to the statutes of the State in force from time to time. The power of alienation and the power of appropriation vested in the Crown in right of a State are also subject to the valid laws of the Commonwealth, including the Racial Discrimination Act. Where a power has purportedly been exercised as a prerogative power, the validity of the exercise depends on the scope of the prerogative and the authority of the purported repository in the particular case.

[...]

95. The plaintiffs seek declarations that the Meriam people are entitled to the Murray Islands -

"(a) as owners

(b) as possessors

(c) as occupiers, or

(d) as persons entitled to use and enjoy the said islands";

that - "the Murray Islands are not and never have been 'Crown Lands' within the meaning of the Lands Act 1962 (Qld) (as amended) and prior Crown lands legislation" and that the State of Queensland is not entitled to extinguish the title of the Meriam people.

96. As the Crown holds the radical title to the Murray Islands and as native title is not a title created by grant nor is it a common law tenure, it may be confusing to describe the title of the Meriam people as conferring "ownership," a term which connotes an estate in fee simple or at least an estate of freehold. Nevertheless, it is right to say that their native title is effective as against the State of Queensland and as against the whole world

Native Title in Australia

unless the State, in valid exercise of its legislative or executive power, extinguishes the title. It is also right to say that the Murray Islands are not Crown land because the land has been either "reserved for or dedicated to public purposes" or is "subject to [...] lease." However, that does not deny that the Governor in Council may, by appropriate exercise of his statutory powers, extinguish native title. The native title has already been extinguished over land which has been leased pursuant to powers conferred by the Land Act in force at the time of the granting or renewal of the lease. Accordingly, title to the land leased to the Trustees of the Australian Board of Missions has been extinguished and title to Dauar and Waier may have been extinguished. It may be that areas on Mer have been validly appropriated for use for administrative purposes the use of which is inconsistent with the continued enjoyment of the rights and interests of Meriam people in those areas pursuant to Meriam law or custom and, in that event, native title has been extinguished over those areas. None of these areas can be included in the declaration.

97. I would therefore make a declaration in the following terms:

Declare -

(1) that the land in the Murray Islands is not Crown land within the meaning of that term in s.5 of the Land Act 1962-1988 (Q.);

(2) that the Meriam people are entitled as against the whole world to possession, occupation, use and enjoyment of the island of Mer except for that parcel of land leased to the Trustees of the Australian Board of Missions and those parcels of land (if any) which have been validly appropriated for use for administrative purposes the use of which is inconsistent with the continued enjoyment of the rights and privileges of Meriam people under native title;

(3) that the title of the Meriam people is subject to the power of the Parliament of Queensland and the power of the Governor in Council of Queensland to extinguish that title by valid exercise of their respective powers, provided any exercise of those powers is not inconsistent with the laws of the Commonwealth.

NATIVE TITLE ACT 1993

(January 1, 1993)

An Act about native title in relation to land or waters, and for related Purposes

128   *The Present Politics of the Past*

Part 1-Preliminary 1 Short title
This Act may be cited as the Native Title Act 1993.

2 Commencement
Commencement of provisions on Royal Assent
(1) Sections 1 and 2 commence on the day on which this Act receives the Royal Assent.
Commencement of provisions by Proclamation
(2) Subject to subsection (3), the remaining provisions of this Act commence on a day or days to be fixed by Proclamation.
Forced commencement of provisions
(3) If a provision referred to in subsection (2) does not commence under that subsection within the period of 9 months beginning on the day on which this Act receives the Royal Assent, it commences on the first day after the end of that period.

3 Objects
Main objects
The main objects of this Act are:
(a) to provide for the recognition and protection of native title; and
(b) to establish ways in which future dealings affecting native title may proceed and to set standards for those dealings; and
(c) to establish a mechanism for determining claims to native title; and
(d) to provide for, or permit, the validation of past acts, and intermediate period acts, invalidated because of the existence of native title.

4 Overview of Act
Recognition and protection of native title
(1) This Act recognises and protects native title. It provides that native title cannot be extinguished contrary to the Act.
Topics covered
(2) Essentially, this Act covers the following topics:
(a) acts affecting native title (see subsections (3) to (6));
(b) determining whether native title exists and compensation for acts affecting native title (see subsection (7)).
Kinds of acts affecting native title
(3) There are basically 2 kinds of acts affecting native title:
(a) past acts (mainly acts done before this Act's commencement on 1 January 1994 that were invalid because of native title); and

Native Title in Australia 129

(b) future acts (mainly acts done after this Act's commencement that either validly affect native title or are invalid because of native title).
Consequences of past acts and future acts
(4) For past acts and future acts, this Act deals with the following matters:
(a) their validity;
(b) their effect on native title;
(c) compensation for the acts.
Intermediate period acts
(5) However, for certain acts (called intermediate period acts) done mainly before the judgment of the High Court in Wik Peoples v Queensland (1996) 187 CLR 1, that would be invalid because they fail to pass any of the future act tests in 47.

5 Act binds Crown
This Act binds the Crown in right of the Commonwealth, of each of the States, of the Australian Capital Territory, of the Northern Territory and of Norfolk Island. However, nothing in this Act renders the Crown liable to be prosecuted for an offence.

6 Application to external Territories, coastal sea and other waters
This Act extends to each external Territory, to the coastal sea of Australia and of each external Territory, and to any waters over which Australia asserts sovereign rights under the Seas and Submerged Lands Act 1973.

7 Racial Discrimination Act
(1) This Act is intended to be read and construed subject to the provisions of the Racial Discrimination Act 1975.
(2) Subsection (1) means only that:
(a) the provisions of the Racial Discrimination Act 1975 apply to the performance of functions and the exercise of powers conferred by or authorised by this Act; and
(b) to construe this Act, and thereby to determine its operation, ambiguous terms should be construed consistently with the Racial Discrimination Act 1975 if that construction would remove the ambiguity.
(3) Subsections (1) and (2) do not affect the validation of past acts or intermediate period acts in accordance with this Act.

8 Effect of this Act on State or Territory laws

This Act is not intended to affect the operation of any law of a State or a Territory that is capable of operating concurrently with this Act.

[...]

An Immediate Priority

The Mining Journal (March 19, 1993) [1]

[...]

The mining industry contributes virtually 50% of Australia's export earnings and many of the major mining and mineral developments are located in areas where Aboriginals may now seek land claims. Mabo raises doubt about the legality of existing mines and could cause of delay or cancellation of new mineral projects. For example, MIM believes it has legal title to its McArthur River lead/zinc/silver project in the Northern Territory and intends to proceed with a $A250 million development but the Northern Land Council, an Aboriginal advisory group, may well file a land claim. The issues are complex. Native title may have been vitiated by mining titles issued before 1975, which effectively transferred ownership of the land into private hands, but since 1975 the introduction of the Racial Discrimination Act prevents the abolition of land claim rights without compensation.

[...]

The Mabo ruling could have far more serious consequences for the mining industry. At least one company has reached agreement with aboriginals, paying compensation in return for a guarantee that no land claim is made, but the fragmented nature of Aboriginal society makes it difficult to gauge whether those making such agreements have the authority to do so. The industry is pressing for urgent action to clarify the existing laws. Unless Mabo is deemed a special case, there seems to be no simple compromise solution and it is a challenge which will tax the ingenuity of the incoming federal government to its fullest extent.

Australia Pushes For Native Title

The Mining Journal (October 22, 1993)[2]

[...]

Meanwhile the biggest lobbying campaign to date over the controversial Mabo decision which triggered Australia's land title debate (MJ, March 9, p.211) has been launched by the Association of Mining and Exploration

Native Title in Australia

Companies (AMEC). In a letter sent to 821 state and federal politicians and to 870 local government authorities, AMEC claims that the question of native title has "such potential for adverse impact" on the economy and social structure of the country that each and every Australian will "suffer in some way" unless the government alters its position and adopts a more conciliatory attitude with the states. Whilst the association has no philosophical objection to Aborigines owning land it does believe that "all Australians are equal before the law" and that there should be no privilege created for particular groups through any statute.

Court clears Aboriginal land rights act

Financial Times-London (March 17, 1995)
By Nikki Tait and AFP

[...]

The long-awaited decision from Australia's highest judicial authority was hailed as a victory for Aboriginal communities, and will have important implications, especially for Australia's mining industry.

It will also throw into immediate question some 8,000-plus land grants made over the past 15 months by the Western Australian government under its own rival 'Land (Titles and Traditional Usage) Act'. This was declared by the High Court yesterday to be unconstitutional. Mr. Richard Court, the Western Australian state premier, vowed to keep fighting the federal government at the political level, although he acknowledged that legal avenues had been exhausted.

[...]

THE WIK PEOPLES V. THE STATE OF QUEENSLAND & OTHERS; THE THAYORRE PEOPLE V. THE STATE OF QUEENSLAND & OTHERS (23 DECEMBER 1996) F.C. 96/044

ORDER

1. Each appeal allowed in part.
2. Set aside the answers given by Drummond J to Question 1B(b), (c) and (d) and Question 1C(b), (c) and (d). Affirm the answers given by Drummond J to Question 1C(a), Question 4 and Question 5.
3. Answer Questions 1B, 1C, 4 and 5 as follows:

132 The Present Politics of the Past

Question 1B

"If at any material time Aboriginal title or possessory title existed in respect of the land demised under the pastoral lease in respect of the Holroyd River Holding a copy of which is attached hereto (pastoral lease):

(a) [not pressed]

(b) does the pastoral lease confer rights to exclusive possession on the grantee? If the answer to (a) is 'no' and the answer to (b) is 'yes':

(c) does the creation of the pastoral lease that has these two characteristics confer on the grantee rights wholly inconsistent with the concurrent and continuing exercise of any rights or interests which might comprise such Aboriginal title or possessory title of the Wik Peoples and their predecessors in title which existed before the New South Wales Constitution Act 1855 (Imp) took effect in the Colony of New South Wales?

(d) did the grant of the pastoral lease necessarily extinguish all incidents of Aboriginal title or possessory title of the Wik Peoples in respect of the land demised under the pastoral lease?"

Answer

(b) No.

(c) Does not arise.

(d) Strictly does not arise but is properly answered No.

Question 1C

"If at any material time Aboriginal title or possessory title existed in respect of the land demised under the pastoral leases in respect of the Mitchellton Pastoral Holding No 2464 and the Mitchellton Pastoral Holding No 2540 copies of which are attached hereto (Mitchellton Pastoral Leases):

(a) was either of the Mitchellton Pastoral Leases subject to a reservation in favour of the Thayorre People and their predecessors in title of any rights or interests which might comprise such Aboriginal title or possessory title which existed before the New South Wales Constitution Act 1855 (Imp) took effect in the Colony of New South Wales?

(b) did either of the Mitchellton Pastoral Leases confer rights to exclusive possession on the grantee?

If the answer to (a) is 'no' and the answer to (b) is 'yes':

(c) does the creation of the Mitchellton Pastoral Leases that had these two characteristics confer on the grantee rights wholly inconsistent with the concurrent and continuing exercise of any rights or interests which might comprise such Aboriginal title or possessory title of the Thayorre People and their predecessors in title which existed before the New South Wales Constitution Act 1855 (Imp) took effect in the Colony of New South Wales?

Native Title in Australia

(d) did the grant of either of the Mitchellton Pastoral Leases necessarily extinguish all incidents of Aboriginal title or possessory title of the Thayorre People in respect of the land demised under either of the Mitchellton Pastoral Leases?"

Answer

(a) No.
(b) No.
(c) Does not arise.
(d) Strictly does not arise but is properly answered No.

Question 4

"May any of the claims in paras 48A to 53, 54 to 58(a), 59 to 61, 61A to 64 and 65 to 68 of the further amended statement of claim [being claims of alleged breach of fiduciary duty and failure to accord natural justice] be maintained against the State of Queensland or Comalco Aluminium Limited notwithstanding the enactment of the Comalco Act, the making of the Comalco Agreement, the publication in the Queensland Government Gazette of 22 March 1958 pursuant to s 5 of the Comalco Act of the proclamation that the agreement authorised by the Comalco Act was made on 16 December 1957 and the grant of Special Bauxite Mining Lease No 1?"

Answer

No.

Question 5

"May any of the claims in paras 112 to 116, 117 to 121, 122 to 124, 125 to 127, 128 to 132, and 141 to 143 of the further amended statement of claim [being claims of alleged breach of fiduciary duty and failure to accord natural justice] be maintained against the State of Queensland or Aluminium Pechiney Holdings Pty Ltd notwithstanding the enactment of the Aurukun Associates Agreement Act 1975, the making of the Aurukun Associates Agreement, the publication in the Queensland Government Gazette of the proclamation of the making of the agreement pursuant to the Act and the grant of Special Bauxite Mining Lease No 9?"

Answer

No.

134 The Present Politics of the Past

4. The respondents who opposed the orders sought in relation to Question 1B(b), (c) and (d) pay the costs of the proceedings in this Court of the Wik Peoples relating to that question.

5. The respondents who opposed the orders sought in relation to Question 1C(b), (c) and (d) pay the costs of the proceedings in this Court of the Thayorre People and the Wik Peoples relating to that question. The Thayorre People pay the costs of the proceedings in this Court of the respondents relating to Question 1C(a).

6. The Wik Peoples pay the respondents' costs of the proceedings in this Court relating to Questions 4 and 5.

7. Remit the matters to the Federal Court with respect to the costs of the proceedings before Drummond J or otherwise in that Court.
23 December 1996

[...]

BRENNAN CJ

[...]

1. Introduction

In proceedings brought in the Federal Court, the Wik Peoples and the Thayorre People claim to be the holders of native title over certain areas of land in Queensland. Those areas include or consist of land known as the Holroyd River Holding and the Mitchellton Pastoral Leases. In 1915 and 1919, pastoral leases had been granted by the Crown to non-Aboriginal lessees over the Mitchellton Pastoral Leases pursuant to The Land Act 1910 (Q) ("the 1910 Act"). In 1945, under the same Act a pastoral lease had been granted by the Crown to non-Aboriginal lessees over the Holroyd River Holding. In 1973, another pastoral lease had been granted over the same area under The Land Act 1962-1974 (Q) ("the 1962 Act")[1]. The Wik Peoples claim that their native title was not extinguished by the granting of pastoral leases but constitutes "a valid and enforceable interest in the land co-existing with the interests of the lessees under the Pastoral Leases and exercisable at all times during the continuation of the Pastoral Leases." The Thayorre People, who were joined as respondents to the Wik Peoples' application filed a cross-claim seeking, inter alia, declarations that:
"On their proper construction and in the events which happened the leases which the Crown granted over the Mitchellton Holding [in] 1915 and again

Native Title in Australia

[in] 1919 allowed the co-existence of use for pastoral purposes only by the lessees with use for the purposes of aboriginal title by the Thayorre people; [...]
Any reversion held by the Crown in respect of the Mitchellton leases was held in trust for the Thayorre people and the exercise by them of their aboriginal title over the claimed land; [and] At all times during the terms of the leases which the Crown granted over the Mitchellton Holding [...] the Thayorre people were entitled to the unimpaired enjoyment and exercise of their aboriginal title over the claimed lands."
[...]

2. The content of the pastoral leases
The first Mitchellton lease, issued under the 1910 Act in 1915, was forfeited for non-payment of rent in 1918. The second lease, issued under the 1910 Act in 1919, was surrendered in 1921. Possession was not taken by the lessees under either lease. Since 12 January 1922 the land has been reserved for the benefit of Aborigines or held for and on their behalf. The first Holroyd lease, issued under the 1910 Act in 1945, was surrendered in 1973. The second lease, issued under the 1962 Act, is for a term of 30 years from 1 January 1974. None of the leases contained an express reservation in favour of Aboriginal people. The power to issue leases under the 1910 Act was vested in the Governor in Council [4] by s 6:
"(1) Subject to this Act, the Governor in Council may, in the name of His Majesty, grant in fee-simple, or demise for a term of years, any Crown land within Queensland.
(2) The grant or lease shall be made subject to such reservations and conditions as are authorised or prescribed by this Act or any other Act, and shall be made in the prescribed form, and being so made shall be valid and effectual to convey to and vest in the person therein named the land therein described for the estate or interest therein stated.
(3) The rights of the Crown in gold and other minerals, and the reservations with respect to the same which are to be contained in all Crown grants and leases, are declared and prescribed in 'The Mining on Private Land Act of 1909.'
(4) In addition to any reservation authorised or prescribed by this Act or any other Act in any grant or lease made after the commencement of this Act, there may be reserved for any public purposes, whether specified or not, a part of the land comprised therein of an area to be specified, but without specifying the part of the land so reserved. And it is hereby declared that all such reservations in all grants and leases made before the commencement of this Act are valid to all intents and purposes."

Similar provisions are contained in s 6 of the 1962 Act, except that the sub-section dealing with the Crown's mineral rights is extended to cover the rights in petroleum declared and prescribed in The Petroleum Acts 1923 to 1958 (Q). "Crown land" was defined by s 4 of the 1910 Act as follows:

"All land in Queensland, except land which is, for the time being -
(a) Lawfully granted or contracted to be granted in fee-simple by the Crown; or
(b) Reserved for or dedicated to public purposes; or
(c) Subject to any lease or license lawfully granted by the Crown: Provided that land held under an occupation license shall be deemed to be Crown land."
An identical definition of the term appeared in s 5 of the 1962 Act.
The leases issued under the 1910 Act recited that the respective lessees were "entitled to a Lease of the Land described in the Schedule endorsed on these Presents for the term, and at the yearly rent, hereinafter mentioned, and with, under, and subject to the conditions, stipulations, reservations, and provisoes in the said Act, and hereinafter contained."
In consideration of the premises and the rent, the Crown did "DEMISE AND LEASE unto the said [lessee] (hereinafter with their Successors in title designated 'the Lessee') and their lawful assigns, ALL THAT portion of Land situated in [name of district] [...] to hold unto the Lessee and their lawful assigns, for pastoral purposes only, for and during the term of [number of years] [...] subject to the conditions and provisoes in Part III, Division I of the said Act, and to all other rights, powers, privileges, terms, conditions, provisions, exceptions, restrictions, reservations, and provisoes referred to [...] in [...] the said Act, and 'The Mining on Private Land Act of 1909'." In addition to the reservations in The Mining on Private Land Act, the second Mitchellton lease included reservations under The Petroleum Act of 1915. Both Holroyd leases included reservations under The Petroleum Act of 1923 (as amended) and the second Holroyd lease included reservations under the Mining Act 1968-1974.
The second Holroyd lease is not expressed to be limited "for pastoral purposes only" but otherwise is in similar terms although granted under the 1962 Act. It contains further express conditions requiring the lessees to erect a manager's residence and effect other improvements on the land (including fencing the land) within 5 years. Although question 1B relates to the operation and effect of the second Holroyd lease, the land title history of both of the parcels of land in question in these proceedings must take account of the operation and effect of the leases issued under the 1910 Act.

Native Title in Australia

137

For reasons that will appear, it is not necessary to examine the effect of the 1962 Act and the second Holroyd lease issued under that Act upon native title. It is sufficient to note that, in all material respects, the operation and effect on native title (if any then subsisted) of the pastoral lease issued under the 1962 Act would be the same as the operation and effect on native title of the pastoral leases issued under the 1910 Act. Hereafter, the references to particular sections are to the sections in the 1910 Act.

Each lease contained reservations with respect to the Crown's mineral rights and a reservation [5] in these terms:

"WE DO FURTHER RESERVE the right of any person duly authorised in that behalf by the Governor of Our said State in Council at all times to go upon the said Land, or any part thereof, for any purpose whatsoever, or to make any survey, inspection, or examination of the same."

The leases under the 1910 Act were issued "pursuant to Part III, Division I" of that Act and were expressed to be subject to "the conditions and provisoes of Part III, Division I." That Division provided for the Minister by notification to declare any Crown land to be open for pastoral lease and to specify "the areas to be leased, the term of the lease [...] and the rent per square mile during the term" [6]. Applications for a pastoral lease were lodged with a land agent and, when issued to a successful applicant, commenced "on the quarter day next ensuing after the date of acceptance of his application" [7]. The term of a lease was divided into 10-year periods, the rent for periods after the first being fixed by the Land Court [8]. Every lease was subject to the condition that the "lessee shall, during the term, pay an annual rent at the rate for the time being prescribed" [9].

The submissions on behalf of the Wik Peoples (the Wik submission) and the Thayorre People (the Thayorre submission) are directed to establishing two basic points: that the pastoral lessees did not acquire a right to exclusive possession of the land the subject of the leases and, even if they did, it is not the right to exclusive possession that extinguished native title but only the exercise of that right to exclude the holders of native title. These basic points were supplemented by two subsidiary arguments, namely, that native title was not extinguished but merely suspended during the term of a lease and that the Crown held any reversion as a fiduciary for the holders of native title. In addition submissions were made specific to the claims made against the mining companies.

The submissions made by the Wik and Thayorre Peoples were supported by some respondents and opposed by others. Leave to intervene was granted without objection to the States of Victoria, Western Australia and South Australia, the Northern Territory and (this being an exceptional case) to cer-

138   *The Present Politics of the Past*

tain Aboriginal Land Councils and representatives of certain other Aboriginal Peoples. The principal issues in the case were raised by the Wik and Thayorre Peoples on the one hand and by the State of Queensland on the other. These issues were addressed by other parties and interveners but it will be convenient to refer chiefly to those parties' submissions as the source of the submissions in the following discussion.

[...]

4. Inconsistency between a lessee's rights and the continued right to enjoy native title

The Wik and Thayorre submissions then raise their second basic point, namely, whether extinguishment of native title is effected by mere inconsistency between the continued right of indigenous inhabitants at common law to the enjoyment of native title and the pastoral lessee's right to exclusive possession created or conferred pursuant to the 1910 Act or whether it is a practical inconsistency between the exercise of those respective bundles of rights that can alone extinguish native title. These submissions contended for the latter view for the reason, it was submitted, that extinguishment required proof of a clear and plain intention to extinguish native title.

As I held in *Mabo* [No 2], native title "has its origin in and is given its content by the traditional laws acknowledged by and the traditional customs observed by the indigenous inhabitants of a territory" [74]. Those rights, although ascertained by reference to traditional laws and customs are enforceable as common law rights. That is what is meant when it is said that native title is recognised by the common law [75]. Unless traditional law or custom so requires, native title does not require any conduct on the part of any person to complete it, nor does it depend for its existence on any legislative, executive or judicial declaration. The strength of native title is that it is enforceable by the ordinary courts. Its weakness is that it is not an estate held from the Crown nor is it protected by the common law as Crown tenures are protected against impairment by subsequent Crown grant. Native title is liable to be extinguished by laws enacted by, or with the authority of, the legislature or by the act of the executive in exercise of powers conferred upon it [76]. Such laws or acts may be of three kinds: (i) laws or acts which simply extinguish native title; (ii) laws or acts which create rights in third parties in respect of a parcel of land subject to native title which are inconsistent with the continued right to enjoy native title; and (iii) laws or acts by which the Crown acquires full beneficial ownership of land previously subject to native title.

Native Title in Australia

A law or executive act which, though it creates no rights inconsistent with native title, is said to have the purpose of extinguishing native title, does not have that effect "unless there be a clear and plain intention to do so" [77]. Such an intention is not to be collected by enquiry into the state of mind of the legislators or of the executive officer but from the words of the relevant law or from the nature of the executive act and of the power supporting it. The test of intention to extinguish is an objective test.

A law or executive act which creates rights in third parties inconsistent with a continued right to enjoy native title extinguishes native title to the extent of the inconsistency, irrespective of the intention of the legislature or the executive and whether or not the legislature or the executive officer adverted to the existence of native title [78]. In reference to grants of interests in land by the Governor in Council, I said in *Mabo* [No 2] [79]:

"A Crown grant which vests in the grantee an interest in land which is inconsistent with the continued right to enjoy a native title in respect of the same land necessarily extinguishes the native title. The extinguishing of native title does not depend on the actual intention of the Governor in Council (who may not have adverted to the rights and interests of the indigenous inhabitants or their descendants), but on the effect which the grant has on the right to enjoy the native title."

Third party rights inconsistent with native title can be created by or with the authority of the legislature in exercise of legislative power but, as the power of State and Territory legislatures is now confined by the Racial Discrimination Act 1975 (Cth), a State or Territory law made or executive act done since that Act came into force cannot effect an extinguishment of native title if the law or executive act would not effect the extinguishment of a title acquired otherwise than as native title [80].

The third category includes laws and acts by which the Crown acquires a full beneficial ownership that extinguishes native title. That may occur by acquisition of native title by or under a statute, in which case the question is simply whether the power of acquisition has been validly exercised. Or the Crown, without statutory authority, may have acquired beneficial ownership simply by appropriating land in which no interest has been alienated by the Crown. (Such an acquisition by the Crown in right of a State or Territory would have occurred, if at all, before the Racial Discrimination Act came into force.) In the latter case, the appropriation of the land gives rise to the Crown's beneficial ownership only when the land is actually used for some purpose inconsistent with the continued enjoyment of native title - for example, by building a school or laying a pipeline. Until such a use takes place, nothing has occurred that might affect the legal status

140 *The Present Politics of the Past*

quo. A mere reservation of the land for the intended purpose, which does not create third party rights over the land, does not alter the legal interests in the land[81], but the Crown's exercise of its sovereign power to use unalienated land for its own purposes extinguishes, partially or wholly, native title interests in or over the land used[82].

In considering whether native title has been extinguished in or over a particular parcel of land, it is necessary to identify the particular law or act which is said to effect the extinguishment and to apply the appropriate test to ascertain the effect of that law or act and whether that effect is inconsistent with the continued right to enjoy native title. In the present case, it would be erroneous, after identifying the relevant act as the grant of a pastoral lease under the 1910 Act to inquire whether the grant of the lease exhibited a clear and plain intention to extinguish native title. The question is not whether the Governor in Council intended or exhibited an intention to extinguish native title but whether the right to exclusive possession conferred by the leases on the pastoral lessees was inconsistent with the continued right of the holders of native title to enjoy that title.

On the issue of a pastoral lease under the 1910 Act, the lessee acquired an estate. There is no legal principle which would defer the vesting of, or qualify, that estate in order to allow the continuance of a right to enjoy native title. Given that the pastoral lessee acquired a right to exclusive possession at latest when the lease was issued, there was an inconsistency between that right and the right of any other person to enter or to remain on the land demised without the lessee's consent. Assuming that access to the land is an essential aspect of the native title asserted, inconsistency arises precisely because the rights of the lessee and the rights of the holders of native title cannot be fully exercised at the same time. As Mahoney J observed in *Hamlet of Baker Lake v Minister of Indian Affairs*[83] with reference to Indian land rights in Canada:

"The coexistence of an aboriginal title with the estate of the ordinary private land holder is readily recognized as an absurdity. The communal right of aborigines to occupy it cannot be reconciled with the right of a private owner to peaceful enjoyment of his land. However, its coexistence with the radical title of the Crown to land is characteristic of aboriginal title."

If a holder of native title had only a non-accessory right, there may be no inconsistency between that right and the rights of a pastoral lessee.

The law can attribute priority to one right over another, but it cannot recognise the co-existence in different hands of two rights that cannot both be exercised at the same time [84]. To postulate a test of inconsistency not between the rights but between the manner of their exercise would be to

Native Title in Australia

141

deny the law's capacity to determine the priority of rights over or in respect of the same parcel of land. The law would be incapable of settling a dispute between the holders of the inconsistent rights prior to their exercise, to the prejudice of that peaceful resolution of disputes which reduces any tendency to self-help. To postulate extinguishment of native title as dependent on the exercise of the private right of the lessee (rather than on the creation or existence of the private right) would produce situations of uncertainty, perhaps of conflict. The question of extinguishment of native title by a grant of inconsistent rights is - and must be - resolved as a matter of law, not of fact. If the rights conferred on the lessee of a pastoral lease are, at the moment when those rights are conferred, inconsistent with a continued right to enjoy native title, native title is extinguished [85].

The submission that inconsistency in the practical enjoyment of the respective rights of the native title holders and of the pastoral lessees, not inconsistency between the rights themselves, determines whether native title has been extinguished is founded on the notion that the 1910 Act and pastoral leases should be given a restrictive operation so as to permit, as far as possible, the continued existence of native title. If that notion is not applied, there is "a significant moral shortcoming in the principles by which native title is recognised," to adopt a dictum of French J [86].

So much can be admitted. The position of the traditional Aboriginal inhabitants of the land demised by the Mitchellton leases is a good illustration. If it be right to hold that the mere grant of those leases extinguished the native title of the traditional Aboriginal inhabitants, the law will be held to destroy the legal entitlement of the inhabitants to possess and enjoy the land on which they are living and on which their forebears have lived since time immemorial. That would be a significant moral shortcoming. But the shortcoming cannot be remedied by denying the true legal effect of the 1910 Act and pastoral leases issued thereunder, ascertained by application of the general law. The questions for decision by this Court are whether, on the issue of the Mitchellton and Holroyd River leases under s 6 of the 1910 Act, there was an inconsistency between the rights of the lessees and the continued right of the Wik and Thayorre Peoples to enjoy their native title and, if there were an inconsistency, which set of rights prevailed. For the reasons stated, the lessees had the right of exclusive possession and that right was inconsistent with native title (except for non-accessory rights, if any) and, as the right of exclusive possession was conferred on the lessees by the Crown as the sovereign power, that right prevailed and the rights of the holders of native title were extinguished.

142   *The Present Politics of the Past*

That does not mean that the holders of native title became trespassers. Their continued presence on the land would have been expected and probably known by the lessees. Unless the lessees took some action to eject them, their presence on the land would have been impliedly consented to. It appears that the holders of native title were never trespassers on the Mitchellton leases and, if their occupation of the Holroyd River Holding was not objected to, they were never trespassers on that land. Nevertheless, consistently with s 6(2), the inhabitants of the land demised became liable to exclusion by the lessee once the lease issued. From this it follows that native title could not co-exist with the leasehold estate.

The holders of native title did not acquire a possessory title. A possessory title arises from possession that is adverse to the title of the true owner. Until the Crown lessees acquired their respective titles, the holders of native title held the land by virtue of that title. After the Crown lessees acquired their titles, the continued occupation by the erstwhile holders of native title is explicable by lessors' consent rather than by possession adverse to the lessors' possession.

The next question is: was native title extinguished on and by the issuing of the leases or was native title merely suspended during the terms of the respective leases? The answer to this question depends on the nature of the Crown's reversion.

5. The nature of the Crown's reversion

In *Mabo* [No 2] I expressed the view [87]:

"If a lease be granted, the lessee acquires possession and the Crown acquires the reversion expectant on the expiry of the term. The Crown's title is thus expanded from the mere radical title and, on the expiry of the term, becomes a plenum dominium."

If this be the correct view, there is no occasion for the revival of native title. The Crown's title to the land on reversion would be inconsistent with a continued right to enjoy native title. The Wik and Thayorre submissions together raise two grounds of challenge to the view I expressed in *Mabo* [No 2]: first, that a pastoral lease is issued in exercise of a statutory power, not in exercise of the Crown's proprietary rights in the land and that the interest of the Crown on reversion is no more than the radical title or, alternatively, no more than the minimum proprietary interest required to support the leasehold interest possessed by the lessee; and second, the rights and interest of the native title holders are suspended only to the extent necessary to admit the interest of the pastoral lessee and, on expiry of the term [88] or earlier determination of the lease, revive [89].

Native Title in Australia

143

The Wik and Thayorre submissions treat the grant of a pastoral lease as no more than an exercise of a statutory power conferring statutory rights, having no significance for the Crown's beneficial interest in the land demised. So viewed, the way is open to contend that native title is merely suspended during the currency of a lease and, when the lease is determined, the Crown has no reversionary interest but only its original radical title burdened by the native title. It is submitted that, although s 135 of the 1910 Act provided that on forfeiture or other determination of a lease prior to expiry of the term "the land shall revert to His Majesty and become Crown land, and may be dealt with under this Act accordingly," that section said nothing as to the Crown's legal and beneficial interest in the land but merely ensured that the Crown dealt with the land after it reverted to His Majesty in accordance with the Act. This argument accounts for the application of s 135 to the expiry of licenses as well as to the determination of leases.

If it were right to regard Crown leaseholds not as estates held of the Crown but merely as a bundle of statutory rights conferred on the lessee, it would be equally correct to treat a "grant in fee simple" not as the grant of a freehold estate held of the Crown but merely as a larger bundle of statutory rights. If the grant of a pastoral lease conferred merely a bundle of statutory rights exercisable by the lessee over land subject to native title in which the Crown (on the hypothesis advanced) had only the radical title, the rights of the lessee would be jura in re aliena: rights in another's property. And, if leases were of that character, an estate in fee simple would be no different. Then in whom would the underlying or residual common law title subsist? Presumably, in the holders of native title. But such a theory is inconsistent with the fundamental doctrines of the common law [90]. And it would equate native title with an estate in fee simple which, ex hypothesi, it is not. To regard interests derived from the Crown as a mere bundle of statutory rights would be to abandon the whole foundation of land law applicable to Crown grants. In Mabo [No 2], Deane and Gaudron JJ declared that the general common law system of land law applied from the establishment of the first Australian colony. Their Honours said [91]:

"It has[...]long been accepted as incontrovertible that the provisions of the common law which became applicable upon the establishment by settlement of the Colony of New South Wales included that general system of land law [92]. It follows that, upon the establishment of the Colony, the radical title to all land vested in the Crown. Subject to some minor and presently irrelevant matters, the practical effect of the vesting of radical title in the Crown was merely to enable the English system of private ownership of estates held of the Crown to be observed in the Colony. In particular, the mere fact that the radical title to all the lands of the Colony was vested in the British Crown did not preclude the preservation and protection, by the domestic law of the new Colony, of any traditional native interests in land which had existed under native law or custom at the time the Colony was established."

The English system of private ownership of estates held of the Crown rests on "two fundamental doctrines in the law of real property" [93], namely, the doctrine of tenure and the doctrine of estates.

By the interlocking doctrines of tenure and estates, the land law provides for the orderly enjoyment in succession of any parcel of land. The doctrine of tenure creates a single devolving chain of title and the doctrine of estates provides for the enjoyment of land during successive periods [94]. The doctrines of tenure (with its incident of escheat [95]) and estates ensure that no land in which the Crown has granted an interest is ever without a legal owner [96]. The creation of a tenure, however limited the estate in the particular parcel of land may be, establishes exhaustively the entire proprietary legal interests which may be enjoyed in that parcel of land. If the interests alienated by the Crown do not exhaust those interests, the remaining proprietary interest is vested in the Crown. In *In re Mercer and Moore* [97], Jessel MR said:

"If a freehold estate comes to an end by death without an heir, or by attainder, it goes back to the Crown on the principle that all freehold estate originally came from the Crown, and that where there is no one entitled to the freehold estate by law it reverts to the Crown."

In this country, the Crown takes either by reversion on expiry of the interest granted or by escheat on failure of persons to take an interest granted. It is unnecessary for present purposes to distinguish between them [98].

By exercise of a statutory power to alienate an estate in land, the Crown creates, subject to statute, a tenure [99] between the Crown and the alienee. It follows that, subject to statute - and all powers of alienation of interests in land in Australia are governed by statute [100] - where a leasehold estate is the only proprietary interest granted by the Crown in a parcel of land [101] and the lessee is in possession, a legal reversionary interest must be vested in the Crown. Such an interest is the necessary foundation for the existence of a right to forfeit for breach of condition [102].

An exercise of the statutory power of alienation of an estate in land brings the land within the regime governed by the doctrines of tenure and estates. Once land is brought within that regime, it is impossible to admit an interest which is not derived mediately or immediately from a Crown grant or which is not carved out from either an estate or the Crown's reversionary title.

Native Title in Australia

Native title is not a tenure [103]; it is not an interest held of the Crown, mediately or immediately. It is derived solely from the traditional laws and customs of the indigenous peoples. Consistently with our constitutional history and our legal system, it is recognised as a common law interest in land provided it has not been extinguished by statute, by a valid Crown grant of an estate inconsistent with the continued right to enjoy native title or by the Crown's appropriation and use of land inconsistently with the continued enjoyment of native title. As the majority judgment in *Western Australia v The Commonwealth*. Native Title Act Case [104] said:

"Under the common law, as stated in *Mabo* [No 2], Aboriginal people and Torres Strait Islanders who are living in a traditional society possess, subject to the conditions stated in that case, native title to land that has not been alienated or appropriated by the Crown."

It was only in respect of unalienated and unappropriated land that native title was recognised as subsisting. Thus I noted in *Mabo* [No 2] [105]:

"As the Governments of the Australian Colonies and, latterly, the Governments of the Commonwealth, States and Territories have alienated or appropriated to their own purposes most of the land in this country during the last two hundred years, the Australian Aboriginal peoples have been substantially dispossessed of their traditional lands. They were dispossessed by the Crown's exercise of its sovereign powers to grant land to whom it chose and to appropriate to itself the beneficial ownership of parcels of land for the Crown's purposes."

Native title is not recognised in or over land which has by alienation become subject to inconsistent rights or which has by Crown use become unavailable for continued enjoyment of native title.

The provisions of the 1910 Act admit of no interest in land the subject of a pastoral lease being held by any person other than the Crown, the lessee and persons taking an interest under the lease. Historically, it is impossible to suppose that Parliament, in enacting the 1910 Act (or, for that matter, the 1962 Act) might have intended that any person other than the Crown should have any reversionary interest in land subject to a pastoral lease. In 1910 (as in 1962), no recognition was accorded by Australian courts to the existence of native title in or over land in Australia. On the contrary, the common understanding was that, from the beginning of colonial settlement, Crown grants were made out of the Crown's proprietary title to all land in the colony [106]. The 1910 Act makes it clear that, on the issue of a pastoral lease, the reversion was held by the Crown. Rent was a debt "due to His Majesty" [107], the Minister was the recipient of a notice of intention to surrender [108] and forfeiture was enforced only if the Governor in Council so decided [109]. On forfeiture, the land reverted to His Majesty [110]; on forfeiture or surrender, improvements to the property were deemed to be vested in the Crown but were to be paid for by the "incoming lessee, selector, or purchaser" [111]; and provision was made for dealing with land "pursuant to a certificate given under 'The Escheat (Procedure and Amendment) Act, 1891'" [112]. The last-mentioned Act provided a simplified procedure for ascertaining "the failure of the heirs or next-of-kin of an intestate, or the alienage of a grantee, or such other facts, as may be necessary to establish the title of Her Majesty in right of the Crown or otherwise" [113]. The procedure was prescribed in order to determine, inter alia, questions arising "as to the title of Her Majesty in right of the Crown to any land or interest in land in any case of escheat or alleged escheat" [114]. Thus, the 1910 Act treated the Crown as having not only the power to issue a lease and thus entitle the lessee to a leasehold estate but also as having the reversionary interest which, under the ordinary doctrines of the common law, a lessor had to possess in order to support and enforce the relationship of landlord and tenant. The 1910 Act also conferred certain statutory rights on pastoral lessees, the exercise of which would require the carving of further proprietary interests out of the reversion. The lessee of a pastoral lease whose term had expired had *a priority* right [115], if the land was then open to selection[116], to apply for a selection, some categories of which conferred a right to acquire the selection in fee simple [117] and others a right to take it on perpetual lease [118]. These interests were clearly intended to be carved out of the Crown's reversionary title, not out of the title of a third party.

The Wik submission then denies the Crown's title to the reversion on the ground that it is not assignable. That objection could as easily be raised to the proprietary interest of the Crown. But the Crown "assigns" a proprietary interest in its land by grant unless the Crown has acquired an interest that is assignable, for example, the interest of a sub-lessor.

It is only by treating the Crown, on exercise of the power of alienation of an estate, as having the full legal reversionary interest that the fundamental doctrines of tenure and estates can operate. On those doctrines the land law of this country is largely constructed. It is too late now to develop a new theory of land law that would throw the whole structure of land titles based on Crown grants into confusion. Moreover, a new theory which undermines those doctrines would be productive of uncertainty having regard to the nature of native title. That is a problem which will be examined in the next section.

Native Title in Australia

6. Temporary suspension of native title

The second limb of the Wik and Thayorre attack on the notion of the Crown's title on reversion limits that title to a nominal period after the determination of the lease. This submission is supported by the thirteenth respondent ("ATSIC") which submits that the Crown should not be taken, upon the granting of a limited estate, to appropriate to itself ownership of the reversion for an unlimited time. At common law, a lessor who grants a leasehold estate needs an estate out of which the leasehold estate is carved [119], else there can be no demise [120]. The lessor needs no more to support the grant than an estate greater (or deemed to be greater) than the estate granted [121]. The demise in a pastoral lease would be supported if the Crown's reversion were limited to some nominal period beyond the term of the lease. That would be a sufficient estate to allow the Crown to enforce conditions binding on the lessee [122].

Must the Crown's title be treated as any greater when the land is subject to a claim of native title? The hypothesis of the submission must be that native title subsists notwithstanding the demise of the land for the term of the pastoral lease and that the Crown acquires no more than a nominal proprietary interest sufficient to support the lease. Upon the determination of the lease, native title revives - assuming there are persons who satisfy the qualifications of native title holders - and burdens the Crown's radical title in the same way as native title burdened that title prior to alienation. Logically, this hypothesis would attribute to the Crown no more than a radical title (that is essentially a power of alienation controlled by statute) whenever there might be a gap in or cesser of the proprietary interest of an alienee. It would treat that proprietary interest as a bundle of statutory rights to which the doctrines of tenure and estates had no necessary application. No land would escheat to the Crown, at least while there were any surviving holders of native title. That cannot be accepted. Even if the grant of a lease were seen merely as an exercise of sovereign power and not as an alienation of property, the land would go back to the Crown on the determination of the lease, if not as a matter of title then as a matter of seigniory [123].

Nevertheless, the hypothesis seems to be internally consistent. But it fails to attribute to the doctrines of tenure and estates their function of maintaining the skeleton of the law of real property unless native title is treated as the equivalent of an estate in remainder, falling into possession on the determination of a prior estate. Of course, native title is not an estate and to treat native title as falling into possession on the determination of a prior estate is to create problems of title not easy to resolve. If the holders of native title were recognised as the owners of an estate in remainder in the land, could the priority right to a selection enjoyed by a lessee [124] be exercised? And would the holders of native title have become liable to pay for the improvements to the land affected during the expired lease? [125] To what extent was the discretion to enforce a forfeiture against a lessee affected by the supposed subsistence of native title in the land? In the unusual event of the determination of an estate in fee simple, would the land revert to the Crown or would it be taken by the holders of native title? And, since the Racial Discrimination Act 1975 (Cth) commenced, would the provisions[126] which annex statutory rights to a pastoral lease (for example, a right to receive an offer of a new lease) be ineffective by reason of s 109 of the Constitution?

These questions indicate some of the problems that arise once the fundamental doctrines that govern the title to land granted by the Crown under the 1910 Act are departed from. In my opinion, the common law could not recognise native title once the Crown alienated a freehold or leasehold estate under that Act. Consequently, the common law was powerless to recognize native title as reviving after the determination of a pastoral lease issued under the 1910 Act. Does equity provide any relief to the erstwhile holders of native title?

7. The claims for equitable relief

The Wik and Thayorre submissions assert the existence of a fiduciary duty owed by the Crown to the indigenous inhabitants of the leased areas. The duty is said to arise from the vulnerability of native title, the Crown's power to extinguish it and the position occupied for many years by the indigenous inhabitants vis-á-vis the Government of the State. These factors do not by themselves create some free-standing fiduciary duty. It is necessary to identify some action or function the doing or performance of which attracts the supposed fiduciary duty to be observed [127]. The doing of the action or the performance of the function must be capable of affecting the interests of the beneficiary and the fiduciary must have so acted [128] that it is reasonable for the beneficiary to believe and expect that the fiduciary will act in the interests of the beneficiary (or, in the case of a partnership or joint venture, in the common interest of the beneficiary and fiduciary [129]) to the exclusion of the interest of any other person or the separate interest of the beneficiary [130].

In the present case the only relevant function performed by the Crown is the exercise of the power of alienation. That is the only power the exercise of which relevantly affects native title. With all respect for the opposing view, I am unable to accept that a fiduciary duty can be owed by the Crown to the

Native Title in Australia

holders of native title in the exercise of a statutory power to alienate land whereby their native title in or over that land is liable to be extinguished without their consent and contrary to their interests.

The exercise of statutory powers characteristically affects the rights or interests of individuals for better or worse. If the exercise of a discretionary power must affect adversely the rights or interests of individuals, it is impossible to suppose that the repository of the power shall so act that the beneficiary might expect that the power will be exercised in his or her interests. The imposition on the repository of a fiduciary duty to individuals who will be adversely affected by the exercise of the power would preclude its exercise. On the other hand, a discretionary power - whether statutory or not - that is conferred on a repository for exercise on behalf of, or for the benefit of, another or others might well have to be exercised by the repository in the manner expected of a fiduciary [131]. Thus in *Guerin v The Queen* [132], the Crown accepted a surrender by an Indian band of native title to land in order that the land be leased by the Crown to a third party. The statutory scheme which provided for the surrender to the Crown and its subsequent dealing with the land imposed on the Crown the duty to act "on the band's behalf" [133], as "the appointed agent of the Indians [...] and for their benefit" [134] or for their "use and benefit" [135]. Similarly, in the United States the statutory scheme for dealing with Indian land requires the sanction of a "treaty or convention entered into pursuant to the Constitution" [136]. The scheme has its origin in the Indian Nonintercourse Act 1790 (US) [137] which, in its successive forms, has been held to impose on the Federal Government "a fiduciary duty to protect the lands covered by the Act" [138].

The power of alienation conferred on the Crown by s 6 of the 1910 Act is inherently inconsistent with the notion that it should be exercised as agent for or on behalf of the indigenous inhabitants of the land to be alienated. Accordingly, there is no foundation for imputing to the Crown a fiduciary duty governing the exercise of the power.

This conclusion precludes the acceptance of a further submission made on behalf of the Wik and Thayorre Peoples. That submission sought to impose a constructive trust in their favour of the Crown's reversionary interest in the leased land. If the constructive trust be viewed as a remedial institution, as Deane J viewed it in *Muschinski v Dodds* [139], it is nevertheless available "only when warranted by established equitable principles or by the legitimate processes of legal reasoning, by analogy, induction and deduction, from the starting point of a proper understanding of the conceptual foundation of such principles" [140]. Given that no fiduciary duty was breached by the Crown in issuing the pastoral leases under s 6 of the 1910 Act and that the issue of those leases destroyed native title, there is no principle of law or equity which would require the imposition of a constructive trust on the reversion to restore what the holders of native title had lost.

The Wik submission raises another equitable basis of relief. It is said that, by reason of the acquiescence of the State and the pastoral lessees in the continued exercise by the Wik Peoples of their native title rights, it would be unconscionable now to hold them liable to ejectment without investigation of the basis or bases on which they have remained in occupation. The propounded basis of relief depends, of course, on contested issues of fact but that basis was not pleaded. Prior to the hearing in this Court, the submission was not argued. It would not be appropriate to express any view on the merits of the submission at this stage. This appeal relates to the answers given by Drummond J to the questions determined as preliminary issues. Those questions turn on the subsistence of native title, not on the existence of an equity which would entitle the Wik Peoples to remain on the land to continue to exercise the rights which they would have been entitled to enjoy if native title still subsisted.

In the result, I would hold the answers given by Drummond J to questions 1B and 1C to be correct. The Wik and Thayorre Peoples' claims fail because native title was extinguished on the issue of the leases under s 6 of the 1910 Act. It is unnecessary to advert to the effect of the 1962 Act. The principles of the law may thus be thought to reveal "a significant moral shortcoming" which can be rectified only by legislation or by the acquisition of an estate which would allow the traditions and customs of the Wik and Thayorre Peoples to be preserved and observed. Those avenues of satisfaction draw on the certainty of proprietary rights created by the sovereign power. Such rights, unlike the rights of the holders of native title, are not liable to extinguishment by subsequent executive action.

8. Claims against Comalco, Pechiney and Queensland

The Commonwealth Aluminium Corporation Pty Limited Agreement Act 1957 (Q) ("the Comalco Act") provided for the making of an agreement between the State of Queensland and Comalco. Section 2 provides:

"The Premier and Chief Secretary is hereby authorised to make, for and on behalf of the State of Queensland, with Commonwealth Aluminium Corporation Pty Limited, a company duly incorporated in the said State and having its registered office at 240 Queen Street, Brisbane, in the said State,

Native Title in Australia 151

the Agreement a copy of which is set out in the Schedule to this Act (herein referred to as 'the Agreement')."

Section 3 provides:

"Upon the making of the Agreement the provisions thereof shall have the force of law as though the Agreement were an enactment of this Act.

The Governor in Council shall by Proclamation notify the date of the making of the Agreement."

The Agreement set out in the schedule required the State, inter alia, to grant to Comalco a Special Bauxite Mining Lease for an initial term of 84 years [141]. The form of lease was prescribed [142]. The Agreement was made on 16 December 1957 and the lease was issued on 3 June 1965 as ML7024.

The Wik submission contends that the Agreement and ML7024 were entered into in disregard of the rules of procedural fairness and in breach of the State's fiduciary duty to the Wik Peoples and that Comalco was a party to that breach. It is further contended that the State and Comalco were unjustly enriched by the breach. Relief is claimed on the footing that the decisions to enter into the Agreement and to grant ML7024 were invalid and that the Agreement and ML7024 are invalid. The relief claimed relates to impairment or loss of the Wik Peoples' enjoyment of native title rights and possessory rights in or over the land leased and the benefits derived by Comalco from exploiting the lease. Comalco's response is that, as s 3 gives the Agreement the force of law, no claim by the Wik Peoples can be based on any irregularity or breach of duty that might have occurred in the course of negotiating or executing the Agreement.

Section 3 was referred to by Dunn J in *Commonwealth Aluminium Corporation Limited v Attorney-General* [143] in these terms:

"By providing, in s 3, that upon the making of the Agreement its provisions 'shall have the force of law as though the Agreement were an enactment of this Act,' legal effect is given to provisions which otherwise would lack such effect, because of such legislation as I have already discussed. The Agreement remains something apart from the Act, however, the legislative artifice adopted in order to give it effect does not make it, in point of law, 'an enactment of this Act'."

This judgment led to the submission that the effect of s 3 was limited to the overriding of particular legislative impediments to the making or implementation of the Agreement. That is too narrow a view of the operation of s 3. To take one example: that view would not admit that mandamus might have gone to compel the granting of the Special Bauxite Mining Lease pursuant to cl 8 of the Agreement, although the State's obligation to grant that lease was the leading purpose of the Comalco Act.

152   *The Present Politics of the Past*

However, the sufficiency of the Comalco response turns on the operation attributed to s 2 as well as to s 3 of the Comalco Act. Although s 2 authorises, but does not command, the Premier and Chief Secretary to make the Agreement, the authorisation it gives is unqualified by any requirement as to the performing of a fiduciary duty or the according of natural justice. So soon as the Agreement is in fact made, s 3 operates to give it the force of law "as though [it] were an enactment of this Act." It follows that, the Agreement having been made, the powers conferred by the Agreement acquire the force of statutory powers. Thus s 3 operates to give validity to what is done in their exercise [144]. Therefore the granting of the Special Bauxite Mining Lease was valid. Moreover, whatever consequences flowed to the Wik Peoples from the granting of that lease could not be actionable loss or damage, for those consequences were the result of an act sanctioned by the Comalco Act.

Nor could relief be granted in relation to the benefits derived by Comalco's exploitation of the lease for those benefits flowed to Comalco from the granting of the lease pursuant to legislative authority.

The Comalco response is thus good in law.

The Wik claim against Aluminium Pechiney Holdings Pty Limited (Pechiney) and the submission in support arise from the making and implementing of an Agreement (the "Associates Agreement") authorised by the Aurukun Associates Agreement Act 1975 (Q). The Associates Agreement provided for the grant of a Special Bauxite Mining Lease [145] for 42 years [146] in a form set out in the Fourth Schedule to that Agreement [147]. The provisions of the Aurukun Associates Agreement Act, the allegations in the statement of claim with respect to the making of the Associates Agreement under that Act and the relief claimed are indistinguishable from the provisions of the Comalco Act and the allegations and the relief claimed against Comalco. Pechiney's response, substantially identical to Comalco's response, is also good in law. The claim against Pechiney seeks relief in respect of an earlier agreement (the "Access Agreement") between the Director of Aboriginal and Islanders' Advancement and certain corporations including Pechiney. The Access Agreement was scheduled to the Associates Agreement, the latter being given the force of law. The third respondent (The Aboriginal and Islander Affairs Corporation) is the statutory successor of the Director and is sued in that capacity. An account is sought against both Pechiney and the third respondent by reason of their entry into the Access Agreement and the obtaining of benefits under it. However, in *The Corporation of the Director of Aboriginal and Islanders Advancement v Peinkinna*[148] the

Native Title in Australia

Privy Council held that the Aurukun Associates Agreement Act ratified the Access Agreement and recognised it as valid and subsisting. There is no reason to dissent from that view, the consequence of which is that neither entry into the Access Agreement nor the obtaining of benefits under it can give rise to a cause of action in the Wik Peoples. It follows that the answers given by Drummond J to questions 4 and 5 were correct.

I would dismiss the appeals and make orders for costs against the Wik Peoples and the Thayorre People in favour of those parties who opposed their claims. I would make no order as to the costs to be paid to or by other parties.

[...]

A Victory for commonsense and fairness

ATSIC Press Release (December 23, 1996) [3]

ATSIC Chairman, Mr. Gatjil Djerrkura, has welcomed today's Decision by the High Court in the Wik Case as confirming the reality of native title in Australian law.

"The decision by the High Court is grounded in common sense." Mr. Djerrkura said. "It is inherently fair, both to native title holders and to others with land interests, including pastoralists."

Mr. Djerrkura said the Decision built on the earlier landmark Decisions by the High Court in Mabo and in this year's Waanyi Case. There is a clear trend in the Decisions to the effect that native title is an integral part of Australian law, which cannot be lightly brushed aside on narrow legalistic or sectional grounds.

"Native title is an important right, and it is clear that indigenous people have to be able to exercise that right, to make claims, and to negotiate in good faith with other parties, such as miners and pastoralists, with interest in native title land.

"Although the Wik decision is confined in its immediate effects to Queensland, it can now reasonably be assumed that native title may also not be extinguished on pastoral leases in other State and Territory jurisdictions, if there is also no clear intent in statutes or leases to exclude traditional indigenous rights."

Mr. Djerrkura said the decision is a great step forward in establishing certainty about native title in Australia. Up to now there had been disagreement about whether native title could co-exist with pastoral leases.

"As pastoral leases cover a considerable portion of the Australian continent this had created some difficulties for all concerned. The situation has now been clarified to a very considerable degree, and the basic uncertainty surrounding the possibility of co-existence of pastoral leases and native title has been settled.

"It is clear that native title claims in respect of pastoral leases are to be taken seriously, with the particulars of any situation depending on the facts of the matter. This is fair and reasonable."

Mr Djerrkura said that Aboriginal native title holders are happy to negotiate with pastoralists and others about the use of native title lands, and to reach co-operative arrangements.

"The Cape York Heads of Agreement provides a good model of how negotiations can lead to agreements of benefit to all parties including miners and pastoralists. As well, overseas experience has shown that there really is no practical alternative but to negotiate with indigenous interests in order to develop positive and constructive arrangements and agreements."

Mr. Djerrkura called on the Government to accept the Wik decision in the spirit of it being a fair and commonsense outcome.

"In respect of the Government's total package of amendments to the Native Title Act, due to be debated by Parliament in February 1997, I propose that, in the light of today's decision, the consideration of the amendments by Parliament be postponed. I urge the Government to meet with indigenous representatives across the negotiating table, with clear ground rules, to identify areas where the operation of the Act can be improved without reducing the rights of native title holders."

Mr. Djerrkura noted that any attempt to reverse the Wik Decision by legislation, either by direct extinguishment or by some form of indirect extinguishment, would be strongly opposed by indigenous Australians and would be inconsistent with the Australian ethos of a fair go - particularly given the historical context of dispossession.

"Any attempt to strip away rights recognised by the highest court in the land would open Australia up to international criticism.

"Today's Wik Decision is an important milestone in the development of an Australian society based on fairness and equity and one which acknowledges the place of Aboriginal and Torres Strait Islanders.

"It is a victory for commonsense and fairness."

Statement by Mr. Gatjil Djerrkura, Chairman ATSIC

ATSIC Press Release (February 14, 1997)[4]

Native Title in Australia

Prime Minister and Delegates:

On behalf of the Indigenous representatives, and the indigenous people of Australia whom we represent today, I would like to thank you, Prime Minister, for convening this meeting to discuss the Wik Decision and other native title matters.

Indigenous people look forward to a positive process of negotiations with industry and with the Commonwealth, State and Territory Governments.

Like others, we will be looking to practical and just resolution of any problems which may exist. To achieve such outcomes we believe negotiations must be inclusive, frank, transparent, and conducted in the spirit of good faith.

The starting point for Indigenous people in this negotiation process is that the decisions of the courts of this land have at last brought recognition of our rights to land. Furthermore, the Australian legal system now acknowledges and protects them.

The Native Title Act 1993 provides a legislative framework for the recognition and protection of native title and for dealings in land where native title may exist. This Act is very important to us.

It may indeed be possible to improve the workability of some of the procedures of the Act. Indigenous representatives are willing to play a constructive role in identifying improved procedures.

However, Indigenous people will not accept any winding back of the rights which are enshrined in the Act, including the right of Indigenous people to negotiate over developments on native title land.

In approaching these negotiations we have identified 7 principles. As you will recall, Prime Minister, in our meeting with you last Thursday we put these forward as the basis of the Indigenous position. I would like to go through these principles again for the benefit of others present. They are:

1. The Commonwealth adopt a non-discriminatory policy in dealing with the property rights of all Australians.
2. There must be no extinguishment or impairment of native title.
3. There must be no implied or direct amendment to the Racial Discrimination Act 1975 or deviation from its principles.
4. The Commonwealth must respect the native title decisions of the High Court of Australia.
5. There must be no amendments to the Native Title Act 1993 which erode existing Indigenous rights, particularly in relation to the right to negotiate and the effective extinguishment or impairment of native title rights by the expansion or conversion of pastoral interests.

156

6. There must be no amendments to erode the Indigenous Land Fund, its functions and its focus.

7. The Commonwealth agree to a process for negotiations with Indigenous people over :

the proposed amendments to the Native Title Act 1993; and the consequences of the Wik decision.

In concluding, I wish to emphasise that we wish to see a real commitment to dealing with our property rights in a non-discriminatory fashion.

As well, we believe the current package of amendments should be set aside until a due process of negotiations about these matters has been concluded. Thank you.

Wik decision courts trouble

ABIX: Australasian Business Intelligence (March 7, 1997 Friday)
By Alan Moran

The High Court has done the Australian economy a disservice by creating Native Title; Native Title is little more than a tax that requires extensive negotiation prior to it being paid; the basis of Native Title is money
[...]

O'Chee Hails Changes To Wik Legislation

AAP NEWSFEED (August 26, 1997)

[...]
"We don't want to have the absurd situation, which we're getting in some places in Queensland at the moment, of people who have never been on the land for two generations lobbing in from Inala (a Brisbane suburb) and saying, 'look, we're going to put a native title claim over this'," Senator O'Chee said.

He said it was bad luck if Aborigines had lost their connection with their land, just as his family was locked out of its property in China when the communists took over.

[...]

Aboriginies Label Wik Bill An Insidious Attack

AAP NEWSFEED (September 4, 1997)

Native Title in Australia

[...]
Spokesman Aden Ridgeway said the group believed the Native Title Amendment Bill would ensure Aborigines continued to be marginalised. "It is designed to achieve the bucket-loads of extinguishment, as described by the Deputy Prime Minister, but I think it will also achieve bucket-loads of litigation," he said.
"It goes far beyond Wik and it is an insidious attack on the indigenous rights of Aboriginal people and Torres Strait Islander people in this country.
[...]
"These amendments will do nothing other than wreck reconciliation because of their unfairness to indigenous Australians," he said.
"This is a bill for everyone except indigenous people in this country."
[...]

Government Suppresses Native Title Legal Submission
AAP NEWSFEED (September 29, 1997)

The federal government had ordered the suppression of an Australian Law Reform Commission (ALRC) submission which argued changes to Wik native title legislation would be unconstitutional, the Sydney Morning Herald said today.
The ALRC also noted the government's proposed Wik legislation would result in Australia being taken to the United Nations for major breaches of our international human rights obligations, the paper said. Commission officers had been forbidden by the government from giving evidence before a parliamentary inquiry into the legislation, the paper said, and the government had barred the submission from appearing.
[...]

Anglicans Urge MPs To Protect Native Title Act
AAP NEWSFEED (October 13, 1997)

[...]
In an impassioned speech, the Reverend Colin Griffiths described changes proposed under Prime Minister John Howard's 10 point Wik plan as "procedural repression."
"The prime minister's plan and subsequent legislation reverses all the work done towards co-existence and is nothing more than procedural repression," Mr. Griffiths said to thunderous applause.

"The bill is steeped in racial discrimination," he said.
"It opens the way for wholesale extinguishment of the property rights of one race only - namely Aboriginal and Torres Strait Islanders."
[...]

Katter says the bush angered at Wik bill's passing
AAP NEWSFEED (October 30, 1997)

People in the bush would not forget their treatment under the federal government's Wik native title legislation, National Party backbencher Bob Katter said today.
[...]
"I would interpret his remarks as providing us with some hope that we might be given ownership of our station properties back and that our wives and kids might be able to live in some form of security."

Wik amendments only just an improvement say Aborigines
AAP NEWSFEED (November 24, 1997)

[...]
Ms. Havnen said the term legal apartheid, expressed yesterday by chairman of the Cape York land council Noel Pearson, was not a bad description of what Aboriginals could end up with.
"The fact that the government is willing to even consider discriminatory legislation, one then could draw that conclusion that it would also form the basis of some kind of legal apartheid.
"That is that our rights are being treated in a much more discriminatory fashion than other rights of other people, and only on the basis of race."

A Vision Based on Rights
ATSIC Press Release (November 24, 1997)

Aboriginal and Torres Strait Islander people have made clear their desire to see ATSIC provide firm leadership, the ATSIC Chairman, Gatjil Djerrkura, said today.
Launching the ATSIC Corporate Plan 1998 – 2001, Mr. Djerrkura said that the document resulted from the Board's consultation over the past year with ATSIC Regional Councils, indigenous peak bodies and communities.

Native Title in Australia 159

"You can hear our people's voices in this third ATSIC corporate plan," Mr. Djerrkura said. "They all sent back a strong message that they want ATSIC to speak out strongly for protection of our rights in this country. ATSIC takes this responsibility very seriously."

Mr. Djerrkura said ATSIC's vision is based firmly on the concept of indigenous rights — the rights due to the original owners of this land.

"I don't want indigenous Australians to go on being defined by our disadvantage. Having rights means having choices about where we live, who we associate with, what sort of work we do and how our children are educated.

"We want our people to have the choice to be educated in our own languages, and to pass on our values to our children. Our people must be free from victimisation on the basis of race.

"Resources need to go back into our communities. We have a right to these resources as our citizenship entitlement. After all, many of our people have been forcibly removed from our lands and therefore from our economic, social, cultural and spiritual base.

"The reality is that governments come and go. But our people have been part of this land for tens of thousands of years. Our spirituality, our laws, our culture, have nurtured this country and sustained its people."

Mr. Djerrkura said that as ATSIC is both part of government and not part of government, there will always be tensions between the Board and the government of the day.

"But these should be creative tensions," he said.

"Other Australians acknowledge our culture sometimes, when they use it to give colour and interest to the national culture. We ask you to extend this recognition to other crucial areas of life and politics.

"We don't need your sympathy. We need government commitment. We seek your respect."

Government wants freehold to extinguish native title

AAP NEWSFEED (November 27, 1997)

[...]

He said he made it clear yesterday that the government understood that freehold did extinguish native title and the bill confirmed that native title was extinguished by freehold. "The real story is why won't the Labor Party support our amendments that provide that freehold extinguishes native title," he said on ABC radio.

160   *The Present Politics of the Past*

"They are refusing to support our amendments that provide that exclusive leasehold tenure extinguishes native title because they think that preempts the common law and will unnecessarily extinguish native title. That will expose 60,000 leases to potential native title claims."
[...]

Address To The Nation by Kim Beazley
AAP NEWSFEED (December 1, 1997)

[...]
"Last night Mr. Howard spoke of the native title debate as a kind of uncomfortable distraction - something we should be getting over with quickly, putting behind us. Moving on to something more important.
But the reason this has become such a big issue for debate is that a great many Australians think it is important, has to be got right - and have still to be persuaded that the government has got it right. They're worried that the government bill simply can't and won't deliver the certainty that everyone is now crying out for. They want the best, and fairest, and most workable balance between all the different interests.
[...]

Dangerous Haste In The Wik Debate
The Canberra Times (December 3, 1997)

[...]
But can it really be beyond the capacity of an intelligent, mature community to accept that two groups, with different but not incompatible needs, might co-exist on the same piece of land, with civility and respect for each other's activities? Such co-existence has been harmoniously going on for generations on many pastoral leases, sometimes with state legislative backing, sometimes at the instigation of individual land-holders and local indigenous groups. Have such arrangements worked? It seems that largely they have. So why is there now such fear? As Opposition Leader, Kim Beazley said in his response to Mr Howard's address to the nation that native title will in many cases mean not much more than the right of access. This single observation injected a greater sense of proportion to the debate than a dozen passionate declarations of justice and reconciliation.
[...]

Native Title in Australia

161

Cape York Mayor Backs Reports Of Arming Over Wik

AAP NEWSFEED (December 4, 1997)
By Steele Tallon

A north Queensland shire mayor said today he had little doubt pastoralists in the region were arming themselves with high-powered weapons to defend their properties from native title.
[...]
Cr. Elmes said many pastoralists in Cape York felt they were losing control of their land as a result of the ongoing indecision over the native title legislation.
"Some people feel as though they're going to be left with nothing," he said.
"We're talking about people who have been on the land for three and four generations and when you see your land prices drop by half, who do you blame?
[...]

One Nation Looks For 'Practical Solution' On Native Title

The Canberra Times (December 30, 1997)
By Aban Contractor

Pauline Hanson's One Nation party will look at the practical ramifications of abolishing native title at a meeting of office-holders in Queensland today. Ms. Hanson's spokesman, David Oldfield, said the party did not believe in native title but recognised that if it held the balance of power there would be some limitations on what could be achieved. "We'll probably look at exactly what stand will be taken and what sort of stand can realistically be taken," he said yesterday.
"We're the only ones officially saying we don't want native title the Nats (National Party) have gone for a watered-down arrangement and the Government would like to abolish it but don't have the guts but we'll be looking for a practical solution."
[...]

Canada knows the value of an apology

ATSIC Press Release (January 8, 1998)[5]

[...]

The Canadian government's action in apologising to its indigenous population further isolates the Australian government as unable to face up to history, the Acting ATSIC Chairperson, Ray Robinson, said today.

"It is significant that the Canadian government has recognised the need to rebuild its relationship with the First Nations communities in Canada," Commissioner Robinson said.

"Our present-day government might not be responsible for implementing past policies but it is responsible for dealing with the history we inherited. [...]

"The Australian government does not have a good relationship with indigenous people in this country at this time. We have no sense of partnership. I urge the Howard government to learn from good examples."

Wik Guide Like Being 'Savaged By Dead Sheep'

The Canberra Times (January 13, 1998)
By Aban Contractor

[...]

"There's nothing new in the document," he said. "It really is just a restatement of the Government's position without attempting to explain it. There's been no attempt to explain the substance of the sticking points and if this is the best the Government can do, it's like being savaged by a dead sheep."

[...]

Aboriginies Denounce Fischer Reconciliation Remarks

AAP NEWSFEED (January 15, 1998)

Aboriginal groups have denounced deputy Prime Minister Tim Fischer's claim that reconciliation would not start until the federal government's native title changes are passed by the Senate.

[...]

But ATSIC acting chairman Ray Robinson said Mr. Fischer should be asked whether he knew what reconciliation was.

"Reconciliation won't be possible without respect for the property rights of indigenous Australians," Mr. Robinson said.

[...]

Native Title in Australia

Wik Does Not Threaten Private Land: Cape York Council
AAP NEWSFEED (January 21, 1998)

Non-Aboriginal Australians would not lose a single square centimetre of their land to native title, contrary to the "very deceitful" claims of National Party politicians, the Cape York Land Council said today.
[...]
"Mr. Borbidge and Mr. Fischer are being very deceitful [...] they're trying to frighten farmers and frighten miners and frighten people in their backyard," Mr. Byrne told ABC Radio. "But I tell those people: you don't need to be afraid because the law protects you.
"It is absolutely impossible, and I have to say since the Native Title Act has come in, not one non-Aboriginal Australian has lost one square centimetre of land.
[...]

Aborigines Barred From Age-Old Tradition Of Hunting
AAP NEWSFEED (February 27, 1998)
By Suzanne Klotz and Malcolm Cole

A landmark Queensland court ruling today effectively barred Aborigines from freely hunting native animals for food - something they have done for thousands of years.
[...]
The court found in a split decision that existing state law overruled the federal Native Title Act, which had been based on the High Court's Mabo ruling. It found in favour of the Queensland Government, which had appealed against a magistrate's ruling in 1996 that Aboriginal activist Murrandoo Yanner was entitled under the Native Title Act to kill two estuarine crocodiles on his tribal land in north-west Queensland.
[...]

Lawyers Say Wik Bill Will Not Bring Certainty
AAP NEWSFEED (March 11, 1998)

A group of eminent lawyers today rejected the federal government's claim that its Wik native title legislation would bring legal certainty.
"This is not true. Even with the amendments which the government has accepted (from Labor and the minor parties), it cannot be said with

164   *The Present Politics of the Past*

confidence that the bill is constitutionally valid," the seven barristers and
professors of law said in a statement. "Thus, far from producing certainty,
the bill in its present form would give rise to protracted litigation."
[...]
"Some aspects of the Native Title Amendment Bill are clearly to the
detriment of Aboriginal people because they involve the lessening or
removal of existing legal rights," the group said.
[...]

Joint statement: Political process fails indigenous people

ATSIC Press Release (April 8, 1998)[6]

The native title legislation before the Senate is unacceptable to Aboriginal
and Torres Strait Islander people and should be voted down.
We agree the National Indigenous Working Group on Native Title has done
its best to communicate its concerns to Parliamentarians but can do no
more.
The legislative package is unfair, unjust and discriminatory. As such, it is setting the foundations for long-term and bitter division in the Australian community. Given the course of the debate so far, any compromise reached in
the Senate today is certain to fall far short of the expectations of indigenous
Australians.
The government has been single-minded in its determination to reverse the
success indigenous people have achieved in the highest court in the land.
Even when succeeding with most of its legislation, the government has come
back to continue the job of destroying the prospects for exercising our
rights.
We face considerable extinguishment of our native title property rights in a
way that goes beyond the common law.
Miners have been rewarded because the states that ignored the federal law
have been allowed to validate mining titles issued without regard for the Native Title Act.
Pastoralists have been rewarded with the potential for a wide range of
diversification despite the terms of their leases. The implications of this go
beyond the concerns of indigenous people.
Let there be no doubt that the legislation as it stands will serve neither the
interests of future generations of indigenous Australians nor non-indigenous
Australians.

Native Title in Australia

It seems we can have no faith in the government to protect our existing rights but we will continue to resist this legislation by all the legal means possible.
Gatjil Djerrkura
Chairman
Commissioner for Native Title
Geoff Clark

What Wik Worry? Nat. Chief's $4M Land Deal

The Canberra Times (June 9, 1998)
By Aban Contractor

National Party chief Don McDonald, who has said native title diminishes property values, has paid an estimated $4 million for a cattle station that is bigger than the ACT.
Opposition Aboriginal affairs spokesman Daryl Melham accused Mr. McDonald of "gross hypocrisy." [...] But the pastoralist who drew last month's sale of Stanbroke Station, north-west Queensland, to the attention of *The Canberra Times*, said he wanted Mr. McDonald to explain why his family would invest in a pastoral lease if it was true their tenure was so insecure. Last year, Mr. McDonald said the uncertainty over farmers' legal rights after the High Court's Wik decision was affecting his family's business.
[...]

End to Aboriginal extortion on way

ABIX: Australasian Business Intelligence (July 16, 1998)
By David Barnett

[...]
The West Australian and Northern Territory Governments are writing legislation under the Australian Government's Wik Native title legislation which will abolish the need to negotiate with Aboriginal groups on land which is claimed by those groups as areas where native title exists. By using the right to negotiate under the Australian Labor Party's legislation, Aboriginal groups have been able to extort large sums of money from developers seeking to use land under claim in native title cases. The application of the native title legislation will allow miners and farmers to initiate developments on their property without fear of native title claims.
[...]

Anger, Fear and Ignorance Drive Australia's Political Direction
ATSIC Press Release (July 28, 1998)[7]

By sending out mixed signals on indigenous affairs and promoting a false debate about accountability, the federal government is feeding the One Nation agenda, ATSIC Chairman Gatjil Djerrkura told an international gathering in Geneva today.

"Australia is a great country and we love our mother land," Mr Djerrkura said.

"However, Australia has lost its political way and direction. Evil has crept into the body politic. It is being fuelled by a cocktail of anger, fear, and ignorance.

"The One Nation agenda is abhorrent but very clear. There is evidence, thankfully, that the more racist elements in One Nation's platform are only important for a minority of those who support the party.

"Regrettably, I have little positive to report in terms of the actions of the national government in the face of this new right wing agenda."

Mr Djerrkura delivered his "review of developments" speech to over 700 indigenous delegates at the 16th Session of the United Nations' Working Group on Indigenous Populations (WGIP). One of only two UN forums that specifically address the issues of indigenous peoples, delegates from around the world gather annually to advise WGIP experts on economic development and social issues.

This year's theme at WGIP is education and language. ATSIC is represented by a small delegation including Mr Djerrkura, the ATSIC Portfolio Commissioner for Education, Mr. David Curtis, and the Acting Chief Executive Officer, Mr Glenn Rees.

Mr Djerrkura said the last twelve months have been difficult for Australia's Aboriginal and Torres Strait Islander peoples who are not only the most disadvantaged people in Australian society but are among the chief scapegoats targeted by an increasingly vocal minority.

One Nation is "tapping into a seemingly rich vein of discontent with the policies of rapid change being pursued by our major political parties," he said.

"Many Australians—particularly in the rural and remote hinterlands—are hurting from the policies of economic rationalism and globalisation. Many of our outback towns want no part of the global village. Many of their residents, fearful about their own future, resent programs for indigenous peoples. They wrongly see them as extra benefits and privileges which they don't have.

Native Title in Australia 167

"The federal government sends out mixed signals on indigenous affairs. It continually undermines ATSIC and the principle of self-empowerment while publicly professing its commitment to the principles of the Commission

"Recently the tabloid press mis-reported the cost of a conference organised by the Kimberley Land Council in West Australia. The government did not wait to check the facts, which showed the cost was within industry guidelines.

"It seized the opportunity to publicly justify a Special Audit of all conferences, seminars and meetings resourced by ATSIC over the last two years.

"The Special Audit is a dangerous and costly act of discrimination against our people. No matter the findings, it will perpetuate the myth that every black dollar somehow ends up in the red."

Mr Djerrkura said other government moves include the quarantining of two thirds of ATSIC's budget from the discretion of the ATSIC Board and taking vital resources from ATSIC to fund its own Office of Indigenous Policy. It has presided over amendments to native title legislation, resulting in substantially reduced indigenous common law property rights, and is threatening to step back from national leadership in the protection of indigenous heritage.

But while its record in respect of indigenous rights is poor, the federal government has taken few initiatives to act on its own priorities—housing, employment, education and health.

"I acknowledge that some Ministers—notably Dr Kemp, Dr Herron and Jocelyn Newman—have fought hard against the odds to protect expenditure on those indigenous programs for which they are responsible," Mr Djerrkura said.

"Dr Wooldridge is to be congratulated on those important initiatives he has been able to take in the health area."

Meanwhile, ATSIC is pursuing several reforms—including a new approach to economic development based on partnerships with the private sector.

"We need to combine indigenous policy making with the skills of the private sector in ensuring that we maximise the use of the resources," Mr. Djerrkura said.

"We have embarked on an ambitious program for the reform of Aboriginal legal services which has received government support.

"We have reviewed the operation of the ATSIC Act. Important recommendations have been made to strengthen the operation of ATSIC at the regional level including through regional agreements and regional authorities. We are working constructively with government to implement the review with a view to ensuring a positive and timely response.

"Indigenous peoples in Australia have been fighting for 200 years for our rights. In the early 1990's we seemed an ace away from achieving justice.

"While there is evil in the body politic there is also good in the majority of Australians.

"Many hundreds of thousands of Australians took part in National Sorry Day on 26th May this year to mark the separation of indigenous children from their families. There has been an immense groundswell of support from the community for the protection of native title rights.

"The people's movement for reconciliation is growing in strength. Its growth demonstrates there is still a strong sense of common decency running through Australian society."

Limits on Native Title

The Canberra Times (September 14, 1998)

THE HIGH COURT's decision on Thursday, holding that a grant of freehold absolutely extinguished native title, was entirely predictable. Members of the court had said so in the Mabo and Wik cases. The court went further, holding that even if land which had once been freehold reverted to the Crown, as the land in question had after a compulsory resumption, native title did not revive. Once taken away, it did not come back. [...]

Statement on 50th Anniversary of UN Declaration on Human Rights: Enjoyment of human rights not yet universal

ATSIC Press Release (December 10, 1998)[8]

On the 50th anniversary of the Universal Declaration of Human Rights, it is right to celebrate progress towards ensuring that all peoples enjoy the protection of their fundamental rights, ATSIC Chairman, Gatjil Djerrkura, said today.

However, it is also important to realise how far we have yet to go.

"Any boasts about Australia's achievements will look foolish without equal recognition of the amount of work still needed to get our own house in order," Mr Djerrkura said.

Native Title in Australia 169

"The Universal Declaration has been the basis for human rights struggles all over the world. It stresses the commonality of all humankind and that there are certain minimum rights that apply to all peoples.

"But we need to keep working towards the international recognition of the rights of indigenous peoples. In Australia, the evidence of this struggle is obvious.

"We are currently seeing the property and cultural rights of indigenous Australians being removed, piece by piece.

"The dismantling of our property rights under changes to the Native Title Act has moved away from national attention, but we are now fighting to retain our rights at the level of state and territory governments.

"At the same time, the federal parliament is currently considering amendments to the Aboriginal and Torres Strait Islander Heritage Protection Act. These further reduce our hopes of guarding what's left of our cultures.

"Australia prides itself on its human rights record, yet we now hold the honour of being the first western country to fall under UN investigation for the direction of its human rights policy."

In August this year, the UN's High Commissioner on Human Rights issued a press release naming Australia, Yugoslavia and the Czech Republic as countries causing concern about their handling of human rights. The UN's Committee on the Elimination of Racial Discrimination has asked Australia to provide information on changes to native title, Aboriginal affairs policy and the role of the Aboriginal and Torres Strait Islander Social Justice Commissioner.

Mr Djerrkura also expressed concern about the government's recent signals that it is seeking to have the term "self-determination" removed from the UN's Draft Declaration on the Rights of Indigenous Peoples.

"There is no right more fundamental for indigenous people than self-determination," he said. "It is an inherent right of all peoples.

"Self-determination is recognised in International Law in the International Covenant on Civil and Political Rights and the International Covenant on Economic, Social and Cultural Rights. Australia is a signatory to both.

"But the government prefers terms such as 'self-empowerment' and 'self-management'.

"It is blatantly discriminatory to proclaim self-determination as a right of all peoples while denying or limiting its application to indigenous peoples.

"ATSIC will use whatever processes are available to us to protect indigenous rights at both the national and international level."

Mr Djerrkura said he was impressed with such initiatives as the Universal Rights Network — a new interactive multi-media site launched today in Melbourne to coincide with the anniversary of the Universal Declaration.

"This gives us all equal access to information about and the words of human rights heroes — people like Pat Dodson, Mahatma Gandhi, Rigberto Menchu, Aung Sun Suu Kyi and many others," he said.

"It profiles the work of human rights agencies such as UNICEF, the United Nations High Commissioner for Refugees, Amnesty International, Greenpeace, Care Australia, the Fred Hollows Foundation and others — including ATSIC.

"I'm proud to be associated with this initiative."

It's Time To Say Yes, Prime Minister
ATSIC Press Release (January 26, 1999)[9]

Australia Day is a perfect opportunity for all Australians to reflect on the past, the present and the future.

We should be looking at where we have been and where we are going.

For most Indigenous Australians today marks the European invasion of their lands and, in many cases, the beginning of an assault on their spiritual and cultural links to that land, which continue to this day.

Many will no doubt be reflecting on this.

I will be.

We are entering a crucial period in our history.

We must all acknowledge the past before looking to the future.

All eyes will be on Australia as we prepare for the Olympic Games next year and the beginning of the new millennium and the Centenary of Federation in 2001.

The concerns of the Aboriginal and Torres Strait Islander peoples, the original owners of this country, will loom large in both domestic and international debate in the lead up to these events.

In this regard we will be looking for a vast improvement in the Federal Government's recognition of our legitimate economic, social, political, cultural and spiritual aspirations.

1998 was a difficult year in the relationship between the Aboriginal and Torres Strait Islander Commission and the Federal Government.

The early signs clearly indicate this year could be the same, particularly in regard to our ongoing quest for true recognition and reconciliation.

Since raising his desire to achieve true reconciliation during the current term of Government the Prime Minister has continued to allow the Australian people to show the leadership on this vital issue.

In recent times the Prime Minister and his Government have said no to self determination for our peoples before the United Nations.

No to a Treaty.

No to ATSIC's bid for additional monies to help address the crying need for more housing and employment.

No to Abstudy.

No to an official Government apology to the Stolen Generations.

No to the ongoing indigenous administration of our spiritual and cultural heritage

No to a Memorial recognising our war dead.

Many Indigenous Australians are now asking; when will you say yes, Prime Minister?

Reprise of the dishonourable silence

ABIX: Australasian Business Intelligence (March 25, 1999)
By Bain Attwood

[...]

More than thirty years ago, anthropologist W.H. Stanner coined the phrase "the great Australian silence." Stanner alluded to the way in which historians had ignored Aboriginal ownership of the land and ignored their dispossession. That silence has emerged again with the draft preamble to the Australian Constitution. Talk about "honouring ancient cultures" presumes that Australian history only began with the arrival of the British in 1770 or 1788. The land now called Australia had other names and was possessed by other peoples before then. Talk about the ancient aboriginal culture supported the idea that Aborigines had no concept of property or ownership of land. They could not survive in a modern Australia. Howard's preamble repeats this argument, and ignores rights recognised by comparable countries such as New Zealand and Canada. It is another retreat from the High Court's Mabo decision and native title. It is immoral and dashes any hope of Reconciliation.

[...]

Government should face up to international scrutiny on native title
ATSIC Press Release (April 30, 1999)[10]

Joint statement: Today's report in *The Age* that the Australian government has warned the United Nations Committee on the Elimination of Racial Discrimination (CERD) against visiting Australia is disappointing but not surprising, according to the ATSIC Commissioners who had issued the invitation.

Commissioners Geoff Clark (Victoria) and Colin Dillon (government appointed) spoke to members of CERD in Geneva last month about the racially discriminatory nature of the government's native title amendments.

Australia is a party to the International Convention on the Elimination of All Forms of Racial Discrimination. In past years, Australia has drawn praise from CERD for its efforts.

Late last year, however, the Australian government became the first western developed nation to receive a "please explain" request from CERD. An official appeared before CERD in mid-March to explain the government's position on native title.

After hearing the government's case, CERD found the amendments to the Native Title Act may be racially discriminatory. It also raised concerns about the lack of effective participation by indigenous communities in the formulation of the amendments and urged the government to suspend them.

"The government can't expect any credibility by arguing that the native title amendments are not racially discriminatory and then slamming the door on a UN committee that wants to check the facts," Commissioner Clark said.

"It should stand by its claims and be open to scrutiny. Accountability in indigenous affairs — isn't this what everyone wants? The government has made its claims and now it should be willing to let other people check them."

Commissioner Dillon said the government could have made all its arguments against a visit and yet still extended a formal invitation as a gesture of goodwill.

"This would have been the gracious thing to do, under the circumstances," he said.

"From my own experience as a police officer, you have to wonder what people are hiding if they refuse a reasonable request for entry."

The Commissioners said that their original invitation to members of CERD still stood.

They said that the native title amendments are aimed squarely at reducing the rights of indigenous people and indigenous people alone. As such, they are undeniably discriminatory.

Landowners should have equal right to negotiate
AAP NEWSFEED (July 20, 1999)

[...]

Independent Gladstone MP Liz Cunningham said the native title regime introduced by the Queensland government last year gave Aborigines more rights than landowners in negotiating with companies keen to mine their land. Mrs. Cunningham's Mineral Resources Amendment Bill aims to make the negotiation process more equitable but landowners will have to demonstrate their connection with the land by proving they have lived and worked on it for a significant part of their lives.

"I am not attempting to gain greater rights to negotiate for non-Aboriginal landowners [...] than given last year to Aboriginal people with a demonstrated interest in land subject to mining lease applications," Mrs Cunningham told parliament.

[...]

Judge made major "legal mistake" over native title
AAP NEWSFEED (August 18, 1999)

The dramatic first day of a land rights appeal was told today that a judge had wrongly insisted that Aborigines must follow the same laws and customs as their ancestors of 1788 if they wanted to prove native title.

Ron Castan, QC, the barrister who won the historic Mabo High Court case, told the full Federal Court that Justice Howard Olney had made a legal mistake "of enormous significance."

The judge's legal test for native title had been, in fact, based on a "frozen-in-time fallacy," Mr Castan told the appeal court. Instead, Aborigines needed only to prove they occupied the same land as their forebears, using laws and customs derived from those handed down over thousands of years, and that the native title had not been extinguished by the granting of other land title, he said.

[...]

Seize the Time - says respected Aboriginal Rights activist Terry O'Shane

ATSIC Press Release (November 5, 1999)[11]

On the eve of the referendum, Terry O'Shane, one of the most senior and respected activists for Aboriginal and human rights for more than 30 years, has issued a passionate and very personal plea to indigenous people to vote "yes" for a republic.

In doing so, he has taken issue with other prominent indigenous leaders who earlier this week issued an open letter to the public and media, urging indigenous people to vote down the republic question.

If we as Aboriginal people oppose racism in all its forms, institutional and direct, then we must raise our voices in unison and vote "YES" for the Republic and "NO" for the preamble.

I fear the continuation of the Monarchy, and all the problems that have arisen from the use of the "Crown. " And I'm concerned we may see its continuation because some of my people are supporting the "NO" vote.

In the list of those people who support a "NO" vote are a lot of my personal friends - people that I have enormous respect for and some whom I consider as my closest friends.

On this issue I'm afraid we'll need to agree to disagree.

It defies understanding that indigenous people may well help maintain a British Monarch as Head of State for "our country" simply because neither party spoke to us about the Republic or the inclusion of our rights in any new Constitution. This is precisely what their advocacy for a "No" vote this Saturday means. If that is the outcome, they are aiding and abetting the perpetuation of the great racism we have been made to live under.

This country was claimed under the doctrine of "Terra Nullius" on behalf of the British Crown. 1992 saw that evil lie exposed in the High Court's decision on "Mabo." Since then, against all opposition, we have been making incremental progress, slowly but surely. The latest step forward was the decision by the UN's CERD committee, criticising the suspension of the Racial Discrimination Act by the Howard Government, when it enacted its 10 point plan.

We need to get rid of the Monarchy and with it the legal fiction of Crown Land. So I am asking all Aboriginal People to vote "YES" for a Republic and "NO" for the preamble on Saturday.

My position is that I will follow the direction that many good people have set for us and continue to set. My life has been dedicated to the elimination of all forms of racism.

Native Title in Australia

175

If I remain silent now I would be complicit in the perpetuation of those things that I have opposed all my life. We will, by increments, develop better quality of life for future generations of Indigenous people, if we attack the evils of racism when the opportunity is with us. This is one of those times. Sieze the Time.

Queensland Indigenous Working Group takes 'strong case' against State Native Title legislation and cultural heritage to Canberra

ATSIC Press Release (February 14, 2000)[12]

The Queensland Indigenous Working Group headed by its Chairman Terry O'Shane and deputy, Les Malezer, and a high powered team of representatives and advisors is in Canberra this week to mount what it says is a 'strong case' against the Queensland government's Native Title legislation.

The Federal government's cultural heritage legislation is also in the sights of the powerful Indigenous body, which represents all of Queensland's Land Councils, ATSIC Regional Councils and the State Aboriginal and Islander Councils.

In a series of meetings QIWG will outline its case and concerns to the Federal Minister for the Environment, Senator Robert Hill, Opposition Leader Kim Beazley, Democrat's spokesman, Senator John Woodley, Green's Senator Bob Brown, independent Senator Brian Harradine and Senator Jan McLucas, a member of the Joint Parliamentary Committee on Native Title. QIWG will also meet with the ATSIC Board of Commissioners. Their week long visit will culminate on Thursday when the indigenous leaders go to Parliament House to attend the Joint Parliamentary Committee on Native Title's inquiry into Australia's international legal obligations under CERD –the international Convention on the Elimination of All Forms of Racial Discrimination, which resumes this week.

Federal Court Decision Throws Serious Doubt Over Queensland's Native Title Extinguishment Law: Massive Compensation Bill Likely

ATSIC Press Release (April 6, 2000)[13]

Statement by the Queensland Indigenous Working Group
Some of Queensland's Native Title legislation is tonight in serious doubt, following a federal court decision yesterday.
Outlining its assessment of the court's decision, the Queensland Indigenous Working Group, the State's peak indigenous negotiating body, warns that

unless the effects of the Beattie government's legislation can be undone, the Beattie Government has indiscriminately extinguished native title, and has needlessly created a massive compensation debt which will burden all Queenslanders.

In *Anderson v. Wilson* the Full Federal Court found that Western Lands Leases in New South Wales do not necessarily extinguish native title.

The QIWG released an opinion on the Federal Court's decision which it says "tends to confirm that Premier Beattie has passed a law which extinguishes native title at least 10 per cent of Queensland."

The QIWG says the Western Lands Lease case is 'a test case by analogy' for Queensland Grazing Homestead Perpetual leases.

In 1998, Premier Beattie passed its own native title legislation to "confirm" the extinguishment of native title over areas of Queensland, including areas covered by Grazing Homestead Perpetual leases.

Before legislation was passed, the QIWG urged Premier Beattie not to proceed with it, and gave the Premier advice from Queen's Counsel, that native title could coexist with Grazing Homestead Perpetual Leases.

Premier Beattie ignored the advice and passed the legislation regardless.

Queensland Grazing Homestead Perpetual leases and New South Wales Western Lands leases are very similar in their likely effect on native title.

The QIWG believes that the Federal Court's decision in Anderson v Wilson confirms that the Beattie Government has extinguished native title over more than 10per cent of Queensland, where Grazing Homestead Perpetual Leases have been granted.

This means that the Beattie Government has effected possibly the largest single act of extinguishment of native title in Queensland's history.

That is a crushing blow for Indigenous Queenslanders whose rights have been taken away by the Beattie Government.

Unless the effect of the Beattie legislation can be undone, it also means that the Beattie Government has needlessly created a massive compensation debt which will burden all Queenslanders.

Indigenous people sold out by Labor deal on Native Title

ATSIC Press Release (August 30, 2000) [14]

Indigenous people have been sold out again by the Federal opposition deal with the Queensland Government to open up as much as 60,000 square kilometres of the state to mining exploration.

Native Title in Australia

This deal cannot even stick unless the Beattie government were re-elected and keeps its word. Its deplorable that political parties can throw away the rights of our people and offer to replace them with more charity.

I fully understand the frustrations that recent events have created across Indigenous communities. The last thing we need is a frustrated Indigenous population at a time when Australia is on show to the rest of the world.

The opposition deal giving the Queensland government a Senate green light on mining and exploration is a typical political scam. Commitments made to Indigenous people have not been kept.

The opposition's Indigenous Affairs spokesman Daryl Melham has been made a sacrificial lamb to allow the deal to go through. Only yesterday the opposition was distancing itself from the Federal Government's hysterical over-reaction to some mild United Nations criticisms of its policies.

A day later the opposition is endorsing a Queensland native title regime based on federal laws found by the UN to be racially discriminatory. Talk about a long time in politics.

The state exploration scheme approved in the Senate can now be used by the Beattie government to allow miners to tear up as much as 60,000 square kilometres of land where native title may exist. It removes any rights of native title holders to have a say in how exploration may occur on their own country.

The deal is also contrary to the relatively principled position Labor took in the 1998 Wik debate and its own Indigenous affairs policy endorsed only last month at its national conference in Hobart.

The Labor Party says it is encouraging consultation and engagement with Indigenous people but how can our leaders be expected to engage with a party with optional policies?

Wik determination a victory for negotiation
ATSIC Press Release (October 3, 2000)[15]

Statement by Commissioner Lester Rosendale,
ATSIC Commissioner for Far North and West Zone
Today's determination recognising the Wik peoples' native title over 6,000 square kilometres of their traditional lands and waters is decisive proof that negotiation is the best way of achieving positive resolution of native title issues.

I congratulate the Wik and Wik Way people on the successful outcome of this part of their claim, and on their persistence and resolve in the face of repeated setbacks.

They have been striving for more than 20 years to formally establish and gain recognition for their traditional rights and use of their country, and the negotiation process available under the Native Title Act has finally given it to them after five years of negotiations.

I think the Queensland Government – which has denied our right to negotiate in many native title claims - should take heed of this outcome as it proves that amicable settlement between competing land users is possible without resorting to costly legal battles.

I only hope that the remaining part of the Wik claim can also be negotiated to a satisfactory outcome.

Today's result should stand as a model for other claims, and persuade those opposed to the idea of negotiated Native Title settlements that they are a positive way forward.

Victorian protocol on native title the first in Australia
ATSIC Press Release (November 3, 2000)[16]

Peak Victorian Indigenous bodies – the Aboriginal and Torres Strait Islander Commission and Mirimbiak Nations Aboriginal Corporation – today signed an historic protocol on native title with the Victorian Government.

The protocol is the first of its type in Australia and commits the parties to negotiating a statewide framework agreement to deal with native title and related issues in Victoria.

The protocol and the subsequent framework agreement are based on the principle of negotiation rather than litigation to settle native title claims.

ATSIC Chairperson, Geoff Clark, said: "This is the first step in reaching an agreement that will ensure communities are able to negotiate with Government on an equal footing. For too long the rights of communities have been ignored.

"It is a process that gives the communities the opportunity to be involved in the negotiations.

"This is also the first time since colonisation that a government is prepared to negotiate with Aboriginal people to obtain their informed consent regarding their rights and interests," Mr Clark said.

Native Title in Australia 179

The statewide framework agreement will not replace native title claims but will provide the mechanism for their resolution if that is the wish of the parties.

Chairperson of Mirimbiak, Damein Bell, said: "Only native title parties can make decisions about their rights. The protocol and the agreement will not affect anyone's rights but will outline how negotiations can take place with everyone on an equal footing. For too long its has been the Aboriginal parties who have had to battle better resourced organisations."

ATSIC Commissioner for Victoria, Marion Hansen, said: "This protocol signifies that this Government is willing to discuss issues of importance to local communities and ATSIC certainly supports such a process. However, this will only work if communities are properly resourced."

Chapter Seven
Native Title in Canada

Too willing to throw in the towel: governments back
natives at historic land-claim appeal [Gitksan &
Wetsuweten bands' appeal on the Delgamuukw case]
British Columbia Report (June 30, 1997)
By Dave Cunningham

With the federal and provincial governments' March 1996 signing of an
agreement in principle with the Nisga'a band, British Columbians could
finally see where the pro-native policies adopted by their governments was
leading: race-based owner ship of land and natural resources, and
apartheid-like self-government. Any remaining doubt about government's
intentions was erased last week inside the Supreme Court of Canada. There,
the country's top jurists heard the Gitksan and Wetsuweten bands' final
appeal on the landmark Delgamuukw case. And there, British Columbians
again saw their governments side with the aboriginals.
[...]
   Vancouver lawyer Norman Mullins says the high court will be loathe to
Balkanize the country by legitimizing the creation of sovereign, self-governing
territories. Indeed, Chief Justice Antonio Lamer grilled native lawyers on
this very point last week. Mr. Mullins says the NDP are trying to put a legal
ribbon on a political gift. "That has backfired," he says, "because the courts
won't have anything to do with it."

DELGAMUUKW V. BRITISH COLUMBIA (11 DECEMBER 1997) 3 S.C.R. 1010

The appellants, all Gitksan or Wet'suwet'en hereditary chiefs, both
individually and on behalf of their "Houses," claimed separate portions of

181

58,000 square kilometres in British Columbia. For the purpose of the claim, this area was divided into 133 individual territories, claimed by the 71 Houses. This represents all of the Wet'suwet'en people, and all but 12 of the Gitksan Houses. Their claim was originally for "ownership" of the territory and "jurisdiction" over it. (At this Court, this was transformed into, primarily, a claim for aboriginal title over the land in question.) British Columbia counterclaimed for a declaration that the appellants have no right or interest in and to the territory or alternatively, that the appellants' cause of action ought to be for compensation from the Government of Canada.

At trial, the appellants' claim was based on their historical use and "ownership" of one or more of the territories. In addition, the Gitksan Houses have an "adaawk" which is a collection of sacred oral tradition about their ancestors, histories and territories. The Wet'suwet'en each have a "kungax" which is a spiritual song or dance or performance which ties them to their land. Both of these were entered as evidence on behalf of the appellants. The most significant evidence of spiritual connection between the Houses and their territory was a feast hall where the Gitksan and Wet'suwet'en people tell and retell their stories and identify their territories to remind themselves of the sacred connection that they have with their lands. The feast has a ceremonial purpose but is also used for making important decisions.

The trial judge did not accept the appellants' evidence of oral history of attachment to the land. He dismissed the action against Canada, dismissed the plaintiffs' claims for ownership and jurisdiction and for aboriginal rights in the territory, granted a declaration that the plaintiffs were entitled to use unoccupied or vacant land subject to the general law of the province, dismissed the claim for damages and dismissed the province's counterclaim. No order for costs was made. On appeal, the original claim was altered in two different ways. First, the claims for ownership and jurisdiction were replaced with claims for aboriginal title and self-government, respectively. Second, the individual claims by each House were amalgamated into two communal claims, one advanced on behalf of each nation. There were no formal amendments to the pleadings to this effect. The appeal was dismissed by a majority of the Court of Appeal.

The principal issues on the appeal, some of which raised a number of sub-issues, were as follows: (1) whether the pleadings precluded the Court from entertaining claims for aboriginal title and self-government; (2) what was the ability of this Court to interfere with the factual findings made by the trial judge; (3) what is the content of aboriginal title, how is it protected by s. 35(1) of the Constitution Act, 1982, and what is required for its proof;

Native Title in Canada

(4) whether the appellants made out a claim to self-government; and, (5) whether the province had the power to extinguish aboriginal rights after 1871, either under its own jurisdiction or through the operation of s. 88 of the Indian Act.

Held: The appeal should be allowed in part and the cross-appeal should be dismissed.

Whether the Claims Were Properly Before the Court

Per Lamer C.J. and Cory, McLachlin, and Major JJ.: The claims were properly before the Court. Although the pleadings were not formally amended, the trial judge did allow a de facto amendment to permit a claim for aboriginal rights other than ownership and jurisdiction. The respondents did not appeal this de facto amendment and the trial judge's decision on this point must accordingly stand.

No amendment was made with respect to the amalgamation of the individual claims brought by the individual Gitksan and Wet'suwet'en Houses into two collective claims, one by each nation, for aboriginal title and self-government. The collective claims were simply not in issue at trial and to frame the case on appeal in a different manner would retroactively deny the respondents the opportunity to know the appellants' case.

A new trial is necessary. First, the defect in the pleadings prevented the Court from considering the merits of this appeal. The parties at a new trial would decide whether any amendment was necessary to make the pleadings conform with the other evidence. Then, too, appellate courts, absent a palpable and overriding error, should not substitute their own findings of fact even when the trial judge misapprehended the law which was applied to those facts. Appellate intervention is warranted, however, when the trial court fails to appreciate the evidentiary difficulties inherent in adjudicating aboriginal claims when applying the rules of evidence and interpreting the evidence before it.

Per La Forest and L'Heureux-Dubé JJ.: The amalgamation of the appellants' individual claims technically prevents a consideration of the merits. However, there is a more substantive problem with the pleadings. The appellants sought a declaration of "aboriginal title" but attempted, in essence, to prove that they had complete control over the territory. It follows that what the appellants sought by way of declaration and what they set out to prove by way of the evidence were two different matters. A new trial should be ordered.

McLachlin J. was in substantial agreement.

184

The Present Politics of the Past

The Ability of the Court to Interfere with the Trial Judge's Factual Findings

Per Lamer C.J. and Cory, McLachlin and Major JJ.: The factual findings made at trial could not stand because the trial judge's treatment of the various kinds of oral histories did not satisfy the principles laid down in R. v. Van der Peet. The oral histories were used in an attempt to establish occupation and use of the disputed territory which is an essential requirement for aboriginal title. The trial judge refused to admit or gave no independent weight to these oral histories and then concluded that the appellants had not demonstrated the requisite degree of occupation for "ownership." Had the oral histories been correctly assessed, the conclusions on these issues of fact might have been very different.

The Content of Aboriginal Title, How It Is Protected by s. 35(1) of the Constitution Act, 1982, and the Requirements Necessary to Prove It

Per Lamer C.J. and Cory, McLachlin and Major JJ.: Aboriginal title encompasses the right to exclusive use and occupation of the land held pursuant to that title for a variety of purposes, which need not be aspects of those aboriginal practices, customs and traditions which are integral to distinctive aboriginal cultures. The protected uses must not be irreconcilable with the nature of the group's attachment to that land.

Aboriginal title is sui generis, and so distinguished from other proprietary interests, and characterized by several dimensions. It is inalienable and cannot be transferred, sold or surrendered to anyone other than the Crown. Another dimension of aboriginal title is its sources: its recognition by the Royal Proclamation, 1763 and the relationship between the common law which recognizes occupation as proof of possession and systems of aboriginal law pre-existing assertion of British sovereignty. Finally, aboriginal title is held communally.

The exclusive right to use the land is not restricted to the right to engage in activities which are aspects of aboriginal practices, customs and traditions integral to the claimant group's distinctive aboriginal culture. Canadian jurisprudence on aboriginal title frames the "right to occupy and possess" in broad terms and, significantly, is not qualified by the restriction that use be tied to practice, custom or tradition. The nature of the Indian interest in reserve land which has been found to be the same as the interest in tribal lands is very broad and incorporates present-day needs. Finally, aboriginal title encompasses mineral rights and lands held pursuant to aboriginal title should be capable of exploitation. Such a use is certainly not a traditional one.

Native Title in Canada 185

The content of aboriginal title contains an inherent limit in that lands so held cannot be used in a manner that is irreconcilable with the nature of the claimants' attachment to those lands. This inherent limit arises because the relationship of an aboriginal community with its land should not be prevented from continuing into the future. Occupancy is determined by reference to the activities that have taken place on the land and the uses to which the land has been put by the particular group. If lands are so occupied, there will exist a special bond between the group and the land in question such that the land will be part of the definition of the group's distinctive culture. Land held by virtue of aboriginal title may not be alienated because the land has an inherent and unique value in itself, which is enjoyed by the community with aboriginal title to it. The community cannot put the land to uses which would destroy that value. Finally, the importance of the continuity of the relationship between an aboriginal community and its land, and the non-economic or inherent value of that land, should not be taken to detract from the possibility of surrender to the Crown in exchange for valuable consideration. On the contrary, the idea of surrender reinforces the conclusion that aboriginal title is limited. If aboriginal peoples wish to use their lands in a way that aboriginal title does not permit, then they must surrender those lands and convert them into non-title lands to do so.

Aboriginal title at common law was recognized well before 1982 and is accordingly protected in its full form by s. 35(1). The constitutionalization of common law aboriginal rights, however, does not mean that those rights exhaust the content of s. 35(1). The existence of an aboriginal right at common law is sufficient, but not necessary, for the recognition and affirmation of that right by s. 35(1).

Constitutionally recognized aboriginal rights fall along a spectrum with respect to their degree of connection with the land. At the one end are those aboriginal rights which are practices, customs and traditions integral to the distinctive aboriginal culture of the group claiming the right but where the use and occupation of the land where the activity is taking place is not sufficient to support a claim of title to the land. In the middle are activities which, out of necessity, take place on land and indeed, might be intimately related to a particular piece of land. Although an aboriginal group may not be able to demonstrate title to the land, it may nevertheless have a site-specific right to engage in a particular activity. At the other end of the spectrum is aboriginal title itself which confers more than the right to engage in site-specific activities which are aspects of the practices, customs and traditions of distinctive aboriginal cultures. Site-specific rights can be made out even if title cannot. Because aboriginal rights can vary with respect to their degree of connection with the land, some aboriginal groups may be unable to make out a claim to title, but will nevertheless possess aboriginal rights that are recognized and affirmed by s. 35(1), including site-specific rights to engage in particular activities.

Aboriginal title is a right to the land itself. That land may be used, subject to the inherent limitations of aboriginal title, for a variety of activities, none of which need be individually protected as aboriginal rights under s. 35(1). Those activities are parasitic on the underlying title. Section 35(1), since its purpose is to reconcile the prior presence of aboriginal peoples with the assertion of Crown sovereignty, must recognize and affirm both aspects of that prior presence—first, the occupation of land, and second, the prior social organization and distinctive cultures of aboriginal peoples on that land.

The test for the identification of aboriginal rights to engage in particular activities and the test for the identification of aboriginal title, although broadly similar, are distinct in two ways. First, under the test for aboriginal title, the requirement that the land be integral to the distinctive culture of the claimants is subsumed by the requirement of occupancy. Second, whereas the time for the identification of aboriginal rights is the time of first contact, the time for the identification of aboriginal title is the time at which the Crown asserted sovereignty over the land.

In order to establish a claim to aboriginal title, the aboriginal group asserting the claim must establish that it occupied the lands in question at the time at which the Crown asserted sovereignty over the land subject to the title. In the context of aboriginal title, sovereignty is the appropriate time period to consider for several reasons. First, from a theoretical standpoint, aboriginal title arises out of prior occupation of the land by aboriginal peoples and out of the relationship between the common law and pre-existing systems of aboriginal law. Aboriginal title is a burden on the Crown's underlying title. The Crown, however, did not gain this title until it asserted sovereignty and it makes no sense to speak of a burden on the underlying title before that title existed. Aboriginal title crystallized at the time sovereignty was asserted. Second, aboriginal title does not raise the problem of distinguishing between distinctive, integral aboriginal practices, customs and traditions and those influenced or introduced by European contact. Under common law, the act of occupation or possession is sufficient to ground aboriginal title and it is not necessary to prove that the land was a distinctive or integral part of the aboriginal society before the arrival of

Native Title in Canada

Europeans. Finally, the date of sovereignty is more certain than the date of first contact.

Both the common law and the aboriginal perspective on land should be taken into account in establishing the proof of occupancy. At common law, the fact of physical occupation is proof of possession at law, which in turn will ground title to the land. Physical occupation may be established in a variety of ways, ranging from the construction of dwellings through cultivation and enclosure of fields to regular use of definite tracts of land for hunting, fishing or otherwise exploiting its resources. In considering whether occupation sufficient to ground title is established, the group's size, manner of life, material resources, and technological abilities, and the character of the lands claimed must be taken into account. Given the occupancy requirement, it was not necessary to include as part of the test for aboriginal title whether a group demonstrated a connection with the piece of land as being of central significance to its distinctive culture. Ultimately, the question of physical occupation is one of fact to be determined at trial.

If present occupation is relied on as proof of occupation pre-sovereignty, there must be a continuity between present and pre-sovereignty occupation. Since conclusive evidence of pre-sovereignty occupation may be difficult, an aboriginal community may provide evidence of present occupation as proof of pre-sovereignty occupation in support of a claim to aboriginal title. An unbroken chain of continuity need not be established between present and prior occupation. The fact that the nature of occupation has changed would not ordinarily preclude a claim for aboriginal title, as long as a substantial connection between the people and the land is maintained. The only limitation on this principle might be that the land not be used in ways which are inconsistent with continued use by future generations of aboriginals.

At sovereignty, occupation must have been exclusive. This requirement flows from the definition of aboriginal title itself, which is defined in terms of the right to exclusive use and occupation of land. The test must take into account the context of the aboriginal society at the time of sovereignty. The requirement of exclusive occupancy and the possibility of joint title can be reconciled by recognizing that joint title can arise from shared exclusivity. As well, shared, non-exclusive aboriginal rights short of aboriginal title but tied to the land and permitting a number of uses can be established if exclusivity cannot be proved. The common law should develop to recognize aboriginal rights as they were recognized by either de facto practice or by aboriginal systems of governance.

Per La Forest and L'Heureux-Dubé JJ.: "Aboriginal title" is based on the continued occupation and use of the land as part of the aboriginal peoples' traditional way of life. This sui generis interest is not equated with fee simple ownership; nor can it be described with reference to traditional property law concepts. It is personal in that it is generally inalienable except to the Crown and, in dealing with this interest, the Crown is subject to a fiduciary obligation to treat the aboriginal peoples fairly. There is reluctance to define more precisely the right of aboriginal peoples to live on their lands as their forefathers had lived.

The approach to defining the aboriginal right of occupancy is highly contextual. A distinction must be made between (1) the recognition of a general right to occupy and possess ancestral lands and (2) the recognition of a discrete right to engage in an aboriginal activity in a particular area. The latter has been defined as the traditional use, by a tribe of Indians, that has continued from pre-contact times of a particular area for a particular purpose. By contrast, a general claim to occupy and possess vast tracts of territory is the right to use the land for a variety of activities related to the aboriginal society's habits and mode of life. As well, in defining the nature of "aboriginal title," reference need not be made to statutory provisions and regulations dealing with reserve lands.

In defining the nature of "aboriginal title," reference need not be made to statutory provisions and regulations dealing specifically with reserve lands. Though the interest of an Indian band in a reserve has been found to be derived from, and to be of the same nature as, the interest of an aboriginal society in its traditional tribal lands, it does not follow that specific statutory provisions governing reserve lands should automatically apply to traditional tribal lands.

The "key" factors for recognizing aboriginal rights under s. 35(1) are met in the present case. First, the nature of an aboriginal claim must be identified precisely with regard to particular practices, customs and traditions. When dealing with a claim of "aboriginal title," the court will focus on the occupation and use of the land as part of the aboriginal society's traditional way of life.

Second, an aboriginal society must specify the area that has been continuously used and occupied by identifying general boundaries. Exclusivity means that an aboriginal group must show that a claimed territory is indeed its ancestral territory and not the territory of an unconnected aboriginal society. It is possible that two or more aboriginal groups may have occupied the same territory and therefore a finding of joint occupancy would not be precluded.

Third, the aboriginal right of possession is based on the continued occupation and use of traditional tribal lands since the assertion of Crown

Native Title in Canada   189

sovereignty. However, the date of sovereignty may not be the only relevant time to consider. Continuity may still exist where the present occupation of one area is connected to the pre-sovereignty occupation of another area. Also, aboriginal peoples claiming a right of possession may provide evidence of present occupation as proof of prior occupation. Further, it is not necessary to establish an unbroken chain of continuity.

Fourth, if aboriginal peoples continue to occupy and use the land as part of their traditional way of life, the land is of central significance to them. Aboriginal occupancy refers not only to the presence of aboriginal peoples in villages or permanently settled areas but also to the use of adjacent lands and even remote territories used to pursue a traditional mode of life. Occupancy is part of aboriginal culture in a broad sense and is, therefore, absorbed in the notion of distinctiveness. The Royal Proclamation, 1763 supports this approach to occupancy.

McLachlin J. was in substantial agreement.

Infringements of Aboriginal Title: The Test of Justification
Per Lamer C.J. and Cory, McLachlin and Major JJ.: Constitutionally recognized aboriginal rights are not absolute and may be infringed by the federal and provincial governments if the infringement (1) furthers a compelling and substantial legislative objective and (2) is consistent with the special fiduciary relationship between the Crown and the aboriginal peoples. The development of agriculture, forestry, mining and hydroelectric power, the general economic development of the interior of British Columbia, protection of the environment or endangered species, and the building of infrastructure and the settlement of foreign populations to support those aims, are objectives consistent with this purpose. Three aspects of aboriginal title are relevant to the second part of the test. First, the right to exclusive use and occupation of land is relevant to the degree of scrutiny of the infringing measure or action. Second, the right to choose to what uses land can be put, subject to the ultimate limit that those uses cannot destroy the ability of the land to sustain future generations of aboriginal peoples, suggests that the fiduciary relationship between the Crown and aboriginal peoples may be satisfied by the involvement of aboriginal peoples in decisions taken with respect to their lands. There is always a duty of consultation and, in most cases, the duty will be significantly deeper than mere consultation. And third, lands held pursuant to aboriginal title have an inescapable economic component which suggests

190   *The Present Politics of the Past*

that compensation is relevant to the question of justification as well. Fair compensation will ordinarily be required when aboriginal title is infringed.

Per La Forest and L'Heureux-Dubé JJ.: Rights that are recognized and affirmed are not absolute. Government regulation can therefore infringe upon aboriginal rights if it meets the test of justification under s. 35(1). The approach is highly contextual.

The general economic development of the interior of British Columbia, through agriculture, mining, forestry and hydroelectric power, as well as the related building of infrastructure and settlement of foreign populations, are valid legislative objectives that, in principle, satisfy the first part of the justification analysis. Under the second part, these legislative objectives are subject to accommodation of the aboriginal peoples' interests. This accommodation must always be in accordance with the honour and good faith of the Crown. One aspect of accommodation of "aboriginal title" entails notifying and consulting aboriginal peoples with respect to the development of the affected territory. Another aspect is fair compensation.

McLachlin J. was in substantial agreement.

Self-Government
Per The Court: The errors of fact made by the trial judge, and the resultant need for a new trial, made it impossible for this Court to determine whether the claim to self-government had been made out.

Extinguishment
Per Lamer C.J. and Cory, McLachlin and Major JJ.: Section 91(24) of the Constitution Act, 1867 (the federal power to legislate in respect of Indians) carries with it the jurisdiction to legislate in relation to aboriginal title, and by implication, the jurisdiction to extinguish it. The ownership by the provincial Crown (under s. 109) of lands held pursuant to aboriginal title is separate from jurisdiction over those lands. Notwithstanding s. 91(24), provincial laws of general application apply proprio vigore to Indians and Indian lands.

A provincial law of general application cannot extinguish aboriginal rights. First, a law of general application cannot, by definition, meet the standard "of clear and plain intention" needed to extinguish aboriginal rights without being ultra vires the province. Second, s. 91(24) protects a core of federal jurisdiction even from provincial laws of general application through the operation of the doctrine of interjurisdictional immunity. That core has been described as matters touching on "Indianness" or the "core of Indianness."

Native Title in Canada

191

Provincial laws which would otherwise not apply to Indians proprio vigore are allowed to do so by s. 88 of the Indian Act which incorporates by reference provincial laws of general application. This provision, however, does not "invigorate" provincial laws which are invalid because they are in relation to Indians and Indian lands.

Per La Forest and L'Heureux-Dubé JJ.: The province had no authority to extinguish aboriginal rights either under the Constitution Act, 1867 or by virtue of s. 88 of the Indian Act.

McLachlin J. was in substantial agreement.

[...]

The judgment of Lamer C.J. and Cory and Major JJ. was delivered by

THE CHIEF JUSTICE —

I. Introduction

1. This appeal is the latest in a series of cases in which it has fallen to this Court to interpret and apply the guarantee of existing aboriginal rights found in s. 35(1) of the Constitution Act, 1982. Although that line of decisions, commencing with *R. v. Sparrow*, [1990] 1 S.C.R. 1075, proceeding through the Van der Peet trilogy (*R. v. Van der Peet*, [1996] 2 S.C.R. 507, *R. v. N.T.C. Smokehouse Ltd.*, [1996] 2 S.C.R. 672, and *R. v. Gladstone*, [1996] 2 S.C.R. 723), and ending in R. v. Pamajewon, [1996] 2 S.C.R. 821, *R. v. Adams*, [1996] 3 S.C.R. 101, and *R. v. Côté*, [1996] 3 S.C.R. 139, have laid down the jurisprudential framework for s. 35(1), this appeal raises a set of interrelated and novel questions which revolve around a single issue—the nature and scope of the constitutional protection afforded by s. 35(1) to common law aboriginal title.

2. In Adams, and in the companion decision in *Côté*, I considered and rejected the proposition that claims to aboriginal rights must also be grounded in an underlying claim to aboriginal title. But I held, nevertheless, that aboriginal title was a distinct species of aboriginal right that was recognized and affirmed by s. 35(1). Since aboriginal title was not being claimed in those earlier appeals, it was unnecessary to say more. This appeal demands, however, that the Court now explore and elucidate the implications of the constitutionalization of aboriginal title. The first is the specific content of aboriginal title, a question which this Court has not yet definitively addressed, either at common law or under s. 35(1). The second is the related question of the test for the proof of title, which, whatever its content, is a right in land, and its relationship to the definition of the aboriginal rights recognized and affirmed by s. 35(1) in *Van der Peet* in terms of activities. The third is whether aboriginal title, as a right in land, mandates a modified

192   *The Present Politics of the Past*

approach to the test of justification first laid down in *Sparrow* and elaborated upon in *Gladstone*.

3. In addition to the relationship between aboriginal title and s. 35(1), this appeal also raises an important practical problem relevant to the proof of aboriginal title which is endemic to aboriginal rights litigation generally—the treatment of the oral histories of Canada's aboriginal peoples by the courts. In *Van der Peet*, I held that the common law rules of evidence should be adapted to take into account the sui generis nature of aboriginal rights. In this appeal, the Court must address what specific form those modifications must take.

4. Finally, given the existence of aboriginal title in British Columbia, this Court must address, on cross-appeal, the question of whether the province of British Columbia, from the time it joined Confederation in 1871, until the entrenchment of s. 35(1) in 1982, had jurisdiction to extinguish the rights of aboriginal peoples, including aboriginal title, in that province. Moreover, if the province was without this jurisdiction, a further question arises—whether provincial laws of general application that would otherwise be inapplicable to Indians and Indian lands could nevertheless extinguish aboriginal rights through the operation of s. 88 of the Indian Act, R.S.C., 1985, c. I-5.

II. Facts

5. At the British Columbia Supreme Court, McEachern C.J. heard 374 days of evidence and argument. Some of that evidence was not in a form which is familiar to common law courts, including oral histories and legends. Another significant part was the evidence of experts in genealogy, linguistics, archeology, anthropology, and geography.

6. The trial judge's decision (reported at [1991] 3 W.W.R. 97) is nearly 400 pages long, with another 100 pages of schedules. Although I am of the view that there must be a new trial, I nevertheless find it useful to summarize some of the relevant facts, so as to put the remainder of the judgment into context.

A. The Claim at Trial

7. This action was commenced by the appellants, who are all Gitksan or Wet'suwet'en hereditary chiefs, who, both individually and on behalf of their "Houses" claimed separate portions of 58,000 square kilometres in British Columbia. For the purpose of the claim, this area was divided into 133 individual territories, claimed by the 71 Houses. This represents all of the Wet'suwet'en people, and all but 12 of the Gitksan Houses. Their claim was originally for "ownership" of the territory and "jurisdiction" over it. (At this Court, this was transformed into, primarily, a claim for aboriginal title over the land in question.) The province of British Columbia counterclaimed for a declaration that the appellants have no right or interest in and to the territory or alternatively, that the appellants' cause of action ought to be for compensation from the Government of Canada.

Native Title in Canada

B. The Gitksan and Wet'suwet'en Peoples

(1) Demography

8. The Gitksan consist of approximately 4,000 to 5,000 persons, most of whom now live in the territory claimed, which is generally the watersheds of the north and central Skeena, Nass and Babine Rivers and their tributaries. The Wet'suwet'en consist of approximately 1,500 to 2,000 persons, who also predominantly live in the territory claimed. This territory is mainly in the watersheds of the Bulkley and parts of the Fraser-Nechako River systems and their tributaries. It lies immediately east and south of the Gitksan.

9. Of course, the Gitksan and Wet'suwet'en are not the only people living in the claimed territory. As noted by both McEachern C.J. at trial (at p. 440) and Lambert J.A. on appeal (at p. 243), there are other aboriginals who live in the claimed territory, notably the Carrier-Sekani and Nishga peoples. Some of these people have unsettled land claims overlapping with the territory at issue here. Moreover, there are also numerous non-aboriginals living there. McEachern C.J. found that, at the time of the trial, the non-aboriginal population in the territory was over 30,000.

(2) History

10. There were numerous theories of the history of the Gitksan and Wet'suwet'en peoples before the trial judge. His conclusion from the evidence was that their ancestors migrated from Asia, probably through Alaska, and spread south and west into the areas which they found to be liveable. There was archeological evidence, which he accepted, that there was some form of human habitation in the territory and its surrounding areas from 3,500 to 6,000 years ago, and intense occupation of the Hagwilget Canyon site (near Hazelton), prior to about 4,000 to 3,500 years ago. This occupation was mainly in or near villages on the Skeena River, the Babine River or the Bulkley River, where salmon, the staple of their diet, was easily obtainable. The other parts of the territory surrounding and between their villages and rivers were used for hunting and gathering for both food and ceremonial purposes. The scope of this hunting and gathering area depended largely on the availability of the required materials in the areas around the villages. Prior to the commencement of the fur trade, there was no reason to travel far from the villages for anything other than their subsistence requirements.

(3) North American Exploration

11. There was little European influence in western Canada until the arrival of Capt. Cook at Nootka on Vancouver Island in 1778, which led to the sea otter hunt in the north Pacific. This influence grew with the establishment of the first Hudson's Bay trading post west of the Rockies (although east of the territories claimed) by Simon Fraser in 1805-1806. Trapping for the commercial fur trade was not an aboriginal practice, but

194 *The Present Politics of the Past*

rather one influenced by European contact. The trial judge held that the time of direct contact between the Aboriginal Peoples in the claimed territory was approximately 1820, after the trader William Brown arrived and Hudson's Bay had merged with the North West Company.

(4) Present Social Organization

12. McEachern C.J. set out a description of the present social organization of the appellants. In his opinion, this was necessary because "one of the ingredients of aboriginal land claims is that they arise from long-term communal rather than personal use or possession of land" (at p. 147). The fundamental premise of both the Gitksan and the Wet'suwet'en peoples is that they are divided into clans and Houses. Every person born of a Gitksan or Wet'suwet'en woman is automatically a member of his or her mother's House and clan. There are four Gitksan and four Wet'suwet'en clans, which are subdivided into Houses. Each House has one or more Hereditary Chief as its titular head, selected by the elders of their House, as well as possibly the Head Chief of the other Houses of the clan. There is no head chief for the clans, but there is a ranking order of precedence within communities or villages, where one House or clan may be more prominent than others.

13. At trial, the appellants' claim was based on their historical use and "ownership" of one or more of the territories. The trial judge held that these are marked, in some cases, by physical and tangible indicators of their association with the territories. He cited as examples totem poles with the Houses' crests carved, or distinctive regalia. In addition, the Gitksan Houses have an "adaawk" which is a collection of sacred oral tradition about their ancestors, histories and territories. The Wet'suwet'en each have a "kungax" which is a spiritual song or dance or performance which ties them to their land. Both of these were entered as evidence on behalf of the appellants (see my discussion of the trial judge's view of this evidence, infra).

14. The most significant evidence of spiritual connection between the Houses and their territory is a feast hall. This is where the Gitksan and Wet'suwet'en peoples tell and retell their stories and identify their territories to remind themselves of the sacred connection that they have with their lands. The feast has a ceremonial purpose, but is also used for making important decisions. The trial judge also noted the Criminal Code prohibition on aboriginal feast ceremonies, which existed until 1951.

[...]

V. Analysis

[...]

B. What is the ability of this Court to interfere with the factual findings made by the trial judge?

[...]

Native Title in Canada 195

80. I recently held, in *Van der Peet*, that these general principles apply to cases litigated under s. 35(1). On the other hand, while accepting the general principle of non-interference, this Court has also identified specific situations in which an appeal court can interfere with a finding of fact made at trial. For example, appellate intervention is warranted "where the courts below have misapprehended or overlooked material evidence": see *Chartier v. Attorney General of Quebec*, [1979] 2 S.C.R. 474, at p. 493. In cases involving the determination of aboriginal rights, appellate intervention is also warranted by the failure of a trial court to appreciate the evidentiary difficulties inherent in adjudicating aboriginal claims when, first, applying the rules of evidence and, second, interpreting the evidence before it. As I said in *Van der Peet*, at para. 68:

In determining whether an aboriginal claimant has produced evidence sufficient to demonstrate that her activity is an aspect of a practice, custom or tradition integral to a distinctive aboriginal culture, a court should approach the rules of evidence, and interpret the evidence that exists, with a consciousness of the special nature of aboriginal claims, and of the evidentiary difficulties in proving a right which originates in times where there were no written records of the practices, customs and traditions engaged in. The courts must not undervalue the evidence presented by aboriginal claimants simply because that evidence does not conform precisely with the evidentiary standards that would be applied in, for example, a private law torts case.

81. The justification for this special approach can be found in the nature of aboriginal rights themselves. I explained in *Van der Peet* that those rights are aimed at the reconciliation of the prior occupation of North America by distinctive aboriginal societies with the assertion of Crown sovereignty over Canadian territory. They attempt to achieve that reconciliation by "their bridging of aboriginal and non-aboriginal cultures" (at para. 42). Accordingly, "a court must take into account the perspective of the aboriginal people claiming the right...while at the same time taking into account the perspective of the common law" such that "[t]rue reconciliation will, equally, place weight on each" (at paras. 49 and 50).

82. In other words, although the doctrine of aboriginal rights is a common law doctrine, aboriginal rights are truly sui generis, and demand a unique approach to the treatment of evidence which accords due weight to the perspective of aboriginal peoples. However, that accommodation must be done in a manner which does not strain "the Canadian legal and constitutional structure" (at para. 49). Both the principles laid down in *Van der Peet*—first, that trial courts must approach the rules of evidence in light of

196   *The Present Politics of the Past*

the evidentiary difficulties inherent in adjudicating aboriginal claims, and second, that trial courts must interpret that evidence in the same spirit—must be understood against this background.

83. A concrete application of the first principle can be found in *Van der Peet* itself, where I addressed the difficulties inherent in demonstrating a continuity between current aboriginal activities and the pre-contact practices, customs and traditions of aboriginal societies. As I reiterate below, the requirement for continuity is one component of the definition of aboriginal rights (although, as I explain below, in the case of title, the issue is continuity from sovereignty, not contact). However, given that many aboriginal societies did not keep written records at the time of contact or sovereignty, it would be exceedingly difficult for them to produce (at para. 62) "conclusive evidence from pre-contact times about the practices, customs and traditions of their community." Accordingly, I held that (at para. 62):

> The evidence relied upon by the applicant and the courts may relate to aboriginal practices, customs and traditions post-contact; it simply needs to be directed at demonstrating which aspects of the aboriginal community and society have their origins pre-contact.

> The same considerations apply when the time from which title is determined is sovereignty.

84. This appeal requires us to apply not only the first principle in *Van der Peet* but the second principle as well, and adapt the laws of evidence so that the aboriginal perspective on their practices, customs and traditions and on their relationship with the land, are given due weight by the courts. In practical terms, this requires the courts to come to terms with the oral histories of aboriginal societies, which, for many aboriginal nations, are the only record of their past. Given that the aboriginal rights recognized and affirmed by s. 35(1) are defined by reference to pre-contact practices or, as I will develop below, in the case of title, pre-sovereignty occupation, those histories play a crucial role in the litigation of aboriginal rights.

85. A useful and informative description of aboriginal oral history is provided by the *Report of the Royal Commission on Aboriginal Peoples* (1996), vol. 1 (Looking Forward, Looking Back), at p. 33:

> The Aboriginal tradition in the recording of history is neither linear nor steeped in the same notions of social progress and evolution [as in the non-Aboriginal tradition]. Nor is it usually human-centred in the same way as the western scientific tradition, for it does not assume that human beings are anything more than one—and not necessarily the most important—element of the natural order of the universe. Moreover, the

Native Title in Canada

Aboriginal historical tradition is an oral one, involving legends, stories and accounts handed down through the generations in oral form. It is less focused on establishing objective truth and assumes that the teller of the story is so much a part of the event being described that it would be arrogant to presume to classify or categorize the event exactly or for all time.

In the Aboriginal tradition the purpose of repeating oral accounts from the past is broader than the role of written history in western societies. It may be to educate the listener, to communicate aspects of culture, to socialize people into a cultural tradition, or to validate the claims of a particular family to authority and prestige....

Oral accounts of the past include a good deal of subjective experience. They are not simply a detached recounting of factual events but, rather, are "facts enmeshed in the stories of a lifetime." They are also likely to be rooted in particular locations, making reference to particular families and communities. This contributes to a sense that there are many histories, each characterized in part by how a people see themselves, how they define their identity in relation to their environment, and how they express their uniqueness as a people.

86. Many features of oral histories would count against both their admissibility and their weight as evidence of prior events in a court that took a traditional approach to the rules of evidence. The most fundamental of these is their broad social role not only "as a repository of historical knowledge for a culture" but also as an expression of "the values and mores of [that] culture": Clay McLeod, "The Oral Histories of Canada's Northern People, Anglo-Canadian Evidence Law, and Canada's Fiduciary Duty to First Nations: Breaking Down the Barriers of the Past" (1992), 30 Alta. L. Rev. 1276, at p. 1279. Dickson J. (as he then was) recognized as much when he stated in *Kruger v. The Queen*, [1978] 1 S.C.R. 104, at p. 109, that "[c]laims to aboriginal title are woven with history, legend, politics and moral obligations." The difficulty with these features of oral histories is that they are tangential to the ultimate purpose of the fact-finding process at trial—the determination of the historical truth. Another feature of oral histories which creates difficulty is that they largely consist of out-of-court statements, passed on through an unbroken chain across the generations of a particular aboriginal nation to the present-day. These out-of-court statements are admitted for their truth and therefore conflict with the general rule against the admissibility of hearsay.

87. Notwithstanding the challenges created by the use of oral histories as proof of historical facts, the laws of evidence must be adapted in order that this type of evidence can be accommodated and placed on an equal footing

with the types of historical evidence that courts are familiar with, which largely consists of historical documents. This is a long-standing practice in the interpretation of treaties between the Crown and aboriginal peoples: Sioui, supra, at p. 1068; *R. v. Taylor* (1981), 62 C.C.C. (2d) 227 (Ont. C.A.), at p. 232. To quote Dickson C.J., given that most aboriginal societies "did not keep written records," the failure to do so would "impose an impossible burden of proof" on aboriginal peoples, and "render nugatory" any rights that they have (*Simon v. The Queen*, [1985] 2 S.C.R. 387, at p. 408). This process must be undertaken on a case-by-case basis. I will take this approach in my analysis of the trial judge's findings of fact.

[...]

(b) Adaawk and Kungax

93. The adaawk and kungax of the Gitksan and Wet'suwet'en nations, respectively, are oral histories of a special kind. They were described by the trial judge, at p. 164, as a "sacred official" litany, or history, or recital of the most important laws, history, traditions and traditional territory of a House. The content of these special oral histories includes its physical representation totem poles, crests and blankets. The importance of the adaawk and kungax is underlined by the fact that they are "repeated, performed and authenticated at important feasts" (at p. 164). At those feasts, dissenters have the opportunity to object if they question any detail and, in this way, help ensure the authenticity of the adaawk and kungax. Although they serve largely the same role, the trial judge found that there are some differences in both the form and content of the adaawk and the kungax. For example, the latter is "in the nature of a song...which is intended to represent the special authority and responsibilities of a chief...." However, these differences are not legally relevant for the purposes of the issue at hand.

94. It is apparent that the adaawk and kungax are of integral importance to the distinctive cultures of the appellant nations. At trial, they were relied on for two distinct purposes. First, the adaawk was relied on as a component of and, therefore, as proof of the existence of a system of land tenure law internal to the Gitksan, which covered the whole territory claimed by that appellant. In other words, it was offered as evidence of the Gitksan's historical use and occupation of that territory. For the Wet'suwet'en, the kungax was offered as proof of the central significance of the claimed lands to their distinctive culture. As I shall explain later in these reasons, both use and occupation, and the central significance of the lands occupied, are relevant to proof of aboriginal title.

Native Title in Canada 199

95. The admissibility of the adaawk and kungax was the subject of a general decision of the trial judge handed down during the course of the trial regarding the admissibility of all oral histories (incorrectly indexed as *Uukw v. R.,* [1987] 6 W.W.R. 155 (B.C.S.C.)). Although the trial judge recognized that the evidence at issue was a form of hearsay, he ruled it admissible on the basis of the recognized exception that declarations made by deceased persons could be given in evidence by witnesses as proof of public or general rights: see Michael N. Howard, Peter Crane and Daniel A. Hochberg, *Phipson on Evidence* (14th ed. 1990), at p. 736. He affirmed that earlier ruling in his trial judgment, correctly in my view, by stating, at p. 180, that the adaawk and kungax were admissible "out of necessity as exceptions to the hearsay rule" because there was no other way to prove the history of the Gitksan and Wet'suwet'en nations.

96. The trial judge, however, went on to give these oral histories no independent weight at all. He held, at p. 180, that they were only admissible as "direct evidence of facts in issue... in a few cases where they could constitute confirmatory proof of early presence in the territory." His central concern that the adaawk and kungax could not serve "as evidence of detailed history, or land ownership, use or occupation." I disagree with some of the reasons he relied on in support of this conclusion.

97. Although he had earlier recognized, when making his ruling on admissibility, that it was impossible to make an easy distinction between the mythological and "real" aspects of these oral histories, he discounted the adaawk and kungax because they were not "literally true," confounded "what is fact and what is belief," "included some material which might be classified as mythology," and projected a "romantic view" of the history of the appellants. He also cast doubt on the authenticity of these special oral histories (at p. 181) because, inter alia, "the verifying group is so small that they cannot safely be regarded as expressing the reputation of even the Indian community, let alone the larger community whose opportunity to dispute territorial claims would be essential to weight." Finally, he questioned (at p. 181) the utility of the adaawk and kungax to demonstrate use and occupation because they were "seriously lacking in detail about the specific lands to which they are said to relate."

98. Although he framed his ruling on weight in terms of the specific oral histories before him, in my respectful opinion, the trial judge in reality based his decision on some general concerns with the use of oral histories as evidence in aboriginal rights cases. In summary, the trial judge gave no independent weight to these special oral histories because they did not accurately convey historical truth, because knowledge about those oral

histories was confined to the communities whose histories they were and because those oral histories were insufficiently detailed. However, as I mentioned earlier, these are features, to a greater or lesser extent, of all oral histories, not just the adaawk and kungax. The implication of the trial judge's reasoning is that oral histories should never be given any independent weight and are only useful as confirmatory evidence in aboriginal rights litigation. I fear that if this reasoning were followed, the oral histories of aboriginal peoples would be consistently and systematically undervalued by the Canadian legal system, in contradiction of the express instruction to the contrary in *Van der Peet* that trial courts interpret the evidence of aboriginal peoples in light of the difficulties inherent in adjudicating aboriginal claims.

(c) Recollections of Aboriginal Life

99. The trial judge also erred when he discounted the "recollections of aboriginal life" offered by various members of the appellant nations. I take that term to be a reference to testimony about personal and family history that is not part of an adaawk or a kungax. That evidence consisted of the personal knowledge of the witnesses and declarations of witnesses' ancestors as to land use. This history had been adduced by the appellants in order to establish the requisite degree of use and occupation to make out a claim to ownership and, for the same reason as the adaawk and kungax, is material to the proof of aboriginal title.

100. The trial judge limited the uses to which the evidence could be put. He reasoned, at p. 177, that this evidence, at most, established "without question, that the plaintiff's immediate ancestors, for the past 100 years or so" had used land in the claimed territory for aboriginal purposes. However, the evidence was insufficiently precise to demonstrate that the more distant ancestors of the witnesses had engaged in specific enough land use "far enough back in time to permit the plaintiffs to succeed on issues such as internal boundaries." In the language of *Van der Peet*, the trial judge effectively held that this evidence did not demonstrate the requisite continuity between present occupation and past occupation in order to ground a claim for aboriginal title.

101. In my opinion, the trial judge expected too much of the oral history of the appellants, as expressed in the recollections of aboriginal life of members of the appellant nations. He expected that evidence to provide definitive and precise evidence of pre-contact aboriginal activities on the territory in question. However, as I held in *Van der Peet*, this will be almost an impossible burden to meet. Rather, if oral history cannot conclusively establish pre-sovereignty (after this decision) occupation of land, it may still

Native Title in Canada

be relevant to demonstrate that current occupation has its origins prior to sovereignty. This is exactly what the appellants sought to do.

[...]

(e) Conclusion

107. The trial judge's treatment of the various kinds of oral histories did not satisfy the principles I laid down in *Van der Peet*. These errors are particularly worrisome because oral histories were of critical importance to the appellants' case. They used those histories in an attempt to establish their occupation and use of the disputed territory, an essential requirement for aboriginal title. The trial judge, after refusing to admit, or giving no independent weight to these oral histories, reached the conclusion that the appellants had not demonstrated the requisite degree of occupation for "ownership." Had the trial judge assessed the oral histories correctly, his conclusions on these issues of fact might have been very different.

108. In the circumstances, the factual findings cannot stand. However, given the enormous complexity of the factual issues at hand, it would be impossible for the Court to do justice to the parties by sifting through the record itself and making new factual findings. A new trial is warranted, at which the evidence may be considered in light of the principles laid down in *Van der Peet* and elaborated upon here. In applying these principles, the new trial judge might well share some or all of the findings of fact of McEachern C.J.

[...]

E.Did the province have the power to extinguish aboriginal rights after 1871, either under its ownjurisdiction or through the operation of s. 88 of the Indian Act?

(1)Introduction

172. For aboriginal rights to be recognized and affirmed by s. 35(1), they must have existed in 1982. Rights which were extinguished by the sovereign before that time are not revived by the provision. In a federal system such as Canada's, the need to determine whether aboriginal rights have been extinguished raises the question of which level of government has jurisdiction to do so. In the context of this appeal, that general question becomes three specific ones. First, there is the question whether the province of British Columbia, from the time it joined Confederation in 1871, until the entrenchment of s. 35(1) in 1982, had the jurisdiction to extinguish the rights of aboriginal peoples, including aboriginal title, in that province. Second, if the province was without such jurisdiction, another question arises—whether provincial laws which were not in pith and substance aimed at the extinguishment of aboriginal rights could have done so nevertheless if they were laws of general application. The third and final question is whether

202   *The Present Politics of the Past*

a provincial law, which could otherwise not extinguish aboriginal rights, be given that effect through referential incorporation by s. 88 of the Indian Act.

(2)Primary Jurisdiction

173. Since 1871, the exclusive power to legislate in relation to "Indians, and Lands reserved for the Indians" has been vested with the federal government by virtue of s. 91(24) of the Constitution Act, 1867. That head of jurisdiction, in my opinion, encompasses within it the exclusive power to extinguish aboriginal rights, including aboriginal title.

"Lands reserved for the Indians"

174. I consider the second part of this provision first, which confers jurisdiction to the federal government over "Lands reserved for the Indians." The debate between the parties centred on whether that part of s. 91(24) confers jurisdiction to legislate with respect to aboriginal title. The province's principal submission is that "Lands reserved for the Indians" are lands which have been specifically set aside or designated for Indian occupation, such as reserves. However, I must reject that submission, because it flies in the face of the judgment of the Privy Council in *St. Catherine's Milling.* One of the issues in that appeal was the federal jurisdiction to accept the surrender of lands held pursuant to aboriginal title. It was argued that the federal government, at most, had jurisdiction over "Indian Reserves." Lord Watson, speaking for the Privy Council, rejected this argument, stating that had the intention been to restrict s. 91(24) in this way, specific language to this effect would have been used. He accordingly held that (at p. 59):

> ... the words actually used are, according to their natural meaning, sufficient to include all lands reserved, upon any terms or conditions, for Indian occupation.

Lord Watson's reference to "all lands" encompasses not only reserve lands, but lands held pursuant to aboriginal title as well. Section 91(24), in other words, carries with it the jurisdiction to legislate in relation to aboriginal title. It follows, by implication, that it also confers the jurisdiction to extinguish that title.

175. The province responds by pointing to the fact that underlying title to lands held pursuant to aboriginal title vested with the provincial Crown pursuant to s. 109 of the Constitution Act, 1867. In its submission, this right of ownership carried with it the right to grant fee simples which, by implication, extinguish aboriginal title, and so by negative implication excludes aboriginal title from the scope of s. 91(24). The difficulty with the province's submission is that it fails to take account of the language of s. 109, which states in part that:

Native Title in Canada

109. All Lands, Mines, Minerals, and Royalties belonging to the several Provinces of Canada ... at the Union ... shall belong to the several Provinces ... subject to any Trusts existing in respect thereof, and to any Interest other than that of the Province in the same.

Although that provision vests underlying title in provincial Crowns, it qualifies provincial ownership by making it subject to the "any Interest other than that of the Province in the same." In *St. Catherine's Milling*, the Privy Council held that aboriginal title was such an interest, and rejected the argument that provincial ownership operated as a limit on federal jurisdiction. The net effect of that decision, therefore, was to separate the ownership of lands held pursuant to aboriginal title from jurisdiction over those lands. Thus, although on surrender of aboriginal title the province would take absolute title, jurisdiction to accept surrenders lies with the federal government. The same can be said of extinguishments—although on extinguishment of aboriginal title, the province would take complete title to the land, the jurisdiction to extinguish lies with the federal government.

176. I conclude with two remarks. First, even if the point were not settled, I would have come to the same conclusion. The judges in the court below noted that separating federal jurisdiction over Indians from jurisdiction over their lands would have a most unfortunate result—the government vested with primary constitutional responsibility for securing the welfare of Canada's aboriginal peoples would find itself unable to safeguard one of the most central of native interests—their interest in their lands. Second, although the submissions of the parties and my analysis have focussed on the question of jurisdiction over aboriginal title, in my opinion, the same reasoning applies to jurisdiction over any aboriginal right which relates to land. As I explained earlier, Adams clearly establishes that aboriginal rights may be tied to land but nevertheless fall short of title. Those relationships with the land, however, may be equally fundamental to aboriginal peoples and, for the same reason that jurisdiction over aboriginal title must vest with the federal government, so too must the power to legislate in relation to other aboriginal rights in relation to land.

"Indians"

177. The extent of federal jurisdiction over Indians has not been definitively addressed by this Court. We have not needed to do so because the vires of federal legislation with respect to Indians, under the division of powers, has never been at issue. The cases which have come before the Court under s. 91(24) have implicated the question of jurisdiction over Indians from the other direction—whether provincial laws which on their face apply to

Indians intrude on federal jurisdiction and are inapplicable to Indians to the extent of that intrusion. As I explain below, the Court has held that s. 91(24) protects a "core" of Indianness from provincial intrusion, through the doctrine of interjurisdictional immunity.

178. It follows, at the very least, that this core falls within the scope of federal jurisdiction over Indians. That core, for reasons I will develop, encompasses aboriginal rights, including the rights that are recognized and affirmed by s. 35(1). Laws which purport to extinguish those rights therefore touch the core of Indianness which lies at the heart of s. 91(24), and are beyond the legislative competence of the provinces to enact. The core of Indianness encompasses the whole range of aboriginal rights that are protected by s. 35(1). Those rights include rights in relation to land; that part of the core derives from s. 91(24)'s reference to "Lands reserved for the Indians." But those rights also encompass practices, customs and traditions which are not tied to land as well; that part of the core can be traced to federal jurisdiction over "Indians." Provincial governments are prevented from legislating in relation to both types of aboriginal rights.

(3)Provincial Laws of General Application

179. The vesting of exclusive jurisdiction with the federal government over Indians and Indian lands under s. 91(24), operates to preclude provincial laws in relation to those matters. Thus, provincial laws which single out Indians for special treatment are ultra vires, because they are in relation to Indians and therefore invade federal jurisdiction: see *R. v. Sutherland*, [1980] 2 S.C.R. 451. However, it is a well-established principle that (Four B Manufacturing Ltd., supra, at p. 1048):

The conferring upon Parliament of exclusive legislative competence to make laws relating to certain classes of persons does not mean that the totality of these persons' rights and duties comes under primary federal competence to the exclusion of provincial laws of general application.

In other words, notwithstanding s. 91(24), provincial laws of general application apply proprio vigore to Indians and Indian lands. Thus, this Court has held that provincial labour relations legislation (Four B) and motor vehicle laws (*R. v. Francis*, [1988] 1 S.C.R. 1025), which purport to apply to all persons in the province, also apply to Indians living on reserves.

180 What must be answered, however, is whether the same principle allows provincial laws of general application to extinguish aboriginal rights. I have come to the conclusion that a provincial law of general application could not have this effect, for two reasons. First, a law of general application cannot, by definition, meet the standard which has been set by this Court for the extinguishment of aboriginal rights without

Native Title in Canada

being ultra vires the province. That standard was laid down in *Sparrow*, supra, at p. 1099, as one of "clear and plain" intent. In that decision, the Court drew a distinction between laws which extinguished aboriginal rights, and those which merely regulated them. Although the latter types of laws may have been "necessarily inconsistent" with the continued exercise of aboriginal rights, they could not extinguish those rights. While the requirement of clear and plain intent does not, perhaps, require that the Crown "use language which refers expressly to its extinguishment of aboriginal rights" (*Gladstone*, supra, at para. 34), the standard is still quite high. My concern is that the only laws with the sufficiently clear and plain intention to extinguish aboriginal rights would be laws in relation to Indians and Indian lands. As a result, a provincial law could never, proprio vigore, extinguish aboriginal rights, because the intention to do so would take the law outside provincial jurisdiction.

181. Second, as I mentioned earlier, s. 91(24) protects a core of federal jurisdiction even from provincial laws of general application, through the operation of the doctrine of interjurisdictional immunity. That core has been described as matters touching on "Indianness" or the "core of Indianness" (*Dick*, supra, at pp. 326 and 315; also see Four B, supra, at p. 1047 and *Francis*, supra, at pp. 1028-29). The core of Indianness at the heart of s. 91(24) has been defined in both negative and positive terms. Negatively, it has been held to not include labour relations (Four B) and the driving of motor vehicles (*Francis*). The only positive formulation of Indianness was offered in *Dick*. Speaking for the Court, Beetz J. assumed, but did not decide, that a provincial hunting law did not apply proprio vigore to the members of an Indian band to hunt and because those activities were "at the centre of what they do and what they are" (at p. 320). But in *Van der Peet*, I described and defined the aboriginal rights that are recognized and affirmed by s. 35(1) in a similar fashion, as protecting the occupation of land and the activities which are integral to the distinctive aboriginal culture of the group claiming the right. It follows that aboriginal rights are part of the core of Indianness at the heart of s. 91(24). Prior to 1982, as a result, they could not be extinguished by provincial laws of general application.

(4) Section 88 of the Indian Act

182. Provincial laws which would otherwise not apply to Indians proprio vigore, however, are allowed to do so by s. 88 of the Indian Act, which incorporates by reference provincial laws of general application: *Dick*, supra, at pp. 326-27; *Derrickson v. Derrickson*, [1986] 1 S.C.R. 285, at p. 297; *Francis*, supra, at pp. 1030-31. However, it is important to note, in Professor Hogg's words, that s. 88 does not "invigorate" provincial laws

206 *The Present Politics of the Past*

which are invalid because they are in relation to Indians and Indian lands (*Constitutional Law of Canada* (3rd ed. 1992), at p. 676; also see *Dick*, supra, at p. 322). What this means is that s. 88 extends the effect of provincial laws of general application which cannot apply to Indians and Indian lands because they touch on the Indianness at the core of s. 91(24). For example, a provincial law which regulated hunting may very well touch on this core. Although such a law would not apply to aboriginal people proprio vigore, it would still apply through s. 88 of the Indian Act, being a law of general application. Such laws are enacted to conserve game and for the safety of all.

183. The respondent B.C. Crown argues that since such laws are intra vires the province, and applicable to aboriginal persons, s. 88 could allow provincial laws to extinguish aboriginal rights. I reject this submission, for the simple reason that s. 88 does not evince the requisite clear and plain intent to extinguish aboriginal rights. The provision states in full:

88. Subject to the terms of any treaty and any other Act of Parliament, all laws of general application from time to time in force in any province are applicable to and in respect of Indians in the province, except to the extent that those laws are inconsistent with this Act or any order, rule, regulation or by-law made thereunder, and except to the extent that those laws make provision for any matter for which provision is made by or under this Act.

I see nothing in the language of the provision which even suggests the intention to extinguish aboriginal rights. Indeed, the explicit reference to treaty rights in s. 88 suggests that the provision was clearly not intended to undermine aboriginal rights.

VI. Conclusion and Disposition

184. For the reasons I have given above, I would allow the appeal in part, and dismiss the cross-appeal. Reluctantly, I would also order a new trial.

185. I conclude with two observations. The first is that many aboriginal nations with territorial claims that overlap with those of the appellants did not intervene in this appeal, and do not appear to have done so at trial. This is unfortunate, because determinations of aboriginal title for the Gitksan and Wet'suwet'en will undoubtedly affect their claims as well. This is particularly so because aboriginal title encompasses an exclusive right to the use and occupation of land, i.e., to the exclusion of both non-aboriginals and members of other aboriginal nations. It may, therefore, be advisable if those aboriginal nations intervened in any new litigation.

186. Finally, this litigation has been both long and expensive, not only in economic but in human terms as well. By ordering a new trial, I do

Native Title in Canada

not necessarily encourage the parties to proceed to litigation and to settle their dispute through the courts. As was said in *Sparrow*, at p. 1105, s. 35(1) "provides a solid constitutional base upon which subsequent negotiations can take place." Those negotiations should also include other aboriginal nations which have a stake in the territory claimed. Moreover, the Crown is under a moral, if not a legal, duty to enter into and conduct those negotiations in good faith. Ultimately, it is through negotiated settlements, with good faith and give and take on all sides, reinforced by the judgments of this Court, that we will achieve what I stated in *Van der Peet*, supra, at para. 31, to be a basic purpose of s. 35(1)—"the reconciliation of the pre-existence of aboriginal societies with the sovereignty of the Crown." Let us face it, we are all here to stay.
[...]

Are B.C.'s Treasury, Economy in Peril of Going for a Song?

The Vancouver Sun (December 19, 1997)
By Owen Lippert,

Last week in Delgamuukw, the Supreme Court of Canada delivered a decision that will plunge B.C.'s economy and public finances into confusion and dysfunction if native leaders unwisely exercise new rights granted them by the court.
[...]
The courts in determining aboriginal title now will follow Lamer's rules of evidence. He ordered that oral evidence, songs and stories, not only be admissible, but placed on a "equal footing" with common law tests of occupation and ownership.
[...]
How does Lamer's decision rate according to economic theory? First, most economists from Adam Smith onwards have shown that land will be better cared for and used if someone owns it. It would make economic sense for aboriginal people to own all provincial Crown land if it were to be held in traditional fee simple ownership. But in his decision, Lamer practically gives control of 95 per cent of the B.C. land mass to about five per cent of the population and then strips away the benefits to economic efficiency and wealth creation.
[...]

B.C. Indian chiefs lay claim to entire province, resources: The provincial government is reviewing a demand by the First Nations Summit for an immediate freeze on any development of land resources anywhere in British Columbia.
The Vancouver Sun (February 2, 1998)
By Rick Ouston

B.C.'s native Indians are laying claim to every tree, every rock, every fish and every animal in the province.
In an unprecedented set of demands, the province's reserve Indians are brandishing a recent Supreme Court of Canada decision they say grants them unfettered control of the entire B.C. land mass, including forests, mines and fish.
[...]

INDIAN CLAIMS
In addition to laying claim to the entire province of B.C., the First Nations Summit is demanding:
-An increase to the $ 350 million "healing fund" announced last month by the federal Indian Affairs minister as compensation for the residential schools program.
- An apology from the premier on behalf of the B.C. government.
- The creation of a public inquiry into the 17 residential schools in B.C. and Alberta where B.C. native children attended.

How to make indian land claims go away: The government of Australia responded to that country's Delgamuukw with legislation extinguishing aboriginal title.
The Vancouver Sun (February 28, 1998)
EDITORIAL
By Trevor Lautens

When the Supreme Court of Canada issued its ruling on the Delgamuukw case concerning Indian rights and land claims in - or rather over - British Columbia, I expected the media to rush to Mel Smith for his reaction. They didn't, apparently on the basis that Smith's take on these issues - as the constitutional adviser to four successive provincial governments - was now irrelevant.
The Vancouver Board of Trade wasn't so dismissive. It invited Smith to talk to its members. In part, Smith said:
[...]

Native Title in Canada

Thus the court "drastically undermined the Crown ownership of 94 per cent of the land mass of B.C." and put "almost insurmountable hurdles" in the way of the province for land resource decisions. [...]
So far, so bad. But what to do? Smith advised: "The prime minister [...] and the premier of B.C. must agree on the following course of action: Suspend the treaty-making process and replace it with a legislative solution, (as) in Australia.... Australia has never signed treaties with its aboriginals."
[...]

Decision discredits the past of Mel Smith: Delgamuukw is a defeat for opponents of the existence of Indian title. Trevor Lautens, take note.
The Vancouver Sun (March 14, 1998)
EDITORIAL
By Felix Grant and Gerald Amos

[...]
Among the points that Smith made in his speech and that Lautens recorded in his column is that the Australian government responded to a ruling similar to Delgamuukw by its judiciary by extinguishing that country's equivalent to aboriginal title in Canada.
[...]

Infringements of aboriginal rights (including title), the Supreme Court of Canada teaches, are only justified if they infringe the right as little as possible. Unilateral extinguishment, it seems to us, infringes aboriginal titles as much as possible.
[...]

The final paragraph in the column, again simply quoting Smith, is especially disturbing. Smith states that "the native leadership... may have to be reminded that their people make up less than three per cent of the population..." Is that a threat? The implication, to us, is that aboriginal peoples are outnumbered and should, therefore, voluntarily hand over our legal title to the newcomers. Or else what? This is dangerous and irresponsible journalism.
[...]

210   *The Present Politics of the Past*

Legislation only hope of settling native land claims
The Vancouver Sun (March 25, 1998)
EDITORIAL
By Mel Smith

Felix Grant's and Gerald Amos's criticisms of my recent speech to the Vancouver Board of Trade do not fairly represent what I said (Decision discredits the past of Mel Smith, Forum, March 14).

I certainly do propose a legislative solution to the aboriginal title question, as was done in Australia, but far from confiscating proven aboriginal interests, those interests would be subject to fair compensation. [...]

The native leadership will resist the legislative approach because it takes the matter out of their hands and places it squarely where it belongs, into the hands of the duly constituted governments of Canada.

[...]

But no one could predict that this distant and cloistered court in Ottawa would be swayed by the sophistry of the Royal Commission on Aboriginal Peoples and its coterie of like-minded academics, create new law on the subject out of thin air and thereby cast aside well-established legal and constitutional principles.

Land claims distract from global demographic realities
The Vancouver Sun (April 2, 1998)
EDITORIAL
By Kurt Preinsperg

[...]

Ten billion people will struggle to survive on our crowded and ravaged planet within a few decades. Attempts to compensate Indian people, who constitute four per cent of Canada's population and already share in the benefits of a relatively prosperous country, are not only a moral irrelevancy. In the face of global injustice they are a distraction from the real issues and a dangerous invitation to a further splintering of the human race.

[...]

A passion for rectifying past injustice is an anachronism which the world can ill afford. It promotes division along ethnic lines which is likely to compound the political obstacles to an effective, coordinated response to shared problems.

[...]

Kurt Preinsperg
Department of Philosophy
Langara College

Native Title in Canada

Land claims talks are a disaster in making: I predict that every Lower Mainland property-owner will eventually be tenants, their rent paid to three bands.
The Vancouver Sun (April 4, 1998)
EDITORIAL
By Trevor Lautens

Let's be clear. One, I strongly wish the Indians of British Columbia well (and I especially advocate the horsewhip for the monsters who abused children in residential schools or anywhere else). Two, I equally strongly believe that this way - the current flow in negotiating Indian issues - lies disaster. For everyone. Perhaps the majority of Indians most of all. Too gloomy? Here, barring any shift from the present course, is my most optimistic projection:

By around 2010 all Greater Vancouver property "owners" will pay ground rent to their three ultimate landlords: the Squamish, Musqueam and Burrard bands. (Other areas will have similar arrangements).

By around 2025 Vancouver, Victoria and British Columbia will no longer bear those names, for the same reason that Rhodesia has been renamed Zimbabwe. The shameful colonial past must be, as totally as possible, expunged. It's started.

[...]

Of course Indian leaders and their lawyers have said repeatedly that only Crown land is sought, that private property is secure. An assurance so emphatic can only be looked upon with the gravest suspicion. I'd say it's plain that that's only a strategic position, to be discarded when timely. [...]

Top Indian advocate responds to Lautens: The $ 147 million two bands accepted for a 50-year-old wrong is a negotiated compromise. Believe it!
The Vancouver Sun (March 28, 1998)
EDITORIAL
By Thomas Berger

[...]
Production of oil and gas began in 1977. The revenues should have been the inheritance of the Blueberry and Doig bands. The federal government knew the oil and gas rights were potentially valuable. Yet they had given them away, without compensating the bands.

The Supreme Court held that the federal government had to pay damages to the bands. The federal government and the bands reached a settlement earlier this month based on the volumes of oil and gas produced since 1977 and the value of future reserves of oil and gas, which should have belonged to the bands. That $147 million is not "unbelievable;" it is a negotiated compromise.
[...]

Folly of Indian-rights decision becoming clear
The Gazette-Montreal (June 20, 1998)
By Andrew Coyne

We are beginning to see the consequences of last December's landmark Supreme Court ruling in the case of *Delgamuukw v. British Columbia*. And the consequences - legal, economic and political - add up to an unholy mess.
[...]
So far, so contentious. Whatever the specific limits of aboriginal title, the idea that the presumptive sovereignty of the Crown must be tempered by fairness to those who were already here - that might is not the only right -is a noble one.
[...]
Myths, legends and other "oral histories" of events long ago are now admissible as evidence - though only in aboriginal cases. No wonder B.C. is in such confusion - more so than usual, I mean.
[...]

AFN Chief Cites Media Intolerance
AFN Press Release (July 23, 1998)[1]

The Assembly of First Nations National Chief is calling on Canadians to speak out against "Indian-bashing" by the country's media.
Phil Fontaine said he is particularly concerned by media references to First Nation milestones in treaty and land rights negotiations as "race-based" policies. "Our nations have been here forever. It is offensive for journalists to suggest that governments are somehow doing us a favour by negotiating to restore lands and rights that were stolen from us in the first place."
The AFN leader, who represents over 600,000 First Nations citizens, referred to Prime Minister Jean Chretien's frequent description of Canada as the best country in the world in which to live. "He talks about how Canadian tolerance for one another's differences sets us apart from the rest

Native Title in Canada 213

of the world. You'd never believe that judging by some of the media reports on Aboriginal issues."

Fontaine cited recent reporting by The Ottawa Citizen newspaper as being particularly offensive. "On Canada Day their front page credited Tecumseh with saving this country from American invaders in the war of 1812. A few days later their editorial page carries an article condemning the Supreme Court's Delgamuukw decision, and in the process, belittles Indian culture and mocks our oral tradition."

"This is the worst kind of stereotyping of First Nations people – to appreciate us only when we're wearing our feathers, but despise us in everyday life. Some journalists and politicians in this country always want to complain about Aboriginal issues, but resent it when we appear to be making headway, like in the negotiating of the Nisga'a treaty."

The national chief noted that Canada's media has yet to respond to major criticisms leveled at them by the Royal Commission on Aboriginal Peoples, including charges that mainstream coverage of native issues was "spotty, misinformed, stereotyped, and sensational."

Fontaine called on the country's six regional press councils to be more pro-active in monitoring bias and unfair journalistic practices by the nation's 105 daily newspapers. "Instead of requiring people to go through a confrontational trial-like process with newspapers that insult them, press councils should be investigating ways to be a deterrent against unfair media practices."

Nisga'a Final Agreement [selections]
(1998)

PREAMBLE

WHEREAS the Nisga'a Nation has lived in the Nass Area since time immemorial;

WHEREAS the Nisga'a Nation is an aboriginal people of Canada;

WHEREAS section 35 of the Constitution Act, 1982 recognizes and affirms the existing aboriginal and treaty rights of the aboriginal peoples of Canada, which the Courts have stated include aboriginal title;

WHEREAS the Nisga'a Nation has never entered into a treaty with Canada or British Columbia;

WHEREAS the Nisga'a Nation has sought a just and equitable settlement of the land question since the arrival of the British Crown, including the preparation of the Nisga'a Petition to His Majesty's Privy Council, dated 21 May, 1913, and the conduct of the litigation that led to the decision of the Supreme Court of Canada in *Calder v. the Attorney-General of British*

Columbia in 1973, and this Agreement is intended to be the just and equitable settlement of the land question;

WHEREAS Canadian courts have stated that the reconciliation between the prior presence of aboriginal peoples and the assertion of sovereignty by the Crown is best achieved through negotiation and agreement, rather than through litigation or conflict;

WHEREAS the Parties intend that this Agreement will result in this reconciliation and establish a new relationship among them;

WHEREAS this Agreement sets out Nisga'a section 35 rights inside and outside of the area that is identified in this Agreement as Nisga'a Lands;

WHEREAS the Parties acknowledge the ongoing importance to the Nisga'a Nation of the Simgigat and Sigidimhaanak (hereditary chiefs and matriarchs) continuing to tell their Adaawak (oral histories) relating to their Ango'oskw (family hunting, fishing, and gathering territories) in accordance with the Ayuuk (Nisga'a traditional laws and practices);

WHEREAS the Parties intend their relationship to be based on a new approach to mutual recognition and sharing, and to achieve this mutual recognition and sharing by agreeing on rights, rather than by the extinguishment of rights; and

WHEREAS the Parties intend that this Agreement will provide certainty with respect to Nisga'a ownership and use of lands and resources, and the relationship of federal, provincial and Nisga'a laws, within the Nass Area; [...]

CHAPTER 2
GENERAL PROVISIONS
NATURE OF AGREEMENT

1. This Agreement is a treaty and a land claims agreement within the meaning of sections 25 and 35 of the Constitution Act, 1982.
AGREEMENT IS BINDING
2. This Agreement is binding on the Parties.
3. The Parties are entitled to rely on this Agreement.
4. Canada and British Columbia will recommend to Parliament and the Legislature of British Columbia, respectively, that settlement legislation provide that this Agreement is binding on, and can be relied on by, all persons.
REPRESENTATION AND WARRANTY
5. The Nisga'a Nation represents and warrants to Canada and British Columbia that, in respect of the matters dealt with in this Agreement, it has the authority to enter, and it enters, into this Agreement on behalf of

Native Title in Canada

all persons who have any aboriginal rights, including aboriginal title, in Canada, or any claims to those rights, based on their identity as Nisga'a.

6. Canada and British Columbia represent and warrant to the Nisga'a Nation that, in respect of the matters dealt with in this Agreement, they have the authority to enter into this Agreement within their respective authorities.

NISGA'A CULTURE AND LANGUAGE

7. Nisga'a citizens have the right to practice the Nisga'a culture, and to use the Nisga'a language, in a manner consistent with this Agreement.

CONSTITUTION OF CANADA

8. This Agreement does not alter the Constitution of Canada, including:

    a. the distribution of powers between Canada and British Columbia;

    b. he identity of the Nisga'a Nation as an aboriginal people of Canada within the meaning of the Constitution Act, 1982; and

    c. sections 25 and 35 of the Constitution Act, 1982.

9. The Canadian Charter of Rights and Freedoms applies to Nisga'a Government in respect of all matters within its authority, bearing in mind the free and democratic nature of Nisga'a Government as set out in this Agreement.

10. There are no "lands reserved for the Indians" within the meaning of the Constitution Act, 1867 for the Nisga'a Nation, and there are no "reserves" as defined in the Indian Act for the use and benefit of a Nisga'a Village, or an Indian band referred to in the Indian Act Transition Chapter, and, for greater certainty, Nisga'a Lands and Nisga'a Fee Simple Lands are not "lands reserved for the Indians" within the meaning of the Constitution Act, 1867, and are not "reserves" as defined in the Indian Act.

APPLICATION OF FEDERAL AND PROVINCIAL LAWS

11. If an authority of British Columbia referred to in this Agreement is delegated from Canada and:

    a. the delegation of that authority is revoked; or

    b. if a superior court of a province, the Federal Court of Canada, or the Supreme Court of Canada finally determines that the delegation of that authority is invalid the reference to British Columbia will be deemed to be a reference to Canada.

12. If an authority of Canada referred to in this Agreement is delegated from British Columbia and:

    a. the delegation of that authority is revoked; or

    b. if a superior court of a province, the Federal Court of Canada, or the Supreme Court of Canada finally determines that the delegation of that authority is invalid the reference to Canada will be deemed to be a reference to British Columbia.

216   *The Present Politics of the Past*

13. Federal and provincial laws apply to the Nisga'a Nation, Nisga'a Villages, Nisga'a Institutions, Nisga'a Corporations, Nisga'a citizens, Nisga'a Lands, and Nisga'a Fee Simple Lands, but:

    a. in the event of an inconsistency or conflict between this Agreement and the provisions of any federal or provincial law, this Agreement will prevail to the extent of the inconsistency or conflict; and

    b. in the event of an inconsistency or conflict between settlement legislation and the provisions of any other federal or provincial law, the settlement legislation will prevail to the extent of the inconsistency or conflict.

14. Any license, permit, or other authorization, including the Commercial Recreation Tenure required to be issued by Canada or British Columbia as a result of this Agreement, will be issued under federal or provincial law, as the case may be, and is not part of this Agreement, but in the event of an inconsistency or conflict between this Agreement and:

    a. that federal or provincial law; or

    b. any term or condition of the license, permit, or other authorization

this Agreement will prevail to the extent of the inconsistency or conflict.

OTHER RIGHTS, BENEFITS, AND PROGRAMS

15. Nisga'a citizens who are Canadian citizens or permanent residents of Canada continue to be entitled to all of the rights and benefits of other Canadian citizens or permanent residents of Canada, applicable to them from time to time.

16. Subject to paragraph 6 of the Fiscal Relations Chapter, nothing in this Agreement affects the ability of the Nisga'a Nation, Nisga'a Villages, Nisga'a Institutions, Nisga'a Corporations or Nisga'a citizens to participate in, or benefit from, federal or provincial programs for aboriginal people, registered Indians or other Indians, in accordance with general criteria established for those programs from time to time.

17. Nothing in this Agreement affects the ability of the Nisga'a Nation, Nisga'a Villages, Nisga'a Institutions, Nisga'a Corporations, or Nisga'a citizens to apply for or bid on any commercial, economic or other activity or project for which they would otherwise be eligible.

18. Subject to the Indian Act Transition Chapter and paragraphs 5 and 6 of the Taxation Chapter, the Indian Act has no application to the Nisga'a Nation, Nisga'a Villages, Nisga'a Institutions, or Nisga'a citizens as of the effective date, except for the purpose of determining whether an individual is an "Indian."

Native Title in Canada 217

Bargaining Away Voting Rights: Nisga'a treaty establishes an ominous precedent
The Financial Post (August 11, 1998)
By David Frum

[...]
By the terms of that agreement, Nisga'a Indians - and only Nisga'a Indians - will possess the right to vote for the new governments of the Nisga'a lands. Non-Nisga'a residents on those lands will be disenfranchised. [...] Normally, in a democracy, we allow the people to be their own judges of what is a significant issue and what is not. But on the Nisga'a lands, the right of non-Nisga'a to be heard will always be contingent and conditional.
[...]

We ought to be integrating Indians into Canadian life [...] Instead, we are carving mini-sovereignties out of Canada, and acquiescing in the demand that those sovereignties, which operate on our soil and are funded by our money, be permitted to run their affairs in something much less than a free and democratic way. The Nisga'a treaty is only the latest incident of that ominous trend - a trend that is day by day corroding the liberty of us all.

Censorship Newest Anti-Indian Tactic
AFN Press Release (September 21, 1998)[2]

The Assembly of First Nations is calling on all Canadians to condemn a British Columbia newspaper chain trying to censor all opinions supporting the signing of the historic Nisga'a Treaty.
"We've been criticized for saying Indians are still the targets of racism," said National Chief Phil Fontaine. "But in recent months we've heard politicians deny our treaty rights, and media commentators contest our inherent right to self-government. Now they're trying to deprive us of our right to free speech. If this isn't racism, I don't know what else to call it."
The spokesman for 633,000 status Indians denounced the action of David Black, who has ordered the editors of his 60 BC weekly newspapers not to publish editorials in support of the Nisga'a treaty due to be ratified by the provincial legislature in six weeks.
"I doubt he would try to suppress the views of any other entire community in British Columbia," the National Chief said. "Let's see Mr. Black refuse

218   *The Present Politics of the Past*

to let members of BC's Chinese or British communities express their viewpoints in his papers."

"The Prime Minister says Canada is the best place in the world in which to live. People like Mr. Black don't want it to be that for First Nations people." Fontaine said British Columbia's press council and Human Rights Commission should be looking into the situation, and urged all right-minded Canadians to send letters to the editors of the Black weeklies expressing concern about the abuse of public trust by the newspaper chain.

Supreme Court Decision Supports First Nations Position on Citizenship and Membership
AFN Press Release (May 20, 1999)[3]

The National Chief of the Assembly of First Nations, Phil Fontaine, says that the decision handed down today by the Supreme Court reinforces First Nations position that they, and not the federal government, should decide on the citizenship and membership of First Nations.

"This case clearly shows that the Indian Act is an antiquated, racist and outdated piece of legislation. The Supreme Court recognizes this and has given the government 18 months to amend it. By the same token, it has also signaled that the government must recognize that First Nations are the ones who are best suited to determine their own laws and governance on this matter," said National Chief Fontaine. "The government must also recognize that they have the legal obligation to provide the financial resources to the communities in light of this decision."

The Supreme Court has also stated quite clearly that First Nations women have been severely disadvantaged by the Indian Act. The ruling states "Aboriginal women, who can be said to be doubly disadvantaged on the basis of both sex and race, are particularly affected by differential treatment of off-reserve band members." This can also be traced back to the discriminatory treatment of First Nations women under the Indian Act and subsequent policies.

The Supreme Court ruling has stated clearly that the government has 18 months to change the Indian Act and allow First Nations citizens, living away from their community, the right to vote in Band elections. The Chiefs-in-Assembly have stated on many occasions that they represent all First Nations citizens, regardless of residency. The Court decision reinforces that and supports, by extension, the inherent right to self-government of First Nations in determining their citizenship.

Native Title in Canada 219

"The Indian Act, a piece of legislation that was created to get rid of the "Indian problem," also divided our communities by imposing a classification among our citizens based on their residency. The government further exacerbated that by also imposing various levels of service and rights on our citizens depending upon residency. This decision states, and I quote, "those affected, or their parents may have left the reserve given historical circumstances such as an often inadequate land base, a serious lack of economic opportunities and housing and the operation of past Indian status and band membership rules imposed by Parliament." This reinforces our position that we are the only ones to determine what's best for all our citizens, regardless of residency," added the National Chief.

The end result, however, is that First Nations are once again victims of this legislation. Although in the short term there may be uncertainty as a result of this decision, it will provide an opportunity for First Nations to address a long-standing problem that has created much division within their communities. "This decision highlights the crucial need for First Nations to create their own legislation in the area of governance. The AFN has already started looking into this issue through the Lands and Trust Services Initiative. We are working with our communities to resolve these issues because we are best suited to manage our own affairs," concluded National Chief Fontaine.

National Chief Applauds Passage of Bill C-49
AFN Press Release (June 11, 1999)[4]

The National Chief of the Assembly of First Nations, Phil Fontaine, applauds the passage of Bill C-49, the First Nations Land Management Act in both Houses of Parliament. Royal Assent is expected in the next 2 weeks. "This is a great day for those 14 First Nations which have persevered in getting this legislation drafted and passed. This legislation will allow these communities to develop economic opportunities and improve the living conditions of their citizens over time, a necessary component on the path to self-determination," stated the National Chief.

This law will provide these First Nations with the opportunity to control, manage and make their own laws with respect to their reserve lands and resources. The Framework Agreement on First Nations Land Management states that the First Nations involved will be able to opt out of the land and resource management sections of the Indian Act. Instead, the First Nations involved will be able to develop their own law on land and

220 *The Present Politics of the Past*

resource management through community developed and ratified Land Codes.

"I have to applaud the federal government in its resolve to push through this legislation in the face of the obstructionist opposition of the Reform Party. The fears they raised amongst the Canadian population in respect to this Act are despicable and show the true colours of this party," added National Chief Fontaine.

It is expected that over the years other First Nations may opt into this process, thereby allowing them to exercise more control over their future and paving the way for improved opportunities for their citizens.

British Columbia Logging: The Westbank First Nation
AFN Press Release (September 29, 1999)[5]

National Chief Phil Fontaine has applauded the victory Monday of the Westbank First Nation in B.C. Supreme Court when a judge declined to force the First Nation to stop logging on land subject to its aboriginal title. The decision, said National Chief Fontaine, sends a clear message to the Government of British Columbia and the Government of Canada that aboriginal title, aboriginal rights and treaty rights must be taken more seriously by the other governments in Canada that has been the case in the past. The Supreme Court of Canada has recognized aboriginal title, together with treaty rights, as providing First Nations in Canada not only with inherent rights of self-government but of the right to deal with, and profit from, their traditional and ancestral lands.

The National Chief observed that the federal government has been slow, as has been the Government of British Columbia and the governments of the Maritime provinces, to meet their legitimate, fair and constitutionally required obligations.

National Chief Fontaine said, "Whether you focus on timber, fish, or any other natural resource the people of Canada traditionally have shown their willingness to share those resources with First Nations people in a spirit of partnership and generosity. The federal and provincial governments must raise their consciousness to those same levels."

National Chief Fontaine said that the Courts decision not to enforce an earlier stop work order at this time was important for a number of reasons. First, he said, that since the judge has asked the Westbank First Nation voluntarily to cease further logging on its land, fairness and equity required that the Government of British Columbia also agree to issue no more timber licenses anywhere in the Province of British Columbia until the issue of

Native Title in Canada 221

aboriginal title and First Nations participation have been meaningfully negotiated between First Nations and the Government of British Columbia. Second, the National Chief said that it is crucial that all governments enter into negotiation processes on resources and governance without the precondition that First Nations extinguish their title, aboriginal rights or treaty rights.

National Chief Fontaine reminded Canadians that, in the Agenda for Action with First Nations promised by Ottawa in 1998, the Government of Canada had proposed a joint process to explore the comprehensive claims process in order to consider and respond to First Nations' concerns. A process had been promised focussing on methods other than surrenders or extinguishments of aboriginal rights or aboriginal title to provide clarity, stability and certainty along with a strategy to deal with lands and resources issues which would encourage co-management and enhancement of the value of reserve lands while increasing access to and ownership of lands and resources by First Nations.

The National Chief said that he, and the Assembly of First Nations, stand ready to assist First Nations and the governments of Canada to achieve equitable and stable results.

National Chief Meets with Manning to Discuss Reform Attacks on First Nations
AFN Press Release (November 24, 1999)[6]

Phil Fontaine, National Chief of the Assembly of First Nations, met with Preston Manning, leader of the Reform Party, on November 23 to discuss his concerns about the tone and level of attacks the Reform Party has been directing against First Nations citizens and governments.

"Mr. Manning and his party have been attacking First Nations at an unprecedented level in the past year. Whether the issue is land claims, the Nisga'a Treaty, the Marshall decision or other key issues related to First Nations, the party has been using particularly mean-spirited language to portray our peoples and our issues. I met with Mr. Manning to ask him to tone down the rhetoric and the personal attacks," stated National Chief Fontaine.

In the fall of 1998, National Chief Fontaine met with the leader of the Reform Party to discuss comments and positions that the party was discussing in public. At the time, an agreement had been reached to avoid using attacks which would cause unnecessary alarm and confusion with Canadians. This agreement has simply not been respected.

"Mr. Manning and certain members of his caucus have increased their attacks and driven the level of discussion on First Nations issues to an all-time low. Using terminology such as race-based policies, attacking the integrity of First Nations governments and claiming that First Nations enjoy 'special rights and privileges' by virtue of their treaties is unwarranted fear-mongering that cause tensions and worry among Canadian citizens. This is a totally unacceptable attitude on the part of a party which also is the Official Opposition and which claims to speak for all Canadians. Obviously, they do not speak for us when they attack us, as First Nations and as a group, in this fashion," concluded National Chief Fontaine.

The National Chief has asked for a meeting with Mike Scott, Aboriginal Affairs critic for the Reform Party, in the near future to again raise his concerns.

National Chief Fontaine Applauds Passage Of Nisga'a Bill
AFN Press Release (December 14, 1999)[7]

Assembly of First Nations National Chief Phil Fontaine praised the Nisga'a People and Tribal Council President Joseph Gosnell for the landmark victory represented by this week's passage of Bill C-9 in the House of Commons.

"This is a watershed moment for Treaty-making in Canada," the National Chief said. "It represents a tribute to Nisga'a persistence and a successful conclusion to a complex and difficult process of negotiation between the three levels of government in Canada. For the first time in Canadian history, the supreme law-making jurisdiction of First Nations governments has been affirmed and recognized by the federal and provincial governments of the land. This victory is the first step towards recognition of self-government powers that will enable First Nation peoples to preserve their heritage and culture while using access to resources to develop their own viable economies."

The National Chief said the Nisga'a bill, once proclaimed into law by the Senate, will give definition to Section 35 of the Constitution Act of 1982. "Section 35 grants Constitutional protection to both existing Aboriginal and Treaty Rights and to those negotiated in modern land claims settlements and treaties," he noted. "It is a mechanism through which the other governments in Canada can and will recognize the inherent right of First Nations to self-government. These rights are not granted by Section 35, since they existed long before European settlement, but are recognized and protected within the fabric of Canadian law by virtue of Section 35."

Native Title in Canada 223

National Chief Fontaine was optimistic that passage of the Nisga'a Treaty bill signals the direction that governments will now take to resolve outstanding land claims and self-government negotiations across Canada. "The spirit of goodwill and open-minded cooperation which made the Nisga'a success possible must be present for the resolution of claims by other First Nations. While the terms of the Nisga'a Treaty were accepted by their citizens, they do not necessarily suit the aspirations of other First Nations. As we move forward, governments must recognize that each First Nation has its own objectives and expectations from the negotiating process," concluded the National Chief.

Address to the Truck Loggers Association Convention
(January 13, 2000)
By Gordon Campbell, Leader of the Official Opposition (BC Liberals)

[...]
There are three things that we are going to do. First, you should understand that unlike this government, we respect private property. We will protect private property, and we will provide fair compensation for all contractual rights that have been adversely affected by government decisions. You will not find us in the midst of a case like the Carrier Lumber case or the Husby Forests Products case, which we currently see.

[...]
We will protect private property in the land claims and treaty negotiations. We will carry out a full, province-wide referendum on the principles that should create a framework for all aboriginal treaties. This will help create a sense of certainty and confidence in people in the forest industry. The way they were treated in the Nisga'a agreement was simply unacceptable. You deserve a vote, and the BC Liberals intend to give you one.
[...]

National Chief Phil Fontaine fully supports Liard First Nation in legal action against Federal Government
AFN Press Release (February 10, 2000)[8]

Phil Fontaine, National Chief of the Assembly of First Nations, condemns the actions by the federal government, which issued timber permits to

224 *The Present Politics of the Past*

logging companies to harvest on land claimed by the Liard First Nation in the Yukon while still in negotiations for a Final Agreement.

"What message does this send to the Liard First Nation and all other First Nations in the concluding steps of their Final Agreement? The expectation is that both parties enter into these negotiations in good faith. This sort of action flies in the face of mutual trust and respect that are the guiding principles in such negotiations," stated the National Chief.

The Liard First Nation is in the process of negotiating its Final Agreement on self-government. The community has also been negotiating for 20 years a land claim that includes the land for which the permits have been granted. The First Nation cannot accept that the government is negotiating an agreement while at the same time signing away the timber rights to land that is clearly within its traditional territory.

"As National Chief, I am concerned that the department would be putting forward one face in negotiations while acting against the interests of the Nation in another area. The government's fiduciary responsibility is all encompassing. The government must act in the best interest of First Nations in all areas that affect them. Obviously, that's not the case here," concluded the National Chief.

The National Chief will be in close contact with the leadership of the Liard First Nation and the Council of Yukon First Nations and will support all actions they undertake.

National Chief concerned with lack of consultation on proposed changes to Indian Act
AFN Press Release (February 14, 2000)[9]

Phil Fontaine, National Chief of the Assembly of First Nations, reacted with concern at the actions of the federal government in introducing changes to the Indian Act without any prior consultations.

"The federal government is unilaterally announcing changes to the Indian Act that will affect all our citizens in Canada. First Nations governments had not received any advance notice as to the extent of the changes, their impact on our communities and the resources required to effect these changes," stated the National Chief.

This is a disturbing gesture by the government. The Federal Government has not responded in a comprehensive manner to various Supreme Court decisions. The decision in Corbiere and now the decision on same-sex benefits have much wider implications for First Nations than the restrictive interpretations that the federal government has chosen to recognize. The way in which the government has chosen to proceed serves to highlight the paternalistic nature of the Indian Act and of the federal government in moving unilaterally in this regard. First Nations citizens and governments must be involved when any changes to the Indian Act are proposed. History has shown us that government actions have led to hardships for First Nations when such piecemeal changes are made. Bill C-31 is a classic example where a further class of First Nations citizens was created without First Nations involvement.

"I am disappointed that neither the Minister of Indian Affairs or the Minister of Justice would give us the courtesy of a call to inform us of this legislative change, except for a notification letter, which contained no details sent to my office late in the day Thursday. I hope this is not the government's new approach to First Nations participation," concluded National Chief Fontaine.

My Name is Sheila and I'm a Hyphenated Canadian
Alliance Party Press Release (May 2, 2000)

Deepak Obhrai, Member of Parliament for Calgary East, said today that Heritage Minister Sheila Copps's visit to Boston promoting Canadian culture contrasts sharply with programs by her department and the Department of Multiculturalism that emphasize differences among us while refusing to let people simply be Canadian.

Heritage Canada, through Statistics Canada, continues to use the national population census as a tool to ask such questions as, "What cultural group did your ancestors belong to?' The list includes French, English, German, Metis, Cree and Canadian among others.

Question 17 and 19 in the 2001 population census continues this trend by seeking information about the ethnic and cultural diversity of Canada's population.

Obhrai has introduced a private member's bill in the House of Commons, C-468, that would ensure that no questions will be asked in a population census about a person's ethnicity. "Our nation is blessed with people from all across the world," said Obhrai. "In addition, this nation has also been blessed with people of the First Nations with their rich heritage. One common thread that holds us together is that we are Canadians and this Minister and her government continue to ignore that fact."

226   *The Present Politics of the Past*

National Chief hopeful of change in Federal Government attitude towards land claims settlement
AFN Press Release (July 5, 2000)[10]

The National Chief of the Assembly of First Nations, Phil Fontaine, expects that the federal government will adopt a more flexible approach to land claims resolution in the near future. In a letter to both the Prime Minister and to the Minister of Indian Affairs, the Honourable Bob Nault, he highlights the government's need to act in accordance to recent Supreme Court decisions in this regard.

"The federal government must start negotiating land claims issues in the spirit of the Delgamuuk'w decision by the Supreme Court. This is ever more important in light of recent developments in land claims negotiations, such as the Agreement-in-principle that some communities within the Innu Nation are expected to announce shortly," stated the National Chief.

The Innu Nation has defined a common approach for the land agreement between the Nation and the Canadian and Quebec governments. This approach is based on the Delgamuuk'w decision and the recognition of Aboriginal Title and the non-extinguishment of Aboriginal Title and Rights when such agreements are reached.

"The role of the Assembly of First Nations is not to dictate to any nation what is acceptable or not in their agreements. However, the Chiefs-in-Assembly have stated that the AFN must ensure that the Delgamuuk'w decision be recognized and respected by governments and that they form the basis of future land claims agreements and I will strive to respect the mandate that the Chiefs have given me. The extinguishment of Aboriginal Rights and Title is just not acceptable to First Nations in Canada and it wasn't to the Supreme Court either," added National Chief Phil Fontaine.

There are currently news reports that some communities within the Innu Nation have accepted an agreement in principle, which falls short of the Delgamuuk'w principles. That decision is one that the communities must make for themselves based on their own needs and expectations and also on other conditions that may exist for the communities.

"First Nations governments act in their own right and authority and these actions are not templates for other communities within their nations or across the country. They must make their own decisions as governments and in consultation with their citizens. That process is a democratic process and we respect that. If the communities have in fact come to an agreement, then I will support them as they strive to finalise

Native Title in Canada

it. I will not allow governments however to seek to impose such agreements on other communities or nations. Each nation has it's own demands and expectations and a template approach is totally unacceptable to First Nations," concluded National Chief Phil Fontaine.

Chapter Eight

Judgements: Indigenous Legal Claims Beyond the Limits of Liberalism

> In the end, however, perhaps the most profound concern ... is the multidimensional nature of the power imbalance that Aboriginal peoples experience. Control ... is not exercised merely through people and institutions. Both are governed by deep-seated global and national tenets that animate and direct the "acceptable" bounds within which people and institutions can exercise power. Aboriginal notions of citizenship with the land are not included among these accredited ideologies.
> John Borrows (Borrows 340)

INTRODUCTION

Although IPMs are often represented as accepting the liberal "rules of the game" in white settler societies, this work has attempted to counter such a view by distinguishing the liberal legal tactics of indigenous land claims from the critical, strategic quality these claims exhibit in relation to liberal governmentality. In these concluding remarks such a writing of indigenous resistance will be read against liberal justifications of native title and self-government. Such a confrontation will help clarify the extent to which liberalism has the resources to respond affirmatively to the claims of indigenous peoples.

A key component of this argument is that indigenous land claims are programmatically incompatible with liberalism. Such a claim must be differentiated from the more commonly accepted notion that native title complicates and modifies the legal systems that recognize such rights. Indeed, much of liberal political theory points to such effects on sovereignty (Maaka and Fleras 93), the nation (Barkan 322), and property (Barkan 336). Yet, this acknowledgement of the novelty of indigenous legal claims

229

has rarely extended to a discussion of the self-sufficiency of *liberal* democracy to manage said claims. When Will Kymlicka writes that it is "legitimate, and indeed unavoidable" to supplement liberal individual rights with minority rights (such as native title and self-government), he is likely unaware of the dangers posed by such supplementarity (Kymlicka 6). Precedents such as those set in the *Mabo* decision have the potential to fundamentally rearrange the structures of power relations precisely because they involve the recognition of alien legal principles that haunt the liberal rule of law (Webber 61, 80-81). However, this radical quality of native title is effaced by liberal political theory.

In chapter two the argument was advanced that mainstream social science depoliticizes IPMs by means of neo-orientalism and neo-ornamentalism. This chapter will illustrate that those self-same processes affect liberal theory's characterization of indigenous rights as well. Other chapters have explored tools for repoliticizing indigenous legal activism. IPM-settler state interaction can be written as (post)coloniality (chapter two), liberalism can be problematized via its genealogy as a complex series of governmentalities (chapter three), and the practice of resistance can be differentiated into its strategic and tactical forms (chapter one). Such discursive moves allow one to write IPMs as articulations of the "present politics of the past" within a shifting field of welfare liberal and neo-liberal techniques of government; they also distinguish indigenous claims produced by a non-liberal system of formation (i.e. the claims of *Tino Rangatiratanga* by the Maori) from those which critically transform claims of liberal descent (i.e. native title and national self-determination by the ATSIC in Australia and the AFN in Canada). What effect does this rewriting of IPMs have when read against liberal theories of indigenous rights?

In discussing liberal approaches to justifying indigenous claims to land and self-government, it is important to make two sets of distinctions. The first is that between those forms of liberalism that exhibit open hostility to group rights, particularly when associated with cultural identities such as indigeneity, and those forms which attempt to justify the recognition of said rights via liberal ideals. Brian Barry's latest work, *Culture and Equality*, exemplifies the former stance in arguing that multiculturalism, the politics of difference, and/or cultural recognition are both indefensible by liberal principles and harmful to the project of a just society through economic redistribution (Barry 8). The latter position, advanced by Will Kymlicka, Jacob T. Levy, Charles Taylor and others, is a more "generous liberalism" with regards to indigenous rights claims. Only the latter will be discussed at length here, for the former position requires no argument to prove its

Judgements

incompatibility with indigenous legal claims. Therefore, one must focus on the different means employed by generous liberalism to justify indigenous rights.

The liberal argument put forward for indigenous rights takes two basic forms: 1) rights as *restitution* for past injustices; and 2) rights as a means to the process of *reconciliation* between indigenous and non-indigenous peoples. Restitution in a strictly legal sense implies the return of unjustly taken belongings, and in this way is directly linked to native title claims; yet, this chapter will use "restitution" in the broader sense of referring to "the entire spectrum of attempts to rectify historical injustices," including reparations (payment for lost belongings) and apologies (Barkan xix). However, and this is the core of the argument made here, the twin depoliticizing strategies of neo-orientalism and neo-ornamentalism that inhabit mainstream social science are even more prevalent in liberal political theory. Thus this chapter is organized according to the matrix in Table 2:

Table 2 Chapter Organization

TACTICS/ JUSTIFICATIONS	Restitution	Reconciliation
Neo-Orientalist	(Barkan)	(Levy, "Three Modes of Incorporating Indigenous Law")
Neo-Ornamentalist	(Anaya)	(Kymlicka)

LIBERAL THEORIES OF INDIGENOUS RIGHTS I: RESTITUTION

The Guilt of Nations by Elazar Barkan is the fullest elaboration of the restitution-orientalist mode of liberal theory, and it is here that one may profitably begin the conversation between indigenous claims and liberalism. Barkan's work is animated with the premise that the legal claims of IPMs "though [their] rhetoric is essentially revolutionary," in both strategy and tactics they resemble "middle-of-the-road liberalism" and adhere to "Enlightenment principles" (Barkan 162-63). This is not altogether surprising given Barkan's second major premise, namely that "we" all are liberals in the 21st century (Barkan xx, 310, 46-47).

> "We" refers to a universe that shares vague liberal political and moral commitments to individual rights as well as to group human rights. This universe is studded with contradictions but increasingly subscribes to a shared political culture. (Barkan x)

That this is an *"Empire*-ial we" (a lá Hardt and Negri) speaking in the voice of a global sovereign in the name of a global pastorate provides the strongest reason for characterizing Barkan's position as neo-orientalist. Such a global political culture is described as one where the "classical liberal notions of the individual have been supplemented [sic] by sociological insights about the place of the community and specific identity in the life of people"—what Barkan terms "Neo-Enlightenment morality" (Barkan 308-09). The argument rests on the lack of acceptable alternatives to such a position. Barkan acknowledges that alternatives do exist, primarily in the form of so-called "national ideologies and religious fundamentalism," but he rejects these positions precisely because they "reject Enlightenment values and liberalism... We embrace tradition but only in its liberal guise" (Barkan xxxix). While it has caught the attention of Barkan that some in the academy are critics of liberalism, they are dismissed as merely participating in "a domestic squabble over how to implement and package these agreed-upon [liberal] principles" (Barkan 311). With these core premises in mind, such a liberal theory proceeds to justify indigenous and other claims to restitution so long as they also satisfy two litmus tests.

In order for group claims to qualify under this "Neo-Enlightenment" scheme of restitution they must abide by two liberal injunctions: 1) to respect individual human rights; and 2) not to threaten the stability of the political-economic structure of the (liberal) status quo. Thus, based on the first litmus test, Jacob T. Levy argues that the common-law mode of incorporating native title claims is the most amenable to liberal values for it "does not attempt to undo historical wrongs (such as conquest), except in so far as it demands compensation for unjust takings of unjust takings of indigenous property in land" (Levy, "Three Modes of Incorporating Indigenous Law" 320). Such incorporation "allows for cultural differentiation without freezing any particular customary understandings or communal affiliations into law" (Levy, "Three Modes of Incorporating Indigenous Law" 317).

Barkan delineates the second test by disqualifying the possibility of giving back the "New World" to the indigenous peoples there, even as "an imaginary gesture" (Barkan 327):

> The restitution plan has to be somehow proportional to the crimes and injustices to be atoned while leaving the political and economic status of the mainstream fundamentally intact. (Barkan 328)

Beyond these two limits of restitution, the neo-orientalist position also maintains that while a group's cultural status may be a relevant fact to be

Judgements   233

considered, groups deserve fair treatment and not special political status as a group *per se* (Levy, "Three Modes of Incorporating Indigenous Law" 318). However, this formulation too introduces the supplement of "moral otherness" via the recognition of indigenous cultural practice within the common law (Webber 77).

In addition to the indigenous objections noted above, this liberal theory of restitution contains two flaws. Barkan admits that while the "choice" implied in the claims of IPMs for liberal rights to property and self-determination is often "shaped by power relations," he gives moral authority to such decisions in writing that "it is often a choice, and not an imposition" (Barkan 332). Any theory that accords a preeminent role to choice patently does not take seriously the political implication of such choices being "shaped by power relations" (Digeser). Also, Barkan often praises the fairness of liberal restitution because such agreements "are not imposed upon the loser by the winner or some third party" (Barkan 317). Yet Derrida gives reason to doubt this very claim. If (with Barkan) we take the two parties to restitution as being the settler society represented by their government and indigenous people then there remains a "third party" required to enact such a settlement—the "we" of neo-liberal Empire. Derrida writes of the practical necessity of such a sovereign "third" in the process of restitution and forgiveness, yet also points to the inherent "impurity" of such an intervention (Derrida, *On Cosmopolitanism and Forgiveness* 59). Such impure interventions are nothing new to indigenous peoples around the world. In the introduction to its 2001/02 Budget Outlook, the Aboriginal and Torres Straits Islander Commission writes about the history of liberal attempts at remedying past injustices:

> It is a deeply embedded characteristic of the culture of migrant Australia, developed over 212 years, that they seek to confer benefits and advantages on Indigenous peoples. That was the justification for the various Protection Acts of the middle and late 19th century, up to the Commonwealth's 1911 legislation. It was the justification for the assimilation policies endorsed at the 1938 Commonwealth/States conference. It was the justification for the Commonwealth policies developed from 1968 to 1972, after the referendum of 1967, and it was the justification for the policies incorporated in the Native Title Act of 1998. On each occasion, the migrant Australia authorities eschewed the misunderstandings and well-meant errors of past policies, announced the New Dawn of enlightened policy, and expected Indigenous peoples to put their experience behind them. Every generation, approximately every thirty years, gets fed the same pap. In all cases, the policies and their avowed benefits were determined by the non-Indigenous

234 The Present Politics of the Past

authorities. No agreement was negotiated with Indigenous peoples or their representatives.

The notions of Indigenous rights, independent of non-Indigenous determination, is quite alien to the social and political culture of non-Indigenous society. That recognition and respect has been beyond its capacity, and directly threatens the notion that what Indigenous people have is conferred on them by migrant Australia. The closest approach to recognition of Indigenous rights was taken by the High Court decision in the Mabo case in 1992, which asserted for the first time that Indigenous peoples held title to the land of Australia prior to non-Indigenous possession of the continent, and that Native Title persisted wherever it had not been extinguished by being alienated by the Crown. That was a significant step forward for non-Indigenous Australia, however tentative and circumscribed it was in actuality. At least, it addressed, for the first time, the fact that Indigenous people owned the land that had been expropriated.

Since all restitution efforts as envisioned by Barkan come from the state, the very apparatus that brought about the injustice in the first place, the self-same institution that remains unquestionably in the hands of the white settlers, there is no way to see such agreements as pure expressions of guilt and acceptance between morally equal partners.

The justification of indigenous legal claims as restitution based upon the tactics of neo-ornamentalism, is not widely found in the literature. However, S. James Anaya provides one example of such an approach in his defense of ethnic group rights (Anaya, "On Justifying Special Ethnic Group Rights: Comments on Pogge"). His position rests on the case of restitution for cultural groups for the specific injustice of cultural discrimination. Since such discrimination is culturally directed, restitution (in the strict sense) requires the subsequent revalorization of the victimized group. Hence Anaya's statement that "indigenous peoples are not alone among groups with strong claims to redress for historical wrongs, but certainly not *all* groups, not all types of groups, can make such a claim" (Anaya, "On Justifying Special Ethnic Group Rights: Comments on Pogge" 229). Anaya treats the expropriation of indigenous self-determination as a particularly egregious example of cultural discrimination. Thus, on his account, contemporary indigenous rights claims are valid under international law to the extent that they propose a redress of past injustice, not to the extent that they return indigenous peoples to a *status quo ante*-colonialism.

Insofar as indigenous peoples have been denied self-determination thus understood, the international indigenous rights regime prescribes remedial measures that may involve changes in the political order, and hence, in

Judgements 235

> keeping with constitutive self-determination, are to be developed in
> accordance with the aspirations of indigenous peoples themselves.
> (Anaya, *Indigenous Peoples in International Law* 87)

It should be noted that Anaya argues this point not as normative theory, but
rather as a description of already existing international legal norms—a
contentious position, to be sure (Kymlicka, *Politics in the Vernacular:
Nationalism, Multiculturalism, and Citizenship* 128).

While Barkan's *The Guilt of Nations* and Anaya's *Indigenous Peoples
in International Law* represent major statements of the restitution approach
to justifying indigenous legal claims, most of the work within generous
liberalism attributes status to such claims via their role in the process of
reconciliation.

LIBERAL THEORIES OF INDIGENOUS RIGHTS II: RECONCILIATION

Despite the amount of time, ink, and energy spent on justifying restitution
for indigenous peoples under a scheme of liberal justice, many if not most
indigenous claims are not limited to redress for past grievances—they are an
attempt to take a more active political role in the present and the future. As
Dale Turner writes:

> The relevant issue for Aboriginal peoples is not whether we ought to rec-
> tify past injustices in order to balance the scales of a liberal distributive
> justice system, but how governments can come to recognize the
> legitimacy of Aboriginal sovereignty in order to renew the political
> relationship on more just foundations. (Turner 146)

Such reorganization requires at a minimum the recognition of group rights
within liberalism. Unlike the adamant "no" to such a possibility given by
liberals like Barry, "generous" liberalism is preoccupied with the questions
of recognizing groups' rights and the ways to balance such rights with the
traditional liberal concern for the individual.

Thomas Pogge gives one a strong and simple statement of a
neo-orientalist argument for group rights under liberalism. Pogge states that
it is sometimes necessary to recognize what he calls the "associative"
component of an individual's identity, in order to promote even-handedness
and provide for the "ideal of treating all citizens as equals" (Pogge 188).
However, he asserts that this public recognition of group membership may
not be restricted to any particular types of groups (i.e. indigenous peoples),

for that would violate the basic liberal principle of equality on which such recognition is justified in the first place (Pogge 199-200). This may be called the "prime directive" of neo-orientalist liberalism—groups' rights may exist only to the extent that they are called for to satisfy basic values of liberalism. This directive leads such thinkers to call for two litmus tests that any group's rights must pass: 1) group rights may not conflict with the basic set of individual rights to equal treatment and political liberty; and, 2) liberal-democratic institutions must serve as the rules of the game from within which conflicts between rights and right-holders are adjudicated. Both of these tests have significant depoliticizing effects for indigenous peoples.

As noted above, under neo-orientalist liberalism indigenous claims must affirm individual rights if they are to gain recognition (Franks 133). This individualism disqualifies many aspects of indigenous claims. Jacob T. Levy argues that the incorporation of indigenous customary law fails just such a test to the extent it limits the individual's choice law enforcement framework to which she is subject (Levy, "Three Modes of Incorporating Indigenous Law" 320, 22). Levy questions the recognition of indigenous sovereignty on similar grounds in that such recognition "leaves the least space for liberal human rights constraints" (Levy, "Three Modes of Incorporating Indigenous Law" 323).

> The case [for indigenous sovereignty] must be made instrumentally in terms of defense of liberal values or protection from violent states, because any general defense of an inherent right to self-government rests on implausible claims about the external reality of some category like "nation." (Levy, "Three Modes of Incorporating Indigenous Law" 324)

For the aforementioned reason, Levy argues that the instances where settler states recognize the sovereignty of indigenous groups should be limited anywhere it has not already been acknowledged (e.g., Australia) (Levy, "Three Modes of Incorporating Indigenous Law" 3244-325). However, others have argued that generous liberalism fails precisely if it cannot accommodate indigenous sovereignty (Turner 137). Dale Turner locates the problem in the disjoint between the ahistorical systems of rights that liberalism presupposes, and the distinctly historical nature of indigenous claims to sovereignty (Turner 145). If the liberal rights litmus test seems impossibly limiting to indigenous claims, the requirement of a liberal-democratic institutional framework to adjudicate conflict is no less so.

The institutions of political liberalism are assumed to be the logical starting point for negotiating multicultural claims because of their supposed

Judgements

lack of definitive answers to the fundamental questions of "human existence and meaning" that may define the "good life" for citizens (Franks 134). C.E.S. Franks go further to argue that indigenous peoples have "progressed" too far to ever go back to their traditional institutional forms—the truly indigenous form of the good life is dead:

> In small-scale traditional Aboriginal societies there was no need for the paraphernalia of courts, rules of justice, representative and accountable government, and formal rules of due process found in Western culture. The economic and social transformation of Aboriginal communities in the twentieth century have been so profound, however, that now Aboriginal self-governments themselves need them as much as governments in the larger nonnative society. (Franks 131)

That such a position reflects a direct continuation of an Orientalist colonial imaginary is difficult to ignore. On the one hand, the manner of indigenous peoples' incorporation into white settler states calls into serious moral question the justice of those liberal-democratic state institutions (Turner 142, 44). On the other hand, it is convenient for settler governments to rely on their own institutions, and most importantly the doctrine of majority rule, in the adjudication of indigenous claims; relying on the existing political framework of such states "legitimizes the fruits of colonialism" (Asch 159).

One can thus see that what indigenous claims must sacrifice under such a system of neo-orientalist liberalism is nothing less than indigeneity itself. First, many if not all of the legal institutions on which liberal-democracy rests in settler states are compromised by the continuing reliance on the legacies of colonialism—the doctrine of *terra nullis* prime among these (Asch 149, 53, 55). Second, the pattern of incorporation via the ideals and institutions of liberalism takes the form of the authoritative allocation of rights and duties to indigenous and non-indigenous peoples. Ideally, such a model should not be an open-ended process of mutual adjustment, but rather a more-or-less precise calculation of interest, claims, and duties (recall the discussion in chapter four on the role of calculation in liberal legal ideology).

> There is often a sense in non-indigenous political life that if there are serious questions of indigenous rights, they should be squarely addressed and exhaustively defined, so that political and economic life can proceed in full *certainty* of what those rights entail. This attitude was abundantly evident in the political debate surrounding *Mabo* and *Wik*, and was effectively harnessed by the Howard government in its campaign to amend the *Native Title Act 1993* [Emphasis added]. (Webber 81)

The governments and settler populations express the need for certainty. Far from being needed by indigenous people, such certainty can only mean the further limitation and depoliticization of their political struggles. The Union of British Columbia Indian Chiefs produced an entire policy document responding to the settler demands for certainty; it reads in part:

> Canada cannot understand our Sacred connection to the Land, our Aboriginal Title. It is "uncertain," because it prevents Indigenous Peoples from viewing the Land as a commodity to be bought, sold or traded. From Canada's perspective, our Aboriginal Title has to be changed, altered, and defined in a treaty so that it fits with Canadian laws and ideas about Land.
> Canada's strive for certainty reflects a desire that Indigenous Peoples assimilate into Canada, that we sever our connection to the Land. Canada asks that we dig up the roots connecting us to the Land and replant them through treaties. This lack of understanding and fear about our connection to the Land is what Canada strives to address through certainty.
> For Indigenous Peoples, our Aboriginal Title and connection to the Land is certain, it is in the bones of our grandmothers buried in the earth, and in the blood which beats in our hearts: Our Sacred connection to the Land is certain. (*Certainty: Canada's Struggle to Extinguish Aboriginal Title*)

Finally, neo-orientalist formulations of generous liberalism all proceed from a common dismissal of what must be considered an important moral and political fact: "most Aboriginal people do not subscribe to political liberalism's justification of their rights as [liberal] minority rights" (Turner 136). Thus, any reconciliation on the terms of liberalism's hegemony must be yet one more chapter in the long history of indigenous peoples' domination and injustice at the hands of white settlers.

There are other liberal theorists, however, who have attempted to find a place for indigenous rights within liberalism despite the fact that indigenous peoples come from outside that tradition of government. Chief among these efforts has been the "multicultural liberalism" of Will Kymlicka. Kymlicka goes beyond the arguments of Pogge and others to justify within liberalism group rights that are tied to the nature of said groups, and indigenous peoples have occupied a central position in his thought. Kymlicka argues that indigenous rights to self-government are not a temporary adjustment to rectify past wrongs (and thus are not restitutive), but rather flow from the status of indigenous peoples having been self-governing communities incorporated into settler states (Kymlicka, *Mul-*

Judgements

ticultural Citizenship). Kymlicka and other neo-ornamentalist liberals justify indigenous rights by reference to whether such groups can be classified as belonging to privileged categories of the Western political tradition—in particular, "civilized peoples" and "nations."

One of the central tropes of the imperial imaginary was the distinction between civilized and barbarous peoples. Both poles of such a distinction could be used to advance the imperial project. Maharajas in India, chiefs in the Americas, and the kings of the Maori all were identified as the responsible governments of civilized peoples, thus making them the legitimate partners in treaties or adversaries in war. The result of either was likely to be the extension of European domination over another set of free peoples. On the other hand, those groups labeled as barbarous need not have been trifled with at all—they simply did not exist. This conjuring trick is at the heart of how territories with indigenous inhabitants could magically become empty under European law. From Australia to Africa, settlers could simply define indigenous peoples as barbarous, declare them not to exist, and appropriate their lands under the full auspices of international law.

Even though either designation could lead to domination, the distinctions had important ramifications for the subsequent status of indigenous peoples in the respective settler state jurisdiction. J.G.A. Pocock points to the definition of the Maori as a "settled people" (capable of agriculture) and Australian Aboriginals as barbarous, as having had a determinant effect on the situation each now faces. In particular, the existence of the Treaty of Waitangi as a founding document for both Maori and Pakeha in Aotearoa/New Zealand (Pocock 27). Key to this distinction is the question of property. Based on a Lockean conception of liberalism, civil government may only emerge out of civil society, and a constituent element of the latter is private property. If the Maori had property, then they could be assumed capable of parting with it. As Pocock writes:

> For its part, the Crown was interested in ascribing to the Maori a capacity to hold property and enter into treaties, in order to acquire sovereignty over the processes of purchase and settlement, over which it did not wish the settlement companies to acquire an authority preceding its own.
>
> The Capacity to hold property, to claim rights in it and to enter into treaties respecting it were understood by Maori in terms of their own concept of *rangatiratanga*. We now see, however, that they implied—and were operated by Pakeha in 1840 so that they should imply—a capacity to alienate property with which Maori were not familiar and which might be hostile to their governing values. (Pocock 29-30)

240   *The Present Politics of the Past*

One might wonder if Pocock is not understating things here; the Maori were assigned a capacity to alienate property (which they did not recognize) precisely in order to get them to agree to turn control over said process to the British Crown. However much weight the distinction between civilized and barbarous people may have carried in the (not so distant) past it is not a tactic that remains easily usable for contemporary liberal theory.

Rather than relying on a people's civilization to judge them worthy of political status, generous liberalism, and Kymlicka's version in particular, turns to the notion of nation. Kymlicka suggests that while all cultural groups can expect some level of protection from a liberal state, "national minorities" have a strong claim to such protection, and only such groups may reasonably expect to exercise their rights in the form of self-government (Kymlicka, *Multicultural Citizenship* 108):

> In a [liberal] democratic society, the majority nation will always have its language and societal culture supported, and will have the legislative power to protect its interests in culture-affecting decisions. The question is whether fairness requires that the same benefits and opportunities should be given to national minorities. The answer, I think, is clearly yes. (Kymlicka, *Multicultural Citizenship* 113)

Thus, for Kymlicka, the recognition of sovereignty rests on the identification of an indigenous group being a nation. Kymlicka uses the example of Hispanics (Mexicans, Cubans, and Puerto Ricans) in the United States to indicate the kind of group that does not qualify as a nation, and hence has no sovereignty. He contends that Hispanics all either plan on assimilating to American society, see themselves as a national people-in-exile (Cubans), or are merely transient labor (Mexicans) headed for their home country at the first chance (Kymlicka, *Multicultural Citizenship* 16). Kymlicka contrasts this with the situation of indigenous peoples whose incorporation into settler states did not involve any such consensual separation or assimilation from mainstream society. Thus, he argues for "involuntary incorporation" as the standard for the recognition of national minorities' self-government rights (Kymlicka, *Multicultural Citizenship* 117).

Why must liberalism afford special status to nations? Kymlicka asserts that such recognition is required by liberalism's own beliefs in individual liberty and equality.

> We have here the two major claims which, I believe, underlie a liberal defence of [national] minority rights: that individual freedom is tied in some important way to membership in one's national group; and that

Judgements   241

> group-specific rights can promote equality between the minority and
> majority. I think these two ideas are essentially correct. (Kymlicka,
> *Multicultural Citizenship* 52)

It is here how one can identify Kymlicka's neo-ornamentalism in dialogue
with a deeper neo-orientalist liberalism. This may seem to be an ungenerous
reading of Kymlicka, the liberal theorist who has arguably gone the farthest
in defending indigenous rights, but upon consideration of his more recent
elaboration of the themes found in *Multicultural Citizenship* one finds this
not to be the case (Kymlicka, *Politics in the Vernacular: Nationalism,
Multiculturalism, and Citizenship*).

Kymlicka stands firm behind the proposition that what is required to
develop a workable theory of multicultural citizenship is a liberal
foundation when he writes, "And in our society, developing a coherent
liberal theory of minority rights is the first priority" [Emphasis in original]
(Kymlicka, *Politics in the Vernacular: Nationalism, Multiculturalism, and
Citizenship* 66). He would like us all to believe (much as Barkan would) that
no real alternatives to a liberal defense of indigenous rights exist. This air of
self-evidence applies to those liberals who resist the justification of
indigenous claims—"[Such] Liberals object to proposals that are not in fact
objectionable from the point of view of liberal principles, and condone
proposals that in fact perpetuate injustices that violate liberal principles"
(Kymlicka, *Politics in the Vernacular: Nationalism, Multiculturalism, and
Citizenship* 63)—as well as nonliberal strategies of justification—"Indeed,
insofar as the postmodernist approach attempts to offer a positive account
of ethnocultural justice, it is not clear how it differs from liberal culturalism"
(Kymlicka, *Politics in the Vernacular: Nationalism, Multiculturalism, and
Citizenship* 44). For Kymlicka, the self-sufficiency exists not only at the level
of theory, but also with regards to existing ethnic group claims.

> There is a real issue here, but I think that many people exaggerate it, and
> misidentify it. First, it is simply untrue that most conflicts between
> ethnocultural groups in the West are over the legitimacy of liberal
> principles. On the contrary, most members of most groups accept liberal
> democratic norms, whether they are immigrants or national minorities.
> (Kymlicka, *Politics in the Vernacular: Nationalism, Multiculturalism,
> and Citizenship* 60)

Leaving the majority of this sweeping claim aside, does Kymlicka's assertion
apply to indigenous groups' claims? He openly admits that it frequently does
not, with numerous indigenous peoples claiming exemptions from liberal
individual rights based upon an inherent communal right to self-government

242   *The Present Politics of the Past*

(Kymlicka, *Politics in the Vernacular: Nationalism, Multiculturalism, and Citizenship* 130). More troubling still is the attitude of Kymlicka when confronted with such tough cases that do not fit his general model. He notes that many of these cases are "the result of, and permeated by, injustice" but rather than accepting this as a call to theoretical action, Kymlicka sounds the retreat:

> Part of the reason is that I really don't know how to reform these relationships to make them more successful. Some of these are genuinely hard cases—the injustices go so deep, and the political obstacles to real reform are so great, that it is difficult not to be discouraged. (Kymlicka, *Politics in the Vernacular: Nationalism, Multiculturalism, and Citizenship* 57)

Thus, Kymlicka sees no alternative than to lump indigenous peoples into the ill-suiting category of "national minorities."

Does treating indigenous peoples as nations serve to depoliticize their claims? On the surface it may not; however, the question of who decides whether someone else is a "nation" remains highly problematic. But on closer scrutiny, even the notion of nation penetrates indigenous politics with the limits of European history. The nation is a construction of the pastoral being interwoven with the modern state—an institution whose genesis is peculiar to Europe. Thus, to use the term nation to designate indigenous peoples is to take it out of context, and also to do violence to indigenous notions of governance (Simpson 119). Yet it is neither surprising nor conceptually problematic to see indigenous peoples asserting their nationhood loudly and often. After all, as Kymlicka argues, being a nation is a necessary first step to being recognized as sovereign.

> References to the Eurocentric term [national] "sovereignty" may not correspond with indigenous mindsets, and thus co-opting indigenous peoples into dialogues that do not reflect their cultures and realities. Nevertheless, indigenous groups may have little choice except to engage in this discourse if they want to *talk the talk that resonates with results.* (Maaka and Fleras 94)

Indeed, when faced with the formula "one must be X to be recognized by the state" it is amazing how quickly "X-ness" becomes a growth industry. Yet, just as one could feel a presence lurking beneath the structure of liberal restitution schemes, here too the role of the state is paramount. For the sovereign state stands at both the point in Western history when political pastorates became nations, and also at the point in indigenous history when peoples must become nations to ensure their very survival. As Audra

Judgements

Simpson writes, "Nationalism is shaped, then, by a relationship with the state" (Simpson 121). In order for indigenous peoples to avoid seeing a repetition of their marginalization as mere "people" and not self-determining "peoples," they had to be *national* peoples (Kymlicka, *Multicultural Citizenship* 21).

Indigenous peoples must play a dangerous game of semantic "Twister" in order to advance their non-violent struggles for recognition and non-domination against the entrenched power of settler populations, which outnumber them ten-to-one, and liberal states, the access to whose rights and institutions is both a challenge and a threat to IPMs. This complicated position is reflected in the four basic principles outlined in the British Columbia Indian Chiefs' position paper on *Aboriginal Title and Rights:*

THE BASIC PRINCIPLES

Self-Determination

First is the principle of self-determination of peoples. The International Covenant of Economic, Social & Cultural Rights and the International Covenant on Civil & Political Rights state that:

"All peoples have the right to self-determination. By virtue of that right they freely determine their political status and freely pursue their economic, social and cultural development."

By virtue of this principle, any alienation of our land or political jurisdiction must carry the consent of the First Nations.

Inherent Sovereignty of the First Nations

The second principle is that of inherent sovereignty of the First Nations. According to this principle, any agreement between the Crown and any First Nation may only be altered or repealed with the consent of that First Nation.

These two basic principles are recognized and confirmed in the first compact between ourselves and the Crown culminating in the passage of the Royal Proclamation of 1763. By the proclamation our Territory and governing institutions are reserved for us until, through a process of informed consent, we choose to surrender them to the Crown.

Our right of self determination is a right which we have not and will not surrender.

Decolonization

The third principle is our right to be decolonized. This principle is recognized in the trust relationship between the Crown and the Indian Nations reflected in section 91(24) of the Constitution Act, 1867.

The World Court has determined that the trust may be devolved only with the attainment of independence and self-determination of the First Nations concerned.

Canada's Conditional Sovereignty

The fourth principle is that Canada's sovereignty is conditional upon Canada protecting forever Crown obligations to the First Nations. Britain insisted that the Canadian Constitution be patriated upon this condition.

Canada remains vested with obligations to assure that the self-determination of First Nations becomes a reality. At the First Minister's Constitutional Conferences, the Federal Government refuses to face its true obligations and the Constitutional position of First Nations to date.

Inherently sovereign, but not independent. Waiting to be decolonized, yet holding the sovereignty of Canada in the palm of their hand. Such are the manifold contradictions of the legal claims of indigenous peoples. Only now has the (neo)liberal state, divorced from its own national sovereignty by the emergence of Empire, been in a position both opened up to challenges from below and yet with heels dug in deep to fight for every last bit of authority and cohesion that remains left to it. Neither the assumption that indigenous peoples join all of "us" in sharing liberal values, nor the representation of their claims by means of images from "our" own past can cover up tensions such as these. Liberalism's gaze must at last recognize its own limited field of view, and accept those who call to it from beyond the shared horizon.

SOME IMPLICATIONS FOR MULTICULTURAL DEMOCRACY

The arts of resistance involved in struggles of freedom to modify the system of internal colonization from within are arguably more important and more effective than the complementary arts of legitimizing and delegitimizing struggles for freedom with which political theorists have been preoccupied.

James Tully (Tully, "The Struggles of Indigenous Peoples for and of Freedom" 58)

What can one hope to learn from listening to the voices of indigenous peoples in their struggles for land rights and self-government? While academic discourses of feminism, poststructuralism, multiculturalism, and postcolonialism have pressed political theory to expand its horizons, the legal claims and political resistance of indigenous peoples concretely "mark the horizon toward which political theory must advance" (Clifford 169). As the preceding discussion has brought to light, liberal political theory, even in its most generous forms, depoliticizes such struggles by the complementary tactics of neo-orientalism and neo-ornamentalism in their treatment of

Judgements

indigenous legal claims. The following brief comments will attempt to put overarching theories of multicultural democracy to a similar test.

If the aforementioned argument about generous liberalism's inability to deal with the political challenge posed by IPMs is credible, then similarly constructed accounts of multicultural democracy also fail. The neo-orientalist assumption of the universality of liberal values leads to the most pernicious form of intolerance among liberal theorists. Chief among these is Jacob T. Levy's "multiculturalism of fear"—a steadfastly neo-orientalist justification of multiculturalism based upon liberal values and a Hobbesian fear of violence (Levy, *The Multiculturalism of Fear*). Michael Walzer's treatment of the indigenous question under the "toleration" regime of the immigrant society functions in much the same way:

> The case of the Aboriginal peoples is harder [than the Quebec case], for it isn't at all clear that their way of life can be sustained, even under conditions on autonomy, within liberal limits: it isn't historically a liberal way of life. (Walzer 46)

In her recent work, *Identity in Democracy*, Amy Gutmann sets out to apply "fair-minded scrutiny" to whether and when the political mobilization of identity groups is compatible with democratic justice (Gutmann 3). One would think that Gutmann was trying to avoid the problems discussed above, until she outlines her own definition of democratic justice:

> I apply the democratic standard of civil equality, broadly understood to include equal freedom and opportunity for all individuals. [...] When I use the term democracy, it signifies a political commitment to the civic *equality* of *individuals* [Emphasis added]. (Gutmann 26)

This definition, encompassing (indeed solely consisting of) the liberal values of egalitarian individualism, would by itself be strong evidence of her neo-orientalism. Yet, Gutmann goes further by suggesting that although the interpretation of democracy varies, any view that does not share her core principles would not count as a "morally defensible democracy" (Gutmann 5). The implications of this are seen in her treatment of the U.S. Supreme Court decision in *Santa Clara Pueblo v. Martinez* 436 U.S. 49 (1978). The case dealt with the question of whether the individual right to equal protection granted in the Indian Civil Rights Act of 1968 supercedes the power of the Santa Clara Pueblo nation to define its membership as a self-governing people (the Court ruled that it did not). Gutmann holds this case up as the paradigm example of a violation of democratic justice (Gutmann 44–51).

Gutmann's reasoning is not tied to that fact that it was the membership policy of a self-governing indigenous people that was being challenged, but instead concludes "pursuing the equal protection of women is a principled reason to limit sovereignty, whether the authority to be limited represents a majority or a minority culture" (Gutmann 47). What this amounts to is treating the liberal goals of limited government and individual rights to equal protection as trumps above the exercise of political power—regardless of whether that power is exercised democratically. No stronger statement of neo-orientalist liberalism is made, even by those (like Barry) who reject multiculturalism tout court.

Possibly the most seductive version of neo-orientalist liberalism is that lately proffered by Seyla Benhabib. Like Gutmann, Benhabib packs dense liberal content into her definition of democracy:

> Democracy, in my view, is best understood as a model for organizing the collective and public exercise of power in the major institutions of society on the basis of the principle that decisions affecting the well-being of the collectivity can be viewed as the outcome of a *procedure* of free and reasoned deliberation among *individuals* considered as moral and political *equals* [Emphasis added]. (Benhabib 105).

Again one may see that this definition puts a premium on the author's normative justification of democracy rather than treating democracy as a normative principle in-itself. This colors all aspects of Benhabib's further investigations. She uses her conception of discourse ethics to judge when the claims of cultural groups may be accepted as valid "public reasons" in democratic discourse. Benhabib goes to great length to distinguish the normative value of consensus-directed discourse from the interested give and take of the law.

> There is no presumption that moral and political dialogues will produce normative consensus, yet it is assumed that even when they fail to do so and we must resort to law to redraw the boundaries of coexistence, societies in which such multicultural dialogues take place in the public sphere will articulate a civic point of view and a civic perspective of "enlarged mentality." The process of "giving good reasons in public" will not only determine the legitimacy of the norms followed; it will also enhance the civic virtues of democratic citizenship by cultivating the habits of mind of public reasoning and exchange. (Benhabib 115)

At face value, this statement implies that legal solutions are not necessarily reliant on discourse ethics for their normative validity. But can those legal

Judgements

247

solutions be considered democratic if they are not? Benhabib lists three key principles as constitutive of pluralist arrangements in multicultural democracies: 1) egalitarian reciprocity, 2) voluntary self-ascription, and 3) freedom of exit and association (Benhabib 131). She writes, "These norms expand on the principles of universal respect and egalitarian reciprocity, which are crucial to a discourse ethic" (Benhabib 132). Thus, the answer to the question above must be no; only those legal and political decisions with an underlying consensus rationally and freely attained can claim democratic status, for only those decisions would satisfy the normative requirements of universal respect and egalitarian reciprocity that Benhabib posits (Benhabib 37). She goes on to argue that the selfsame principles of universalism and egalitarianism are part and parcel of the "rule of law" itself (Benhabib 128). Indeed, Benhabib is willing to place justice under the heading of those concepts derivative of discourse ethics' norms as well. She writes "for claims of justice aspire to impartiality in order to represent what 'is in the best interests of all considered as equally worthy moral beings'" (Benhabib 125). By this point her earlier distinction between legal solutions to multicultural accommodation and the requirements of public dialogue within civil society has collapsed entirely.

There is a contradiction here. Benhabib argues that the normative justification of not only free and rational public discussion, but also democracy, justice, and the rule of law as well, is conditional upon the principles of discourse ethics. Yet, her definition of the ethical is that "which concerns what is appropriate for us insofar as we are members of a specific collectivity, with its unique history and tradition" (Benhabib 40). How then can the requirements of discourse *ethics* be rightly said to underlie the justifications of democracy, justice, and the law across different collectivities with divergent histories and traditions—multicultural societies? Benhabib's answer is that today's "globalized world we are inhabiting compels cultural traditions" to accept her modern, liberal, and deliberative conceptions as their own (Benhabib 40).

One can see the ramifications of this neo-orientalist doctrine in Benhabib's brief comments about native title in Canada. She wants to convince that discourse ethics only governs the "syntax" but not the "semantics" or content of potential claims made by cultural minorities in liberal democratic states (Benhabib 140-141). Her example, fortuitously, is the acceptance of the native title claims of the Gitxan people by the Canadian Supreme Court. She writes, "What lent legitimacy to the Canadian court's decision was precisely their recognition of a specific group's claims to be in the *best* interests of *all* Canadian citizens" [Emphasis in original] (Benhabib 141). After reading all of the material contained in the dossier on native title in Canada, it is nearly impossible to accept Benhabib's assertions that the Gitxan people's claim was couched in such universalistic language, that the Canadian court made its ruling on a weighing of the benefits for all Canadians rather than the requirements of the law, or that the white majority in British Columbia accepted the claims and the ruling as directed at their own best interests. Benhabib's best-case scenario turns out to be strong evidence to prove the limitations of her vision of multicultural democracy.

Neo-ornamentalist conceptions provide similar problems in their requirements of *national* self-determination. Charles Taylor's much discussed "politics of recognition" only transcends a neo-orientalist, procedural liberalism to the extent that it validates the installation of liberalism as a thick view of the good life pursued by national communities (Taylor 61). Kymlicka's arguments, in so far as they represent a comprehensive doctrine of multicultural democracy, are in the same mold as Taylor's—the pitfalls of the national minorities thesis having been discussed at length above.

Some may claim that this is an unfairly simplistic account of these nuanced thinkers, and to some extent this is undoubtedly true. Yet, much of the complexity of thinkers like Kymlicka and Walzer comes from their willingness to combine neo-orientalist and neo-ornamentalist impulses. Bhikhu Parekh argues that Kymlicka's extension of self-government rights to national minorities exhibits such tensions: "[Kymlicka] expects Amerindians, Inuits, Orthodox Jews and others to view and relate to their cultures in the same way that the liberal does to his, and defends them only to the extent that they behave as respectable liberals" (Parekh 107-08). Walzer is more explicit:

> This means that we can never be consistent defenders of multiculturalism or individualism; we can never be simply communitarians or liberals, or modernists or postmodernists, but must be now one, now the other, as the balance requires. (Walzer 112)

By this point it is well substantiated that many formulations of (neo)liberal politics retain the flexibility to co-opt the language of multiculturalism through the twin tactics of neo-orientalism and neo-ornamentalism (Hale). Yet, what is left for democracy if one rejects the above tactics of depoliticization? There are others who seek to divorce democratic theory and practice

Judgements 249

from their liberal shackles. Transforming democracy requires rethinking the liberal notions of sovereignty, nation, and property.

In the discussions of liberal restitution and reconciliation, one could detect how the sovereign state often tips the scale of justice towards liberal ends. In fact, most liberal theories begin by assuming the modern state-form to be the *sine non qua* of political institutions. However, the practice of indigenous claims should make one wary of this starting point:

> The modern state makes good sense in a society that is culturally homogenous or willing to become so. In multi-ethnic and multinational societies whose constituent communities entertain different views on its nature, power and goals, have different histories and needs, and cannot therefore be treated in an identical manner, the modern state can easily become an instrument of injustice and oppression and even precipitate the very instability and secession it seeks to prevent. (Parekh 185)

Parekh suggests that we abandon the notion of sovereignty as "a single and unitary system" for an alternative model of authority where "overlapping jurisdictions" make policy be means of negotiation and compromise (Parekh 194). Putting aside the empirical challenge that this describes how modern states actually function, as opposed to how political theory sees them, this formulation is most radical when Parekh adds the proviso that "the constituent communities might never have alienated their customary rights of self-determination to the state as the individuals in the state of nature are deemed to have done in the traditional contractualist account of the sovereignty of the state" (Parekh 195). Certainly this statement resonates with the claims of indigenous groups that they have remained self-determining peoples throughout the process of colonization by settler states. Yet, this experience seems to get lost in Parekh's account of what such a (post)sovereign authority would look like. Indeed, his account seems to be little more than another version of procedural liberalism when he argues for the removal of substantive principles of justice from the state (Parekh 207), and an instrumental account of the value of cultural membership (Parekh 219).

Iris Marion Young's conception of self-determination as non-domination may be a better framework. Young argues that self-determination in this new sense requires the following elements: 1) a presumption of non-interference; 2) "recognized and settled institutions" to adjudicate conflicts within a community; and, 3) "that the peoples have the right to participate in designing and implementing intergovernmental institutions aimed at minimizing domination" (Young, *Inclusion and Democracy* 265). Not only does this significantly resemble actual indigenous claims, but it also serves as a justification for indigenous peoples' right to both be included in the larger constitutional conversation of settler states, while also being afforded a sphere of nonintervention.

Changes in the structure of authority must be matched by a transition in one's conception of the political community (i.e. the nation) as well. Young is potentially useful in this regard too. She argues that rather than seeing groups, national or otherwise, in terms of a shared identity, one can identify "groupness" via the relations to others and the state that similarly structures people's political subjectivity (Young, *Inclusion and Democracy* 91). While the general move towards a more relational notion of politics is to be applauded, Young undermines her own position by reverting to a non-relational categorization of structured versus cultural difference (Young, *Inclusion and Democracy* 106).

Such a distinction (like James C. Scott's between *infrapolitics* and co-optation) can only rest upon an authoritative claim to know peoples' true interests, or at the least to authoritatively delimit the political from the private sphere. Such distinctions are the stock and trade of traditional political theory (including liberalism), and thus should be avoided by a critical theory of democracy. The reason for such an avoidance can be drawn from the history of indigenous peoples' experience with having their "true interests" defended by the liberal state.

Of the three major elements of liberal governmentality, notions of property are the most clearly challenged by indigenous claims. If much of the substance of Native Title claims consists of decentering the assumptions about alienability, commodification, and individualization that liberal property rights entail, indigenous relations with the land (as opposed to mere property) pose an even greater ideal of transformation—the conception of "land as citizen." John Borrows writes:

> Assertions of Aboriginal control of [settler state] affairs will encounter a matrix of power that works to exclude notions of "land as citizen." This will be especially evident when its economic implications are understood. In some cases the application of indigenous traditions might require that Aboriginal people share the wealth of the land with other [settlers]; in others it may mean that a proposed use would have to be modified or terminated. A reorientation of this magnitude is not likely to occur without substantial opposition from those who benefit from the prevailing ideologies currently allocating power. (Borrows 340)

Judgements 251

Such claims then far surpass the impact that they would have in purely distributional terms, and may serve as a manner of resisting the further commodification of life associated with neo-liberal Empire.

All of these transformations require that one recast democracy as a constitutional form into the mold of intercultural dialogue. Dialogue in this sense need not be an intentional, face-to-face conversation (as envisioned by Habermasian discourse ethics), nor need it be a normative injunction at all. Rather, it may be though of as a nominal description of what necessarily goes on in the everyday process of "being in the world with others" (Falzon). Such a notion of dialogue is not a choice; it is the state of contemporary politics in settler states—the claims of indigenous peoples are an ever-present reminder of this fact. The intercultural aspect of this dialogue need not pose the opposition between rational evaluation and cultural relativism that many theorists would impose on it. As Parekh writes:

> This is where monists and culturalists go wrong. The former argue that since some culture are superior, they have a right to impose themselves on others, making the mistake of concentrating on the content of the culture and not the basic respect owed to each culture. Culturalists make the opposite mistake of assuming that since every community has aright to its culture, we are not entitled to judge, criticize or press for changes in it. (Parekh 177)

How then should one proceed in the face of differing cultural standards of political interaction? Indigenous peoples may lie at the center of answering that very question.

Canadian political theorist James Tully uses indigenous artist Bill Reid's sculpture "The Spirit of Haida Gwaii" as a metaphor for such an intercultural ship of state. The sculpture (which resides in the Canadian Embassy in Washington, D.C.) depicts a wide cast of both mythical and human characters thrown together in a canoe. Tully sees the canoe as a representation of Canada (or any settler state) where peoples must exist in dialogue whether they like it or not. He writes:

> The questioning, contestation and renegotiation of their cultural identities seem plain for all to see. Is this not the constitutional game they are playing as they vie and squabble for position, both in the canoe and in Haida mythology? The chief signals this Derridean feature because, although a Haida chief is usually a man, he is called *laana augha*, village mother, so he must act like a mother in caring for the common good if s/he is to secure respect and authority. All the passengers are Metis, exhibiting the non-identity of cultural identities: the dogfish and mouse women, the bear mother who is part human, the wolf with his human forepaws and

> the others, for they are other-than-human persons who take off their
> furs and feathers at home and converse like human persons. (Tully,
> *Strange Multiplicity: Constitutionalism in an Age of Diversity* 25)

If this seems like an unworkably limited and limiting account of democracy, it is indeed what is required by the (post)colonial situation in settler states. One can see the violence done to indigenous peoples when even the most generous definition of liberal democracy is imposed upon them. The more limited and mediated model of social dialogue that Tully proposes is beyond our current grasp, and yet is the situation that indigenous and non-indigenous people thrown together in the "canoes" of the contemporary world find themselves. As Tully argues, "if this view of constitutionalism came to be accepted, the allegedly irreconcilable conflicts of the present would not have to be the tragic history of our future." (Tully, *Strange Multiplicity: Constitutionalism in an Age of Diversity* 211)

To advance the notion of democracy beyond the horizon of liberalism, one must listen carefully to the long-neglected voice of indigenous political experience. For this condition of radical interconnectedness is not new to native peoples; indeed, in large part it defines "indigeneity":

> In many Aboriginal narratives this harmonious diversity was disrupted
> by the invasion and occupation of strangers whose restless mode of life
> is out of tune with the ways of this continent. Nonetheless, harmony will
> be restored in the long run. It will win out because it is "indigenous,"
> both in the descriptive sense that it is embodied in the ecology,
> Aboriginal peoples, and ways of North America and in the normative
> sense that it is appropriate or fitting for this place. Harmony will be
> restored by gradually infusing the diverse ways of both Aboriginal and
> non-Aboriginal peoples and the relations among them. So, someday, we
> all, Aboriginal and non-Aboriginal, will be indigenous. (Tully, "A Just
> Relationship between Aboriginal and Non-Aboriginal Peoples of
> Canada" 70-71)

One could reasonably claim that this view of the future is not only hyper-optimistic, but indeed, impossible. It may well be. Yet, as Derrida suggests, the impossibility of such a view also holds out the very possibility of justice. It is to this end that the voices of the world's indigenous people call political theory.

Notes

NOTES TO CHAPTER ONE

1. Such a reading of poststructural theory runs counter to Thiele's claim that Foucault's account of subjectivation relies on freedom as mastery, and thus fails to "acknowledge and affirm the limitations and contingencies that constitute Being-in-the-world" according to Heidegger, Leslie Paul Thiele, *Timely Meditations: Martin Heidegger and Postmodern Politics* (Princeton, NJ: Princeton UP, 1995) 71.
2. This is a less-essentialized version of Alain Touraine's classic typology of *principe d'identité, principe d'opposition,* and *principe de totalité.* Rather than assuming that all three characteristics of social movements are self-evident, this approach analyses "indigenous peoples" as the product of *subjectification* influenced by the diagram of adversarial forces and the archive of a group's statements. Manuel Castells, *The Power of Identity,* The Information Age: Economy, Society, and Culture, vol. 2, 3 vols. (Oxford: Blackwell, 1997).
3. See, for example, Drucilla Cornell, "Time, Deconstruction, and the Challenge to Legal Positivism: The Call for Judicial Responsibility," *Legal Studies as Cultural Studies: A Reader in (Post)Modern Critical Theory,* ed. Jerry Leonard (Albany, NY: SUNY Press, 1995).; and Peter Fitzpatrick, ed., *Dangerous Supplements: Resistance and Renewal in Jurisprudence* (Durham, NC: Duke UP, 1991).
4. Including the work of Will Kymlicka, Michael Walzer, Charles Taylor, Iris Marion Young and Bhikhu Parekh.

NOTES TO CHAPTER TWO

1. Guntram F.A. Werther's *Self-Determination in Western Democracies: Aboriginal Politics in Comparative Perspective* (Westport, CT: Greenwood Press, 1992) and Franke Wilmer's *The Indigenous Voice in World Politics: Since Time Immemorial,* (Newbury Park, CA: Sage Publications, 1993) stand as notable exceptions to the lack of sustained social scientific reflection on indigenous politics.

254 *Notes to Chapter Two*

2. See for example Barbara F. Walter and Jack Snyder, *Civil Wars, Insecurity, and Intervention* (New York: Columbia UP, 1999).

3. See the case sketches on the indigenous people of Amazonian Ecuador (96-99) and Bolivia (178-182) in *Peoples versus States*.

4. See Doug McAdam's discussion of the "signifying work" done by movement tactics for the position that tactics do determine strategy. Doug McAdam, "The Framing Function of Movement Tactics," *Comparative Perspective on Social Movements*, eds. Doug McAdam, John D. McCarthy and Meyer Zald (Cambridge: Cambridge UP, 1999) 341.

5. The problematic aspects of postcolonialism/post-colonialism/(post) colonialism as a label have been pointed out many times before Chadwick Allen, "Postcolonial Theory and the Discourse of Treaties," *American Quarterly* 52.1 (2000), Leela Gandhi, *Postcolonial Theory: A Critical Introduction* (New York: Columbia UP, 1998), Bob Hodge and Vijay Mishra, "What Is Post(-)Colonialism?," *Textual Practice* 5.3 (1991), Anne McClintock, "The Angel of Progress: Pitfalls of the Term 'Post-Colonialism'," *Social Text* 31/32 (1992), Bart Moore-Gilbert, *Postcolonial Theory: Contexts, Practices, Politics* (London: Verso, 1997), Ella Shohat, "Notes on the 'Post-Colonial'," *Social Text* 31/32 (1992). Following Shohat, I find the term more appropriate when designating a stage of intellectual production, rather than a historical era. Shohat, "Notes on the 'Post-Colonial'," 101, 08. (Post)colonialism refers to an approach to the study of former imperial possessions with an explicit view to how that past continues to play a constitutive role in the present, and therefore expressly does not refer to an age "past" colonialism. Throughout, the use of the parenthetical "(post)colonialism" rather than the hyphenated "post-colonialism" highlights this distinction.

6. Another, albeit preliminary, mainstream attempt at writing IPMs as a "postliberal" challenge can be found in the work of Deborah J. Yashar (1999). Yashar, like Werther, argues that native title claims amount to a serious challenge to the liberal rules of the political game, "This is more than just a call for more land, although that is certainly a core component of the demand. Rather, it is a demand that the state recognize indigenous political jurisdiction over that land, including the right of indigenous legal systems and authorities to process and adjudicate claims. In this regard, diversified state structures would coincide with some form of legal pluralism." This being said, Yashar's normative assessment of the situation betrays a return to liberal neo-orientalism. She praises indigenous struggles for "local autonomy (a liberal good)" while she worries about "decreased local tolerance (an illiberal outcome)." Thus, while her descriptive analysis holds the potential for a repoliticization of indigenous resistance, the normative framework of liberalism that she continues to apply renders any such outcome stillborn. Deborah J. Yashar, "Democracy, Indigenous Movements, and the Postliberal Challenge in Latin America," *World Politics* 52.1 (1999): 95.

7. Cannadine writes further that the other settler dominions were even more conservative than the United States: "the dominions of settlement (and

Notes to Chapter Three   *255*

settler's Kenya) were far more traditionalist in their attitudes than were the United States of America. They had their anti-royal, anti-title, anti-hierarchy revolution in 1776; the dominions desired no such rupture. They might be moving towards greater democracy and political freedom, but socially, culturally, and significantly, economically, they remained in thrall to a certain vision of the mother country" David Cannadine, *Ornamentalism: How the British Saw Their Empire* (Oxford: Oxford UP, 2001) 40.

NOTES TO CHAPTER THREE

Some material in this chapter has been adapted and developed from my "The Kantian Peace Through a Radical Theoretic Lens." (with Kirk Bowman) *New Approaches to Comparative Politics: Insights from Political Theory.* Ed. Jennifer S. Holmes. Lanham, MD: Lexington Books, 2003. 111–123.

1. The two most common critiques of the governmentality approach are that it assumes a position of subjective idealism in the determination of historical development, and that it eschews juridical language only to "enthrone" the economic mentality of the market. Throughout this chapter I will attempt to articulate an account of governmentality that falls into neither of these traps. For the former critique see: Danica Dupont and Frank Pearce, "Foucault Contra Foucault: Rereading the 'Governmentality' Papers," *Theoretical Criminology* 5.2 (2001). For the latter see: Derek Kerr, "Beheading the King and Enthroning the Market: A Critique of Foucauldian Governmentality," *Science and Society* 63.2 (1999).

2. For the argument that liberalism should not be seen as hegemonic because of these diverse practices see: Rogers M. Smith, "Beyond Tocqueville, Myrdal, and Hartz: The Multiple Traditions in America," *American Political Science Review* 87.3 (1993).

3. Thus Jean-Jacques Rousseau, who shows so much affinity for both Hobbes' definition of sovereign power and the classical, pastoral emphasis on citizen participation, must be distinguished from the aforementioned modes of government in his adherence to the necessity of the free subject. In this manner Rousseau is to be considered a liberal thinker. Mitchell Dean, *Governmentality: Power and Rule in Modern Society* (London: Sage Publications, 1999) 165.

4. See: Peter Miller and Nikolas Rose, "Governing Economic Life," *Economy and Society* 19.1 (1990), Peter Miller and Nikolas Rose, "Political Power Beyond the State: Problematics of Government," *British Journal of Sociology* 43.2 (1992).

5. See for example: Kenichi Ohmae, *The End of the Nation State: The Rise of Regional Economies* (New York: The Free Press, 1995).

6. For a variety of perspectives on globalization and the state see: Peter Evans, "The Eclipse of the State? Reflections on Stateness in a Globalizing World," *World Politics* 50.1 (1995), Richard Rosecrance, "The Rise of the Virtual State," *Foreign Affairs* (1993), James Rosenau, *State and Sovereignty in a Globalizing World* (Stockholm: Swedish Ministry for Foreign Affairs, 1998),

Hendrik Spruyt, *The Sovereign State and Its Competitors* (Princeton, NJ: Princeton UP, 1996), Susan Strange, *The Retreat of the State: The Diffusion of Power in the World Economy* (Cambridge: Cambridge UP, 1996).

NOTES TO CHAPTER FOUR

1. It must be made clear that Allen is attempting to read indigenous discourse against postcolonial theory, while I am attempting to read them together.
2. See the discussion of the repercussions of Hanson's article 'The Making of the Maori: Cultural Invention and its Logic', Joane Nagel, *American Indian Ethnic Renewal* (New York: Oxford UP, 1997) 67.

NOTES TO CHAPTER SIX

1. Reprinted by permission of *The Mining Journal*, London.
2. Reprinted by permission of *The Mining Journal*, London.
3. Reprinted by permission of the Aboriginal and Torres Strait Islander Commission.
4. Reprinted by permission of the Aboriginal and Torres Strait Islander Commission.
5. Reprinted by permission of the Aboriginal and Torres Strait Islander Commission.
6. Reprinted by permission of the Aboriginal and Torres Strait Islander Commission.
7. Reprinted by permission of the Aboriginal and Torres Strait Islander Commission.
8. Reprinted by permission of the Aboriginal and Torres Strait Islander Commission.
9. Reprinted by permission of the Aboriginal and Torres Strait Islander Commission.
10. Reprinted by permission of the Aboriginal and Torres Strait Islander Commission.
11. Reprinted by permission of the Aboriginal and Torres Strait Islander Commission.
12. Reprinted by permission of the Aboriginal and Torres Strait Islander Commission.
13. Reprinted by permission of the Aboriginal and Torres Strait Islander Commission.
14. Reprinted by permission of the Aboriginal and Torres Strait Islander Commission.
15. Reprinted by permission of the Aboriginal and Torres Strait Islander Commission.
16. Reprinted by permission of the Aboriginal and Torres Strait Islander Commission.

NOTES TO CHAPTER SEVEN

1. Reprinted by permission of the Assembly of First Nations.
2. Reprinted by permission of the Assembly of First Nations.
3. Reprinted by permission of the Assembly of First Nations.
4. Reprinted by permission of the Assembly of First Nations.
5. Reprinted by permission of the Assembly of First Nations.
6. Reprinted by permission of the Assembly of First Nations.
7. Reprinted by permission of the Assembly of First Nations.
8. Reprinted by permission of the Assembly of First Nations.
9. Reprinted by permission of the Assembly of First Nations.
10. Reprinted by permission of the Assembly of First Nations.

Bibliography

Adams, Howard. *Prisons of Grass: Canada from the Native Point of View*. Toronto: New Press, 1975.

Alford, C. Fred. *Whistleblowers: Broken Lives and Organizational Power*. Ithaca, NY: Cornell UP, 2001.

Allen, Chadwick. "Postcolonial Theory and the Discourse of Treaties." American Quarterly 52.1 (2000): 59–89.

Anaya, S. James. *Indigenous Peoples in International Law*. Oxford: Oxford UP, 1996.

Anaya, S. James. "On Justifying Special Ethnic Group Rights: Comments on Pogge." *Ethnicity and Group Rights*. Eds. Ian Shapiro and Will Kymlicka. Vol. 39. Nomos. New York: New York UP, 1997. 222–31.

Anderson, Benedict. *Imagined Communities*. 1983. London: Verso Books, 1991.

Asch, Michael. "First Nations and the Derivation of Canada's Underlying Title: Comparing Perspectives on Legal Ideology." *Aboriginal Rights and Self-Government: The Canadian and Mexican Experience in North American Perspective*. Eds. Curtis Cook and Juan D. Lindau. Montreal & Kingston: McGill-Queen's UP, 2000. 148–67.

Ashcroft, Bill, Gareth Griffins, and Helen Tiffin, eds. *The Post-Colonial Studies Reader*. London: Routledge, 1997.

Baird-Olson, Karren. "Reflections of an Aim Activist: Had It All Been Worth It?" *Red Power: The American Indians' Fight for Freedom*. Eds. Josephy, Jr., Alvin, Joane Nagel, and Troy Johnson. 2nd ed. Lincoln, NE: University of Nebraska Press, 1999.

Barkan, Elazar. *The Guilt of Nations: Restitution and Negotiating Historical Injustices*. Baltimore, MD: The Johns Hopkins University Press, 2000.

Barry, Brian. Culture and Equality: An Egalitarian Critique of Multiculturalism. Cambridge, MA: Harvard UP, 2001.

Bartowski, Frances. "Epistemic Drift in Foucault." *Feminism and Foucault: Reflections on Resistance*. Eds. Irene Diamond and Lee Quimby. Boston, MA: Northeastern UP, 1988. 43–58.

Behrendt, Larissa. "Blood from a stone: the real goal of 'practical reconciliation' is indigenous disempowerment, and ATSIC is once again a target. Now it's being subject to a massive disinformation campaign. It won't get the real attention it needs until a genuine commitment to Indigenous rights is made." *Arena Magazine* (August–September 2002): 32–35.

260   *Bibliography*

Benhabib, Seyla. *The Claims of Culture: Equality and Diversity in the Global Era.* Princeton: Princeton UP, 2002.

Borrows, John. "'Landed Citizenship': Narratives of Aboriginal Political Participation." *Citizenship in Diverse Societies.* Eds. Will Kymlicka and Wayne Norman. Oxford: Oxford UP, 2000. 326–42.

Bradford, Neil. "Governing the Canadian Economy: Ideas and Politics." *Canadian Politics in the 21st Century.* Eds. Michael Whittington and Glen Williams. Scarborough, ON: Nelson Thompson Learning, 2000. 193–216.

Brown, Richard Harvey, and Beth Davis-Brown. "The Making of Memory: The Politics of Archives, Libraries and Museums in the Construction of National Consciousness." History of the Human Sciences 11.4 (1998): 17–32.

Brownlie, Ian. *Treaties and Indigenous Peoples.* Oxford: Clarendon Press, 1992.

Brubaker, Rogers. *Citizenship and Nationhood in France and Germany.* Cambridge, MA: Harvard UP, 1992.

Burchell, Graham. "Civil Society and 'the System of Natural Liberty'." *The Foucault Effect: Studies in Governmentality.* Eds. Graham Burchell, Colin Gordon, and Peter Miller. Chicago: University of Chicago Press, 1991. 119–50.

Burchell, Graham, Colin Gordon, and Peter Miller, eds. *The Foucault Effect: Studies in Governmentality.* Chicago: University of Chicago Press, 1991.

Cannadine, David. *Ornamentalism: How the British Saw Their Empire.* Oxford: Oxford UP, 2001.

Castells, Manuel. *The Power of Identity.* The Information Age: Economy, Society, and Culture. Vol. 2. 3 vols. Oxford: Blackwell, 1997.

Certainty: *Canada's Struggle to Extinguish Aboriginal Title.* Vancouver and Kamloops, BC: Union of British Columbia Indian Chiefs, 1998.

Clifford, Michael. *Political Genealogy after Foucault: Savage Identities.* New York and London: Routledge, 2001.

Colwell, C. "Deleuze and Foucault: Series, Event, Genealogy." *Theory and Event* 1.2 (1997).

Cornell, Drucilla. "Time, Deconstruction, and the Challenge to Legal Positivism: The Call for Judicial Responsibility." *Legal Studies as Cultural Studies: A Reader in (Post)Modern Critical Theory.* Ed. Jerry Leonard. Albany, NY: SUNY Press, 1995. 231–66.

de Certeau, Michel. "History: Science and Fiction." Trans. Brian Massumi. *Heterologies: Discourse on the Other.* 17 ed. Theory and History of Literature. Minneapolis, MN: University of Minnesota Press, 1986. 199–221.

de Certeau, Michel. "The Laugh of Michel Foucault." Trans. Brian Massumi. *Heterologies: Discourse on the Other.* Theory and History of Literature. Minneapolis, MN: University of Minnesota Press, 1986. 193–98.

de Certeau, Michel. "The Politics of Silence: The Long March of the Indians." *Heterologies: Discourse on the Other.* Minneapolis, MN: University of Minnesota Press, 1997.

de Certeau, Michel. *The Practice of Everyday Life.* Berkeley, CA: University of California Press, 1984.

Dean, Mitchell. *Critical and Effective Histories: Foucault's Methods and Historical Sociology.* London: Routledge, 1994.

Bibliography

Dean, Mitchell. *Governmentality: Power and Rule in Modern Society*. London: Sage Publications, 1999.

Deleuze, Gilles. *Foucault*. Minneapolis, MN: University of Minnesota Press, 1988.

Deleuze, Gilles. "Post-Scriptum Sur Les Societes De Controle." *Pourparlers*. Paris: Minuit, 1990.

Deleuze, Gilles, and Michel Foucault. "Intellectuals and Power: A Conversation between Michel Foucault and Gilles Deleuze." *Language, Counter-Memory, Practice*. Ed. Donald F. Bouchard. Ithaca, NY: Cornell UP, 1977.

Deloria, Jr.,Vine. *Behind the Trail of Broken Treaties: An Indian Declaration of Independence*. 1974. Austin, TX: University of Texas Press, 1999.

Deloria, Jr.,Vine. *Red Earth, White Lies: Native Americans and the Myth of Scientific Fact*. New York: Scribner, 1995.

Deloria, Jr., Vine, and Clifford Lytle. *The Nations Within: The Past and Future of Native American Sovereignty*. New York: Pantheon, 1984.

Derrida, Jacques. "A Discussion with Jacques Derrida." *Theory and Event 5.1* (2001).

Derrida, Jacques. "Force of Law: The 'Mystical Foundation of Authority'." *Deconstruction and the Possibility of Justice*. 1990. Eds. Drucilla Cornell, Michel Rosenfeld and David Gray Carlson. London: Routledge, 1992. 3–67.

Derrida, Jacques. *On Cosmopolitanism and Forgiveness*. Trans. Mark Dooley and Michael Hughes. Thinking in Action. Eds. Simon Critchley and Richard Kearney. London: Routledge, 2001.

Derrida, Jacques. *Specters of Marx: The State of the Debt, the Work of Mourning, and the New International*. Trans. Peggy Kamuf. New York: Routledge, 1994.

Digeser, Peter. "The Fourth Face of Power." *The Journal of Politics* (1992).

Donzelot, Jacques. "The Mobilization of Society." *The Foucault Effect: Studies in Governmentality*. Eds. Graham Burchell, Colin Gordon, and Peter Miller. Chicago: University of Chicago Press, 1991. 169–80.

Dupont, Danica, and Frank Pearce. "Foucault Contra Foucault: Rereading the 'Governmentality' Papers." *Theoretical Criminology* 5.2 (2001): 123–58.

Edkins, Jenny. *Poststructuralism in International Relations: Bringing the Political Back In*. Boulder, CO: Lynne Rienner Publishers, 1999.

Elkin, Stephen L. "The Constitutional Theory of the Commercial Republic." *Fordham Law Review* 69 (2001): 1933–68.

Eudaily, Seán Patrick, and Kirk Bowman. "The Kantian Peace Through a Radical Theoretic Lens." *New Approaches to Comparative Politics: Insights from Political Theory*. Ed. Jennifer S. Holmes. Lanham, MD: Lexington Books, 2003. 111–123.

Evans, Peter. "The Eclipse of the State? Reflections on Stateness in a Globalizing World." *World Politics* 50.1 (1995): 62–87.

Falzon, Christopher. *Foucault and Social Dialogue: Beyond Fragmentation*. London and New York: Routledge, 1998.

Fish, Stanley. "Play of Surfaces: Theory and the Law." *Legal Hermeneutics: History, Theory, and Practice*. Ed. Gregory Leyh. Berkeley, CA: University of California Press, 1992. 297–316.

Fitzpatrick, Peter, ed. *Dangerous Supplements: Resistance and Renewal in Jurisprudence*. Durham, NC: Duke UP, 1991.

Foucault, Michel. *The Archaeology of Knowledge*. New York: Pantheon Books, 1972.

Foucault, Michel. "The Birth of Biopolitics." *Ethics: Subjectivity and Truth*. Ed. Paul Rabinow. Vol. 1. The Essential Works of Michel Foucault, 1954–1984. New York: The New Press, 1994. 73–80.

Foucault, Michel. "The Eye of Power." *Power/Knowledge: Selected Interviews and Other Writings, 1972–1977*. Ed. Colin Gordon. New York: Pantheon Books, 1980. 146–65.

Foucault, Michel. "Governmentality." Trans. Colin Gordon. *The Foucault Effect: Studies in Governmentality*. 1978. Eds. Graham Burchell, Colin Gordon, and Peter Miller. Chicago: University of Chicago Press, 1991. 87–104.

Foucault, Michel, ed. Herculine Barbin: Being the Recently *Discovered Memoirs of a Nineteenth-Century Hermaphrodite*. New York: Knopf, 1980.

Foucault, Michel, ed. *The History of Sexuality, Volume I: An Introduction*. 1978. New York: Vintage, 1990.

Foucault, Michel, ed. I, *Pierre Riviére, Having Slaughtered My Mother, My Sister, and My Brother...: A Case of Parricide in the 19th Century*. Lincoln, NE: University of Nebraska Press, 1975.

Foucault, Michel, ed. "Nietzsche, Genealogy, History." *Language, Counter-Memory, Practice*. Ed. Donald F. Bouchard. Ithaca, NY: Cornell UP, 1977. 139–64.

Foucault, Michel, ed. "On the Government of the Living." *Ethics: Subjectivity and Truth*. Ed. Paul Rabinow. Vol. 1. The Essential Works of Michel Foucault, 1954–1984. New York: The New Press, 1994. 81–86.

Foucault, Michel, ed. "Politics and Reason." *Politics, Philosophy, Culture: Interviews and Other Writings 1977–1984*. Ed. L.D. Kritzman. London: Tavistock, 1988.

Foucault, Michel, ed. "Politics and the Study of Discourse." *The Foucault Effect: Studies in Governmentality*. 1968. Eds. Graham Burchell, Colin Gordon, and Peter Miller. Chicago: University of Chicago Press, 1991. 53–72.

Foucault, Michel, ed. "Power and Strategies." *Power/Knowledge: Selected Interviews and Other Writings, 1972–1977*. Ed. Colin Gordon. New York: Pantheon Books, 1980.

Foucault, Michel, ed. "Questions of Method." *The Foucault Effect: Studies in Governmentality*. 1980. Eds. Graham Burchell, Colin Gordon, and Peter Miller. Chicago: University of Chicago Press, 1991. 73–86.

Foucault, Michel, ed. "Revolutionary Action: 'until Now'." *Language, Counter-Memory, Practice*. Ed. Donald F. Bouchard. Ithaca, NY: Cornell UP, 1977.

Foucault, Michel, ed. "Society Must Be Defended." *Ethics: Subjectivity and Truth*. Ed. Paul Rabinow. Vol. 1. The Essential Works of Michel Foucault, 1954–1984. New York: The Free Press, 1994. 59–66.

Foucault, Michel, ed. "Theatrum Philisophicum." *Language, Counter-Memory, Practice*. Ed. Donald F. Bouchard. Ithaca, NY: Cornell UP, 1977.

Foucault, Michel, ed. "Two Lectures." *Power/Knowledge: Selected Interviews and Other Writings, 1972–1977*. Ed. Colin Gordon. New York: Pantheon Books, 1980.

Foucault, Michel, ed. "'What Is Enlightenment?'" Trans. Catherine Porter. *The Foucault Reader*. Ed. Paul Rabinow. New York: Pantheon Books, 1984. 32–50.

Bibliography 263

Franks, C.E.S. "Rights and Self-Government for Canada's Aboriginal Peoples." *Aboriginal Rights and Self-Government: The Canadian and Mexican Experience in North American Perspective*. Eds. Curtis Cook and Juan D. Lindau. Montreal & Kingston: McGill-Queen's UP, 2000. 101–34.

Fried, Morton H. *The Notion of Tribe*. Menlo Park, CA: Cummings, 1975.

Gandhi, Leela. *Postcolonial Theory: A Critical Introduction*. New York: Columbia UP, 1998.

Gordon, Colin. "Governmental Rationality: An Introduction." *The Foucault Effect: Studies in Governmentality*. Eds. Colin Gordon, Graham Burchell, and Peter Miller. Chicago: University of Chicago Press, 1991.

Guha, Ranajit. *Dominance without Hegemony: History and Power in Modern India*. Convergences: Inventories of the Present. Ed. Edward W. Said. Cambridge, MA: Harvard UP, 1997.

Gurr, Ted Robert. *Peoples Versus States: Minorities at Risk in the New Century*. Washington, D.C.: United States Institute of Peace Press, 2000.

Gutmann, Amy. *Identity in Democracy*. Princeton: Princeton UP, 2003.

Hacking, Ian. "How Should We Do the History of Statistics?" *The Foucault Effect: Studies in Governmentality*. Eds. Graham Burchell, Colin Gordon, and Peter Miller. Chicago: University of Chicago Press, 1991. 181–96.

Hale, Charles R. "Does multiculturalism menace?: Governance, cultural rights and the politics of identity in Guatemala." *Journal of Latin American Studies* 34.3 (2002): 485–525.

Hardt, Michael, and Antonio Negri. *Empire*. Cambridge, MA: Harvard UP, 2000.

Harrison, Linda. "On Cultural Nationalism." *The Black Panthers Speak*. Ed. Philip S. Foner. New York: Da Capo Press, 1995. 151–54.

Heidegger, Martin. "The Question Concerning Technology." *Basic Writings*. 1977. Ed. David Farrell Krell. San Francisco, CA: Harper Collins, 1993. 311–41.

Heisler, Martin O. "Ethnicity and Ethnic Relations in the Modern West." *Conflict and Peacemaking in Multiethnic Societies*. Ed. Joseph V. Montville. Lexington, MA: D.C. Heath and Company, 1990. 27–28.

Hexter, J.H. "The Historical Method of Christopher Hill." *On Historians: Reappraisals of Some of the Masters of Modern History*. Cambridge, MA: Harvard UP, 1979. 227–54.

Hill, Ronald Paul. "Blackfellas and Whitefellas: Aboriginal Land Rights, the Mabo Decision, and the Meaning of Land." *Human Rights Quarterly* 17.2 (1995): 303–22.

Hindess, Barry. "Neo-Liberalism and the National Economy." *Governing Australia: Studies in Contemporary Rationalities of Government*. Eds. Barry Hindess and Mitchell Dean. Cambridge: Cambridge UP, 1998. 21–226.

Hobsbawm, Eric J. Nations and Nationalism since 1780: *Programme, Myth and Reality*. 1990. Cambridge: Cambridge UP, 1992.

Hodge, Bob, and Vijay Mishra. "What Is Post(-)Colonialism?" *Textual Practice* 5.3 (1991): 399–413.

Hopkins, A.J. "Development and the Utopian Ideal, 1960–1999." *Oxford History of the British Empire: Volume V, Historiography*. Ed. Robin W. Winks. Vol. 5. Oxford History of the British Empire. Oxford: Oxford UP, 1999. 635–52.

Jackson, Robert H. Quasi-States: *Sovereignty, International Relations and the Third World*. Cambridge: Cambridge UP, 1990.

Jaimes, M. Annette. "Federal Indian Identification Policy." *Red Power: The American Indians' Fight for Freedom*. Eds. Troy Johnson, Josephy, Jr., Alvin, and Joane Nagel. Lincoln, NE: University of Nebraska Press, 1999.

Josephy, Jr., Alvin, Troy Johnson, and Joane Nagel. Red Power: *The American Indians' Fight for Freedom*. Lincoln, NE: University of Nebraska Press, 1999.

Kerr, Derek. "Beheading the King and Enthroning the Market: A Critique of Foucauldian Governmentality." *Science and Society* 63.2 (1999): 173–202.

Krasner, Stephen D. *Sovereignty: Organized Hypocrisy*. Princeton, NJ: Princeton UP, 1999.

Kymlicka, Will. *Multicultural Citizenship: A Liberal Theory of Minority Rights*. Oxford Political Theory. Oxford: Clarendon Press, 1995.

Kymlicka, Will. *Politics in the Vernacular: Nationalism, Multiculturalism, and Citizenship*. Oxford: Oxford UP, 2001.

Leonard, Jerry. "Foucault and (the Ideology of) Genealogical Legal Theory." *Legal Studies as Cultural Studies: A Reader in (Post)Modern Critical Theory*. Ed. Jerry Leonard. Albany, NY: SUNY Press, 1995. 133–51.

Levy, Jacob T. *The Multiculturalism of Fear*. Oxford: Oxford UP, 2000.

Levy, Jacob T. "Three Modes of Incorporating Indigenous Law." *Citizenship in Diverse Societies*. Eds. Will Kymlicka and Wayne Norman. Oxford: Oxford UP, 2000. 297–325.

Lichbach, Mark I. *The Rebel's Dilemma*. Ann Arbor, MI: University of Michigan Press, 1995.

Maaka, Roger, and Augie Fleras. "Engaging with Indigeneity: Tino Rangatiratanga in Aotearoa/New Zealand." *Political Theory and the Rights of Indigenous Peoples*. Eds. Duncan Ivison, Paul Patton, and Will Sanders. Cambridge: Cambridge UP, 2000. 89–109.

May, Todd. *Between Genealogy and Epistemology: Psychology, Politics, and Knowledge in the Thought of Michel Foucault*. State College, PA: Penn State UP, 1993.

McAdam, Doug. "The Framing Function of Movement Tactics." *Comparative Perspective on Social Movements*. Eds. Doug McAdam, John D. McCarthy, and Meyer Zald. Cambridge: Cambridge UP, 1999.

McAdam, Doug, Sidney Tarrow, and Charles Tilly. *Dynamics of Contention*. 2001.

McClintock, Anne. "The Angel of Progress: Pitfalls of the Term 'Post-Colonialism'." *Social Text* 31/32 (1992): 84–97.

McCormick, John P. "Derrida on Law; or, Poststructuralism Gets Serious." *Political Theory* 29.3 (2001): 395–423.

McHugh, P.G. "Constitutional Theory and Maori Claims." *Waitangi: Maori and Pakeha Perspectives on the Treaty of Waintangi*. Ed. I.H. Kawharu. Auckland: Oxford UP, 1989.

Means, Russell. "Fighting Words on the Future of Mother Earth." *Mother Jones* December 1980.

Mercer, Kobena. "Black Hair/Style Politics." *New Formations* 3 (1987): 140–65.

Bibliography

Meredyth, Denise. "Corporatising Education." Governing Australia: Studies in Contemporary Rationalities of Government. Eds. Mitchell Dean and Barry Hindess. Cambridge: Cambridge UP, 1998. 20–46.

Miller, Peter, and Nikolas Rose. "Governing Economic Life." Economy and Society 19.1 (1990): 1–31.

Miller, Peter, and Nikolas Rose. "Political Power Beyond the State: Problematics of Government." British Journal of Sociology 43.2 (1992): 173–205.

Moore-Gilbert, Bart. Postcolonial Theory: Contexts, Practices, Politics. London: Verso, 1997.

Nagel, Joane. American Indian Ethnic Renewal. New York: Oxford UP, 1997.

Norrie, Alan. "From Critical to Socio-Legal Studies: Three Dialectics in Search of a Subject." Social and Legal Studies 9.1 (2000): 85–113.

Ohmae, Kenichi. The End of the Nation State: The Rise of Regional Economies. New York: The Free Press, 1995.

O'Malley, Pat. "Indigenous Governance." Governing Australia: Studies in Contemporary Rationalities of Government. Eds. Mitchell Dean and Barry Hindess. Cambridge: Cambridge UP, 1998.

Parekh, Bhikhu. Rethinking Multiculturalism: Cultural Diversity and Political Theory. Cambridge, MA: Harvard UP, 2000.

Pasquino, Pasquale. "Theatrum Politicum: The Genealogy of Capital." The Foucault Effect: Studies in Governmentality. Eds. Graham Burchell, Colin Gordon, and Peter Miller. Chicago: University of Chicago Press, 1991. 105–18.

Pocock, J.G.A. "Waitangi as Mystery of State: Consequences of the Ascription of Federative Capacity to the Maori." Political Theory and the Rights of Indigenous Peoples. Eds. Duncan Ivison, Paul Patton, and Will Sanders. Cambridge: Cambridge UP, 2000. 25–35.

Pogge, Thomas W. "Group Rights and Ethnicity." Ethnicity and Group Rights. Eds. Ian Shapiro and Will Kymlicka. Vol. 39. Nomos. New York: New York UP, 1997. 187–221.

Rosecrance, Richard. "The Rise of the Virtual State." Foreign Affairs (1993): 78–87.

Rosenau, James. State and Sovereignty in a Globalizing World. Stockholm: Swedish Ministry for Foreign Affairs, 1998.

Runstrom, Robert A. "American Indian Placemaking on Alcatraz, 1969–1971." American Indian Activism. Eds. Troy Johnson, Joane Nagel and Duane Champagne. Urbana, IL: University of Illinois Press, 1997.

Said, Edward W. Orientalism. New York: Vintage Books, 1978.

Schelling, Thomas C. The Strategy of Conflict. 1960. 2nd ed. Cambridge, MA: Harvard UP, 1980.

Scott, James C. Domination and the Arts of Resistance: Hidden Transcripts. New Haven, CT: Yale UP, 1990.

Shohat, Ella. "Notes on the 'Post-Colonial'." Social Text 31/32 (1992): 99–113.

Simpson, Audra. "Paths toward a Mohawk Nation: Narratives of Citizenship and Nationhood in Kahnawake." Political Theory and the Rights of Indigenous Peoples. Eds. Duncan Ivison, Paul Patton, and Will Sanders. Cambridge: Cambridge UP, 2000. 113–36.

Smith, Rogers M. "Beyond Tocqueville, Myrdal, and Hartz: The Multiple Traditions in America." American Political Science Review 87.3 (1993): 549–66.

Sorrenson, M.P.K. "Towards a Radical Reinterpretation of New Zealand History." *Waitangi: Maori and Pakeha Perspectives on the Treaty of Waitangi*. Ed. I.H. Kawharu. Auckland: Oxford UP, 1989.

Spivak, Gayatri Chakravorty. "Constitutions and Cultural Studies." *Legal Studies as Cultural Studies: A Reader in (Post)Modern Critical Theory*. Ed. Jerry Leonard. Albany, NY: SUNY Press, 1995. 155–73.

Spivak, Gayatri Chakravorty. *A Critique of Postcolonial Reason: Toward a History of the Vanishing Present*. Cambridge, MA: Harvard UP, 1999.

Spivak, Gayatri Chakravorty. "Marginality in the Teaching Machine." *Outside in the Teaching Machine*. New York: Routledge, 1993.

Spivak, Gayatri Chakravorty. "More on Power/Knowledge." *Outside in the Teaching Machine*. London: Routledge, 1993. 25–51.

Spruyt, Hendrik. *The Sovereign State and Its Competitors*. Princeton, NJ: Princeton UP, 1996.

Stavenhagen, Rodolfo. "Indigenous Peoples and the State in Latin America: An Ongoing Debate." *Multiculturalism in Latin America: Indigenous Rights, Diversity and Democracy*. Ed. Rachel Sieder. New York: Palgrave MacMillan, 2002. 24–44.

Strange, Susan. *The Retreat of the State*: The Diffusion of Power in the World Economy. Cambridge: Cambridge UP, 1996.

Taylor, Charles. "The Politics of Recognition." *Multiculturalism: Examining the Politics of Recognition*. Ed. Amy Gutmann. Princeton, NJ: Princeton UP, 1994. 25–74.

Teubner, Gunther. "The King's Bodies: The Self-Deconstruction of Law's Hierarchy." *Law and Society Review* 31.4 (1997): 763–88.

Thiele, Leslie Paul. *Timely Meditations: Martin Heidegger and Postmodern Politics*. Princeton, NJ: Princeton UP, 1995.

Tully, James. "A Just Relationship between Aboriginal and Non-Aboriginal Peoples of Canada." *Aboriginal Rights and Self-Government: The Canadian and Mexican Experience in North American Perspective*. Eds. Curtis Cook and Juan D. Lindau. Montreal & Kingston: McGill-Queen's UP, 2000. 39–71.

Tully, James. *Strange Multiplicity: Constitutionalism in an Age of Diversity*. Cambridge: Cambridge UP, 1995.

Tully, James. "The Struggles of Indigenous Peoples for and of Freedom." *Political Theory and the Rights of Indigenous Peoples*. Eds. Duncan Ivison, Paul Patton, and Will Sanders. Cambridge: Cambridge UP, 2000. 36–59.

Turner, Dale. "Liberalism's Last Stand: Aboriginal Sovereignty and Minority Rights." Aboriginal Rights and Self-Government: *The Canadian and Mexican Experience in North American Perspective*. Eds. Curtis Cook and Juan D. Lindau. Montreal & Kingston: McGill-Queen's UP, 2000. 135–47.

Unger, Roberto Mangabeira. *The Critical Legal Studies Movement*. 1983. 2nd ed. Cambridge, MA: Harvard UP, 1986.

Walker, R.J. "The Treaty of Waitangi as the Focus of Maori Protest." *Waitangi: Maori and Pakeha Prespectives on the Treaty of Waitangi*. Ed. I.H. Kawharu. Auckland: Oxford UP, 1989.

Walter, Barbara F., and Jack Snyder. *Civil Wars, Insecurity, and Intervention*. New York: Columbia UP, 1999.

Bibliography

Walzer, Michael. *On Toleration*. New Haven, CT: Yale UP, 1997.

Webber, Jeremy. "Beyond Regret: Mabo's Implications for Australian Constitutionalism." *Political Theory and the Rights of Indigenous Peoples*. Eds. Duncan Ivison, Paul Patton and Will Sanders. Cambridge: Cambridge UP, 2000. 60–88.

Werther, Guntram F.A. *Self-Determination in Western Democracies*: Aboriginal Politics in a Comparative Perspective. Westport, CT: Greenwood Press, 1992.

Whitaker, Re.g., "Politics Versus Administration: Politicians and Bureaucrats." *Canadian Politics in the 21st Century*. Eds. Michael Whittington and Glen Williams. Scarborough, ON: Nelson Thompson Learning, 2000. 55–78.

Wilmer, Franke. *The Indigenous Voice in World Politics: Since Time Immemorial*. Newbury Park, CA: Sage Publications, 1993.

Winks, Robin W. "The Future of Imperial History." *Oxford History of the British Empire: Volume V, Historiography*. Ed. Robin W. Winks. Vol. 5. Oxford History of the British Empire. Oxford: Oxford UP, 1999. 653–68.

Yashar, Deborah J. "Democracy, Indigenous Movements, and the Postliberal Challenge in Latin America." *World Politics* 52.1 (1999): 76–104.

Young, Iris Marion. *Inclusion and Democracy*. Oxford: Oxford UP, 2000.

Young, Iris Marion. *Justice and the Politics of Difference*. Princeton, NJ: Princeton UP, 1990.

Table of Authorities

A

A. Raptis and Son v. South Australia (1977) 138 CLR 346; 93

Adeyinka Oyekan v. Musendiku Adele (1957) 1 WLR 876; 112

Advisory Opinion on Western Sahara (1975) 1 ICJR 12; 95, 102

Advocate-General of Bengal v. Ranee Surnomoye Dossee (1863) 15 ER 811; 98

Amodu Tijani (1921) 2 AC; 111, 112, 115

Attorney-General v. Brown (1847) 1 Legge 312; 88, 92, 104, 118

Attorney-General v. Nissan (1970) AC 179; 111

Attorney-General for New South Wales v. Butterworth and Co. (Australia) Ltd. (1938) 38 SR (NSW) 195; 109

Australia Act, 1986 (Cth); 91

Australian Conservation Foundation v. The Commonwealth (1980) 146 CLR 493; 117

Australian Courts Act, 1828 (Imp) 9 Geo IV c.83; 100

Australian Consolidated Press Ltd. v. Uren (1967) 117 CLR 221; 91

B

Baker Lake, Hamlet of v. Minster of Indian Affairs and Northern Development (1979) 107 DLR (3d); 120, 140

Beaumont v. Barrett (1836) 12 ER 733; 96

Blankard v. Galdy (1693) 90 ER 1089; 96, 97

Bonser v. La Macchia (1969) 122 CLR 177; 93

Buchanan v. The Commonwealth (1913) 16 CLR 315; 97

Burmah Oil Co. Ltd. V. Lord Advocate (1965) AC 75; 111

C

Calder v. Attorney-General of British Columbia (1973) SCR 313; 105–6, 112, 120, 122, 213

Calvin's Case (1608) 77 ER 377; 99

Campbell v. Hall (1774) 98 ER 848; 96–7, 98, 99

Case of Tanistry, The (1608) 80 ER; 115

Chartier v. Attorney-General of Quebec (1979) 2 SCR 474: 195

Coe v. The Commonwealth (1979) 53 ALJR 403; 93

Colonial Act, The, 6 Wm IV No. 16 (1836); 89

Colonial Boundaries Act, 1895 (Imp) 58 and 59 Vict c 34; 87, 92

Commonwealth, The v. Tasmania (1983) 158 CLR 1; 108

Commonwealth Aluminum Corporation Pty. Limited Agreement Act, The, 1957 (Queensland); 150–52

Communal Services (Torres Strait) Act, 1984–1990 (Queensland); 117–8

Cook v. Cook (1986) 162 CLR 376; 91

Cook v. Sprigg (1899) AC 572; 110

Cooper v. Stuart (1889) 14 App Cas 286; 28, 95, 98, 100

Constitution Act, 1867, ss. 91(24); 190–1, 202, 203, 204, 205, 206, 215, 243

Constitution Act, 1982, s. 35(1); 182, 185, 186, 188, 191, 192, 196, 201, 204, 205, 213, 214, 222

Corporation of the Director of Aboriginal and Islanders Advancement v. Peinkinna (1978) 52 ALJR 286; 122, 152

Crown Lands Alienation Act, 1876 (Queensland); 120, 121

Cudgen Rutile (No. 2) Ltd. v. Chalk (1975) AC 520; 119

D

Delgamuukw v. British Columbia, [1997] 3 S.C.R. 1010; 18, 79, 181–207, 208, 209, 212, 213, 226

Derrickson v. Derrickson (1986) 1 SCR 285; 205

Dick v. The Queen (1985) 2 SCR 309; 205, 206

Donegani v. Donegani (1835) 12 ER 571; 99

E

Ex parte Lye (1967) 2 QB 153; 93

F

Falkland Islands Co. v. The Queen (1863) 15 ER 902; 99

Ffrost v. Stevenson (1937) 58 CLR 528; 93

First Nations Land Management Act, 1999 (Canada); 219–20

Forbes v. Cochrane (1824) 2 B and C 448; 96

Four B Manufacturing Ltd. V. United Garment Workers of America (1980) 1 SCR 1031; 204

Freeman v. Fairlie (1828) 18 ER 117; 97

G

Gerhardy v. Brown (1985) 159 CLR 970; 104

Guerin v. The Queen (1984) 13 DLR (4th) 321; 116, 149

I

Idewu Inasa v. Oshodi (1934) AC 99; 117

Indian Act, RSC, 1985, c. I-5, ss. 18, 88; 183, 190, 192, 201, 202, 206, 216, 218–9, 224–5

Indian Nonintercourse Act, 1790 (U.S.); 149

In re Southern Rhodesia (1919) AC 211; 101, 102, 103, 111, 113, 114

International Covenant on Civil and Political Rights (16 December 1966) 999 U.N.T.S. 171; 169, 243

International Covenant on Economic, Social, and Cultural Rights (16 December 1966) 993 U.N.T.S. 3; 243

International Convention on the Elimination of All Forms of Racial Discrimination (21 December 1965) 660 U.N.T.S. 195; 172

"Indian Chief," The (1801) 2 C Rob 12; 97, 169

Indian Civil Rights Act, 1968 (U.S.); 28, 245

J

John v. Federal Commissioner of Taxation (1989) 166 CLR 417; 91

Johnson v. McIntosh 21 U.S. 240 (1823); 94, 104, 116

Joint Tribal Council of the Passemaquoddy Tribe v. Morton (1975) 528 Fed. 2d 370; 118

Jones v. The Commonwealth (1987) 61 ALJR 348; 91

Table of Authorities

K

Khoo Hooi Leong v. Khoo Chong Yeok (1930) AC 346; 97

Kielley v. Carson (1842) 13 ER 225; 98, 99

Kruger v. The Queen (1978) 1 SCR 104; 197

L

Land Act, 1910 (Queensland); 120, 134, 135–38, 140–41, 145–46, 148, 150

Land Act, 1962 (Queensland); 120, 126, 127, 134, 135, 137, 145, 150

Lauderdale Peerage, The (1885) App Cas 692; 98

Lipan Apache Tribe v. Unites States (1967) 180 Ct Cl 487; 120

Liquidators of Maritime Bank of Canada v. Receiver-General (New Brunswick) (1892) AC 437; 90

Lyons (Mayor of) v. East India Co. (1836) 12 ER 782; 98, 99

M

Mabo v. Queensland (1988) 166 CLR 186; 90, 109, 123

Mabo v. Queensland (1992) 175 O.L.R. 1; 18, 28, 68, 79, 83–127, 130, 138–39, 142–43, 145, 153, 163, 168, 171, 173, 174, 230, 234, 237

Madzimbamuto v. Lardner-Burke (1969) 1 AC 645; 109

McKinney v. The Queen (1991) 171 CLR 468; 91

Milirrpum v. Nabalco Pty. Ltd. (1971) 17 FLR 141; 100, 107

Mining Act, The, 1968–1974 (Australia); 136

Mining on Private Land Act, The, 1909 (Australia); 136

Muschinski v. Dodds (1985) 160 CLR 583; 149

N

National Provincial Bank Ltd. v. Ainsworth (1965) AC 1175; 107

Native Title Act, 1993 (Australia); 127–30, 155–56, 237

Native Title Act, 1998 (Australia); 154, 157, 158, 163, 164–65, 172, 177–78, 233

Natural Parents v. Superintendent of Child Welfare (1976) 2 SCR 751;

New South Wales v. The Commonwealth ("the Seas and Submerged Lands Case") (1975) 135 CLR 337; 90, 92, 93, 109, 122

New South Wales Constitution Act, 1855 (Imp) 18 and 19 Vict c 54; 86, 132

Nisga'a Final Agreement (Nisga'a Treaty), (1998), 18, 213–6, 217, 221, 223

O

Optional Protocol to the International Covenant on Civil and Political Rights (16 December 1966) 999 U.N.T.S. 302; 103–4

Onus v. Alcoa of Australia Ltd. (1981) 149 CLR 27; 117

P

Pacific Islanders Protection Act, 1872 (Imp) 36 Vict c 19 (P9/579); 86

Pacific Islandes Protection Act, 1875 (Imp) 38 and 39 Vict c 51; 86

Petroleum Acts, The, 1923–1958 (Queensland); 136

Post Office v. Estuary Radio Ltd. (1968) 2 QB 740; 93

Privy Council (Limitation of Appeals) Act, 1968 (Cth); 91

Privy Council (Appeals from the High Court) Act, 1975 (Cth); 91

Q

Queensland Coast Islands Act, 1879; 87, 100

R

Racial Discrimination Act, 1975 (Australia); 83, 109, 123, 126, 129, 139, 148, 155, 174

Randwick Corporation v. Rutledge (1959) 102 CLR 54; 89, 104

Re Loh Toh Met (1961) 27 MLJ 234; 97

Re.g. v. Adams (1996) 3 SCR 101; 191

Re.g. v. Côté (1996) 3 SCR 139; 191

Re.g. v. Francis (1988) 1 SCR 1025; 204, 205

Re.g. v. Gladstone (1996) 2 SCR 723; 190, 192, 205

Re.g. v. Kidman (1915) 20 CLR 425; 90

Re.g. v. N.T.C. Smokehouse Ltd. (1996) 2 SCR 672; 191

Re.g. v. Pamajewon (1996) 2 SCR 821; 191

Re.g. v. Sparrow (1990) 1 SCR 1075; 120, 191, 192, 205, 207

Re.g. v. Sutherland (1980) 2 SCR 451; 204

Re.g. v. Symonds (1847) NZPCC 387; 108, 116

Re.g. v. Taylor (1981) 62 CCC (2d) 227; 198

Re.g. v. Van der Peet (1996) 2 SCR 507; 184, 191, 192, 195, 196, 200, 201, 205, 207

Re.g. v. Wedge (1976) 1 NSWLR 581; 100

Re.g. v. Willans (1858) 3 Kyshe 16; 97

Royal Proclamation, 1763, R.S.C., 1985, App. II, No. 1; 184, 189, 243

Ruding v. Smith (1821) 161 ER 774; 97

S

Sabally and N'Jie v. H.M. Attorney-General (1965) 1 QB 273; 97, 99

Sakariyawo Oshodi v. Moriamo Dakolo (1930) AC 667; 112

Sammut v. Strickland (1938) AC 678; 97, 99

Santa Clara Pueblo v. Martinez 436 U.S. 49 (1978); 245

Schwartz v. Canada (1996) 1 SCR 254;

Secretary of State in Council of India v. Kamachee Boye Sahaba (1859) 19 ER 388; 111

Secretary of State for India v. Bai Rajbai (1915) LR 42 Ind App 229; 110

Secretary of State for India v. Sardar Rustam Khan (1941) AC 356; 110

Simon v. The Queen (1985) 2 SCR 387; 198

Sobhuza II. v. Miller (1926) AC 518; 93, 112

St. Catherine's Milling and Lumber Co. v. The Queen (1888) 14 App Cas, aff'g St. Catherine's Milling and Lumber Co. v. The Queen (1887) 13 SCR 577; 116, 202, 203

State Government Insurance Commission v. Trigwell (1979) 142 CLR 617; 97

State of South Australia, The v. The State of Victoria (1911) 12 CLR 667; 109

T

Te Weehi v. Regional Fisheries Officer (1986) 1 NZLR 680; 120

Tee-Hit-Ton Indians v. United States (119) 348 U.S. 272; 119

Treaty with the Sioux – Brulé, Oglala, Miniconjou, Yanktonai, Hunkpapa, Blackfeet, Cuthead, Two Kettle, Sans Arsc, and Santee – and Arapaho(Fort Laramie Treaty), 1868 (U.S.); 70

U

United States v. Sante Fe Pacific Railroad Company (1941) 314 U.S. 339; 119, 120

Table of Authorities

Universal Declaration of Human Rights (10 December 1948) G.A. Res. 217 A(III); 168

Universal Declaration on Indigenous Rights: Working Group on Indigenous Populations (1988) U.N. Doc. E/CN.4/SUB.2/1988/25; 169

Uukw v. R. (1987) 6 WWR 155; 199

V

Vajesingji Joravarsingji v. Secretary of State for India (1924) LR 51 Ind App; 110–2

Viro v. The Queen (1978) 141 CLR 88; 91

W

Wade v. New South Wales Rutile Mining Co. Pty. Ltd. (1969) 121 CLR 177; 89

Waitangi, Treaty of, (Te Tiriti O Waitangi), 1840 (Aotearoa/New Zealand); 71, 239

Western Australia vs. The Commonwealth (Native Title Act Case) (1995) 183 CLR 373; 145

Wi Parata v. Bishop of Wellington (1877) 3 NZ(Jur) NS 72; 119

Wik Peoples v. The State of Queensland & Others, The; The Thayorre Peoples v. The State of Queensland & Others, (23 December 1996) F.C. 96/044; 18, 68, 129, 131–153, 154, 155–56, 157, 165, 168, 237

Williams v, Attorney-General for New South Wales (1847) 1 Legge; 90

Williams v. Attorney-General for New South Wales (1913) 16 CLR 404; 104, 108

Wilson v. Anderson (2002) HCA 29; 176

Winfat Ltd. V. Attorney-General (1985) AC 733; 110, 111

Worchester v. Georgia 31 U.S. 350 (1832); 94

Y

Yeap Cheah Neo v. Ong Cheng Neo (1875) 6 LR 381; 97

Index

A

Aboriginal, See *indigenous*

Aboriginal Land Councils, 138, 167, 175

Aboriginal and Torres Strait Islander Commission, 74, 147, 153–156, 158–59, 161–62, 164–65, 166–71, 172–73, 174–79, 230, 233, 256n. 6.3–16.

adaawk, 182, 194, 198–200, 214

Adams, Howard, 70

Alexie, Sherman, 70

Allen, Chadwick, 27, 70, 72, 256n. 4.1.

American Indian Movement (AIM), 2, 31

Amnesty International, 56

Amos, Gerald, 210

Anaya, S. James, 234, 235

Anderson, Benedict, 40, 42

Ango'oskw, 214

Aotearoa/NewZealand, 1, 21, 69, 70, 71, 73, 171, 239

Ashcroft, Bill, 26

Association of First Nations, 212–3, 217–25, 226–7, 230, 257n. 7.1–10.

Australia, 1, 17, 18, 21, 28, 29, 52, 53, 61, 68, 69, 72, 77, 79, 83–179, 209, 210, 230, 233, 236
  New South Wales, 86, 87, 88, 89, 98, 99, 100, 101, 143, 176
  Northern Territory, 130, 137, 165
  Queensland, 83, 86, 87, 95, 118, 119, 123, 126, 127, 133, 135–36, 150, 153, 156, 161, 163, 165, 173, 175–178
  South Australia, 137
  Victoria, 137, 178–79
  Western Australia, 131, 137, 165, 167

Ayuuk, 214

B

Baird-Olson, Karen, 31

Barkan, Elazar, 231–5

Barry, Brian, 230, 235, 246

Beazley, Kim, 160, 175

Benhabib, Seyla, 246–8

biopolitics, biopower, 2, 48, 54, 57

Blueberry Band, *See indigenous*

Borrows, John, 250

British Columbia, *See Canada*

British Empire, 32, 71, 79

Brown, Richard Harvey, 78

Brubaker, Rogers, 41, 56

Busby, James, 71

C

Canada, 1, 17, 18, 21, 52, 53, 69, 70, 77, 79, 161–62, 171, 181–227, 230, 238, 244, 247–8, 251
  British Columbia, 18, 181, 182, 189–90, 192, 201, 206, 207, 208, 209, 211, 212, 214–6, 217, 220–1, 223, 248
  Quebec, 226

Cannadine, David, 31, 254n. 2.7.

Castan, Ron, 173

Chrétien, Jean, 53, 212

Citizenship, 75, 218–9, 241, 246, 250

Clark, Geoff, 165, 172, 178

Clausewitz, Baron von, 58
Clifford, Michael, 82
colonialism, *See imperialism*
Commentaries on the Law of England, 95, 97, 106
Cornell, Drucilla, 63, 68
Court, Richard, 131
Culture and Equality, 230
Cunningham, Liz, 173

D

Davis-Brown, Beth, 78
de Certeau, Michel, 3, 8–10, 11, 72
Dean. Mitchell, 37
deconstruction, 17, 25–6, 27, 72, 76
    and law, 61–70
    and justice, 61–64, 68, 247
    ethics of, 18, 61, 63, 65
    See also supplement
    See also trace
Deleuze, Gilles, 2–4, 7, 8–10, 15, 57
Deloria, Jr., Vine, 25, 26, 73
Democracy, 244–52
    theories of, 18, 76, 248, 250
Derrida, Jacques, 3, 27–30, 61–70, 72, 233, 251, 252
Dillon, Colin, 172
Djerrkura, Gatjil, 153–56, 158–59, 165, 166–71
discipline, disciplinary power, 48
Discipline and Punish, 48
Doig Band, *See indigenous*
Donzelot, Jacques, 49

E

economy, 44–7
    and biopower, 48
    and Chicago School, 51
    and classical political economy, 46–7
    and globalization, 54
    and welfare liberalism, 49–50
    Aristotle's concept of, 44
Eighteenth Brumaire of Louis Bonaparte, The, 4
Edkins, Jenny, 24

Elkin, Stephen L., 35–36
Empire, 54–8
episteme (knowledge), of
    governmentality, 37, 47
    of liberalism, 17, 46, 79, 237
    of neo-liberalism, 50, 51, 54
    of pastoral power, 39–40, 43
    of *raison d'etat* (reason of state), 42, 43–4, 46
    of sovereignty, 43
    of welfare liberalism, 50
    See also knowledge
ethos (ethics), of governmentality, 37, 47
    of deconstruction, 18, 61, 63, 65
    of genealogy, 5–7, 10, 62, 77–8, 82
    of liberalism, 47–50, 248
    of neo-liberalism, 50, 53, 56–7
    of pastoral power, 39–40
    of sovereignty, 45
    of welfare liberalism, 49

F

First Indian on the Moon, 70
First Nations (Canada), *See indigenous*
Fish, Stanley, 17
Fischer, Tim, 162, 163
Fontaine, Phil, 212–3, 217–25, 226–7
Foucault, Michel, 2–18,36–7, 39–40, 47–8, 50, 54, 57, 58, 67, 77–8, 81, 82, 253n. 1.1.
Franks, C.E.S., 237
freedom, 253n. 1.1.
    and neo-liberalism, 52
Fukuyama, Francis, 28

G

genealogy, 5, 8, 18, 67, 77, 81
    and *episteme* (knowledge), 67
    and governmentality, 11
    and history, 6–7, 78, 81
    and power, 7–10, 67
    and subjectivity, 67
    ethics of, 5–7, 10, 62, 77–8, 82
    of liberalism, 47–58, 230
Gitksan (Gitxan), *See indigenous*

Index

277

government, governmentality, 17, 33, 36–58, 255n. 3.1.
  analytics of, 36–7, 54, 58
  and resistance, 57, 58
  as "conduct of conduct", 36–7
  defined, 37
  episteme (knowledge) of, 37
  ethos (ethics) of, 37
  international/global, 54
  liberal, 17, 38
  neo-liberal, 50–8
  pastoral power, 39–42, 43
  police, 42–5
  raison d'etat (reason of state), 42–5
  sovereignty, 38–9, 43
  techne (technology) of, 37
  welfare liberalism, 49–50
Grant, Felix, 210
"Greenstone Patu, The", 72
Griffiths, Colin, 157
Griffins, Gareth, 26
Guilt of Nations, The, 231, 235
Gurr, Ted Robert, 21, 23, 25, 33
Gutmann, Amy, 245–6

H

Haida, *See indigenous*
Hanson, Allen, 71, 256n. 4.2.
Hanson, Pauline, 161
Hardt, Michael, 54, 56, 57, 58, 232
hauntology, 29–30, 69, 72, 75, 76, 230
Hayek, F.A., 51
Heidegger, Martin, 7–10, 64, 253n. 1.1.
Heisler, Martin O., 23
Hill, Ronald Paul, 72
Hindess, Barry, 54
Hobbes, Thomas, 40, 255n. 3.3.
Hobsbawm, Eric, 40–1
Hobson, Lieutenant-General, 71
Hodge, Bob, 26, 27
homo economicus (economic man), 45–6, 49
  and liberalism, 46–7
  as subjectivity, 45
Hopkins, A.G., 79
Howard, John, 69, 157, 160, 162

I

Identity in Democracy, 245
Ihimeara, Witi, 72
imperialism, 22, 26–33, 54–8, 69, 70, 71, 72, 73, 74, 76, 211, 237
Indians of All Tribes, 70
indigenous
  American Indians, Amerindians 2, 13, 25, 71, 73, 74, 75, 119, 239, 248
  and colonialism, 69
  Australians, 2, 28, 53, 72, 73, 100, 101, 157, 158, 164, 166, 168, 170, 173, 233
  Blueberry Band, 211
  culture, 184, 195
  definitions, 1–2, 74, 75, 76
  Doig Band, 211
  First Nations (Canada), 2, 18, 162, 208, 211, 212–3, 218, 219–21, 222, 223, 224, 225, 226–7, 243, 244
  Gitksan (Gitxan), 181–2, 183, 192–4, 198–200, 206, 247–8
  government, 75
  groups, 74, 184
  Haida, 75, 251
  Inuit, 2, 248
  Innu Nation, 226
  land rights, 72, 73, 74, 75
  law, 237
  legal activism/claims, 3, 16, 17, 31, 32, 36, 37, 60, 61, 67, 72, 77, 79–81, 208, 221, 226, 229–31, 234–7, 241, 244, 245, 247, 249, 250, 251
  Liard First Nation, 223–4
  Maori, 2, 71, 72, 73, 230, 239–40
  Metis, 70, 251
  Murray Islanders, 83, 84–6
  nations, 71, 242, 243
  Nisga'a, 181, 213–6, 217, 222
  Oglala Lakota (Sioux), 75
  peoples, 18, 22, 26, 27, 28, 29–33, 68, 72, 74, 75, 81, 164, 166, 169, 173, 174, 176, 186, 188, 189, 190, 203, 209, 233, 234, 235, 236, 238,

241, 243, 244, 245, 250, 251, 252, 253n. 1.2, 254n. 2.3.
peoples' movements (IPMs), 21-6, 29-33, 36, 58, 60, 61, 69, 71, 72, 74, 75, 76, 229, 230, 233, 243, 245
resistance, 33, 229, 244
rights, 24, 25, 29, 36, 69, 76, 104, 155, 159, 162, 172, 173, 174, 183, 184-7,188, 189, 195-6, 203-4, 206, 208, 226, 230, 234, 237-8, 239, 241, 243, 250
Santa Clara Pueblo, 245
self-determination, self-government, 23, 169, 181, 182, 183, 219, 229, 230, 233, 234, 236, 238, 240, 241, 243-4, 245-6, 248, 249
sovereignty, 28, 31, 71, 76, 181, 186-7, 189, 207, 214, 217, 235, 236, 242, 243-4, 246
Torres Strait Islanders, 2, 28, 157, 164, 166, 170
Westbanks First Nation, 220-1
Wet'suwet'en (Wetsueten), 181-2, 183, 192-4, 198-200, 206
Indigenous Peoples in International Law, 235
Inuit, *See indigenous*
Inuu Nation, *See indigenous*

J

Jaimes, M. Annette, 75
Johnson, Lyndon Baines, 28
jurisprudence, 61, 63, 64, 65, 66, 67, 68, 184
justice
and law, 61-4, 68, 247
and deconstruction, 61, 62
and reconciliation, 69, 162, 168, 171, 230, 235-44, 249
and restitution, 230, 231-5, 242, 249
for indigenous peoples, 69, 230, 242, 245

K

Katter, Bob, 158
Keynes, John Maynard, 51

knowledge, 81
and liberalism, 17
and power, 7-10, 12
See also episteme
Krasner, Stephen, 38
kungax, 182, 194, 198-200
Kymlicka, Will, 230, 238, 239, 240-2, 248, 253n. 1.4.

L

Labor Party (Australia), 159, 163, 165, 176-77
Lamer, Antonio, 181, 207
Lautens, Trevor, 209
law
and justice, 61-4, 68, 247
and sovereignty, 55, 60, 66
Australian, 29, 83-130
British Common, 160, 184, 187, 195, 233
Canadian, 181-207, 215, 222
Constitutional, 23, 29, 33, 35-6, 63, 79, 171, 184, 195, 215, 252
Critical theories of, 18, 60-4, 65
indigenous, 184
international, 23, 32, 67, 169, 234, 239, 243
right of conquest, 28-9, 94
rule of, 230, 247
systems of, 16, 60, 64, 65, 229
terra nullis (empty land), 28-9, 94-5, 97-100, 102-4, 113, 174, 237
violence of, 61-3, 66-7, 68
Western, 18, 31
Liard First Nation, *See indigenous*
Liberal Party (British Columbia), 223
liberalism, liberal governmentality, 1, 3, 12, 13, 16-9, 47-58, 76, 79, 80, 250, 252
and indigenous peoples, 1, 17, 21, 23-33, 36, 38, 67, 71, 74, 79, 81, 229, 230, 231-44, 246, 250, 254n. 2.6.
and law, 66, 67
and pastoral power, 58
and police, 58
and rights, 23, 29, 69, 70, 72, 73, 74, 229, 230, 231, 233, 235, 236, 241, 246

Index

and social science, 25–6, 38, 80
and sovereignty, 31, 46, 48, 51, 58, 79, 229, 249
episteme (knowledge) of 17, 46, 79, 237
ethos (ethics) of, 47–50, 248
nationalism, 31, 79, 229, 240–1, 248, 249
techne (technology) of, 50, 236–7, 243
telos (goal) of, 48
See also neo-liberalism, welfare liberalism
Levy, Jacob T., 230, 232, 236, 245
Locke, John, 33
London Missionary Society, 86, 94–5, 100, 116
Luhman, Niklas, 68

M

Machiavelli, Niccolo, 39, 40, 42
Manning, Preston, 221–2
Maori, *See indigenous*
Marx, Karl, 4, 28
McAdam, Doug, 11, 60, 254n. 2.4.
McCormick, John, 66, 67
McDonald, Don, 165
Means, Russell, 2
Médicins sans Frontières (Doctors without Borders), 56
Metis, *See indigenous*
Miller, Peter, 52
Mining Journal, The (London), 130–131, 256n. 6.1–2.
Mishra, Vijay, 26, 27
Moore-Gilbert, Bart, 26
multicultural(ism), multiethnic, 225, 230, 244, 246, 248
democracy, 18, 244–252
liberalism, 238, 245
Multicultural Citizenship, 241
Murray Islanders, *See indigenous*

N

Nagel, Joanne, 1, 74
National Democratic Party (Canada), 181

National Party (Australia), 158, 161, 165
nationalism, 13, 40–2, 250
and indigenous peoples, 31, 242, 243, 247
and pastoral power, 40–2, 242
civic, 41, 56
ethnic, 41
French, 41–2, 56
German, 41–2
liberal, 31, 79, 229, 240–1, 248, 249
theories of, 40–2
native title, *See title*
Negri, Antonio, 54, 56, 57, 232
neo-liberalism, neo-liberal governmentality, 2, 49, 50–8, 248, 251
and globalization, 50, 54–58
and pastoral power, 56, 232
and police, 54, 55, 56
and social capital, 52, 53, 54, 56
and sovereignty, 51, 53, 54–5, 56, 232, 233, 244
as government at a distance, 52, 54
episteme (knowledge) of, 50, 51, 54
ethos (ethics) of, 50, 53, 56–7
Ordo-liberalism, 51
techne (technology) of, 50, 52, 53, 55, 57, 230
telos (goal) of, 51, 52–3, 54, 57
neo-orientalism, *See Orientalism*
neo-ornamentalism, *See ornamentalism*
New South Wales, *See Australia*
New Zealand, *See Aotearoa/New Zealand*
Nietzsche, Friedrich, 5
Nisga'a, *See indigenous*
Northern Territory, *See Australia*

O

Obhrai, Deepak, 225
Oglala Lakota (Sioux), *See indigenous*
Oldfield, David, 161
Olney, Howard, 173
O'Malley, Pat, 57
O'Shane, Terry, 174–75
One Nation Party (Australia), 161, 166
ontology, 7–9, 29–30, 69, 71, 72, 73, 75, 76
Orientalism, 22, 31, 237

neo-orientalism, 21–6, 230, 231–44, 245, 246, 247, 248, 254n. 2.6.
ornamentalism, 31–2
   Ornamentalism, 31
   neo-ornamentalism, 32, 230, 231–44, 248
Oxfam, 56

P

Parekh, Bhikhu, 248, 249, 251, 253n. 1.4.
pastoral power, 39–42, 43, 48, 49
   and nationalism, 40–2, 48
   and neo-liberalism, 56, 232
   and sovereignty, 39, 40
   episteme (knowledge) of, 39–40, 43
   ethos (ethics) of, 39–40
   techne (technology) of, 39–40
   telos (goal) of, 39–40
Pearson, Noel, 158
Pine Ridge Reservation (South Dakota), *See United States*
Pocock, J.G.A., 239–40
Pogge, Thomas, 235, 238
political theory, 2, 18, 32, 35, 38, 66, 229, 230, 231–52
police, 42–5, 47
   and neo-liberalism, 54, 55
   science of *(Polizeiwissenschaft)*, 43–4, 45, 46, 48
(post)colonial, (post)coloniality, 2, 16–8, 31, 33, 76, 78, 79, 230, 251, 254n. 2.5.
   approach, 26
   states, 69
   theory, 17, 26, 33, 244
Post-Colonial Studies Reader, The, 26
poststructuralism, 2, 4, 18, 31, 33, 54, 65, 67, 244
power, 8–10, 12, 14–6, 17
   four faces of, 7
property
   and indigenous peoples, 72–4, 164, 201, 211, 238, 239–40, 250
   and liberalism, 73, 79, 223, 229, 233, 239, 249, 250

Q

Quebec, *See Canada*
Queensland, *See Australia*

R

Raison d'etat (reason of state), 42–5
   episteme (knowledge) of, 42, 43–4, 46
   techne (technology) of, 43–4, 47, 50
   telos (goal) of, 44, 48
Reform Party (Canada), 220, 221–2, 225
Reid, Bill, 251
resistance, 10–6, 33, 76
   and governmentality, 57
   and law, 60
   strategic, 11–2, 14–5, 24–5, 30, 60
   tactical, 11–4, 24–5, 60
   theories of, 11
Ridgeway, Aden, 157
Robinson, Ray, 162
Rose, Nikolas, 52
Rousseau, Jean-Jacques, 255n. 3.3.
Runstrom, Robert A., 71

S

Said, Edward, 22
Santa Clara Pueblo, *See indigenous*
Schelling, Thomas C., 14
Schmitt, Carl, 55, 64
Scott, James C., 11, 13, 60
self-determination, *See indigenous*
settler
   and indigenous peoples, 26–7, 32, 69, 230, 250
   societies, 26–7, 80, 229, 233, 237, 238
   states, 16–7, 19, 21, 26–7, 28, 29, 30, 67, 69, 73, 75, 76, 77, 79, 238, 240, 249, 250, 251, 252, 254n. 2.7.
Sigidimhaanak, 214
Shohat, Ella, 27
Simgigat, 214
Simpson, Audra, 242–3
Smith, Adam, 46, 48, 51, 207
Smith, Mel, 208–9, 210

Index

Specters of Marx, 27–8
spectropolitics, 27–30
"Spirit of Haida Gawaii, The", 251
Spivak, Gayatri Chakravorty, 3–4, 7, 9–10
social science, 21–2, 24–5, 29, 30–3, 35, 37–8, 76, 80, 230
South Australia, *See Australia*
sovereignty, 87, 88–9, 93, 97, 106–8, 109, 110, 111, 113, 114, 118, 123, 125, 184, 186–7, 189, 207, 212, 214, 217, 249–50
    as governmentality, 38–9
    and law, 55, 60, 66
    and liberalism, 31, 48, 49, 50, 70, 72, 242
    and neo-liberalism, 51, 53, 54–5, 56, 232, 233
    and pastoral power, 39, 40
    and police, 43
    episteme (knowledge) of, 43
    ethos (ethics) of, 45
    techne (technology) of, 39, 47, 55
    telos (goal) of, 39
Stolen Generations, 171
strategic space, 15–6, 29
Strategy of Conflict, The, 14
supplement(ality), 17, 61, 64, 69, 72–5, 230
    See also deconstruction

T

Tarrow, Sidney, 11, 60
Taylor, Charles, 230, 248, 253n. 1.4.
techne (technology), 37, 47
    of liberalism, 50, 236–7, 243
    of neo-liberalism, 50, 52, 53, 55, 57, 230
    of pastoral power, 39–40
    of *raison d'etat* (reason of state), 43–4, 47, 50
    of sovereignty, 39, 47, 55
    of welfare liberalism, 50, 230
terra nullis (empty land), *See law*
terrorism/terrorist, 56
Theile, Leslie Paul, 7, 253n. 1.1.
Tiffin, Helen, 26

Tilly, Charles, 11, 60
Tino Rangatiratanga, 230, 239
title
    communal, 115
    native, 17, 18, 73, 80, 110–54, 155, 156, 159–60, 164, 165, 172–73, 174–79, 181–207, 209, 212, 226, 229, 230, 234, 238, 243, 247–8, 250
    radical, 113–4, 140, 143
Torres Strait Islanders, *See indigenous*
Touraine, Alain, 253n. 1.2.
trace, 17, 61, 69, 71
    See also deconstruction
treaties, 18, 70, 71, 72, 76, 171, 2113–6, 217, 221, 222, 223, 239
Tully, James, 251–2
Turner, Dale, 235, 236

U

Union of British Columbia Indian Chiefs, 238, 243
United Nations, 25, 28, 55, 74, 157, 166, 168–70, 171, 172, 177
United States, 1, 13, 21, 28, 29, 55, 56, 69, 70, 73, 74, 75, 240, 254–5n. 2.7.
    Pine Ridge Reservation (South Dakota), 75

V

Victoria, *See Australia*

W

Walzer, Michael, 245, 248, 253n. 1.4.
Wealth of Nations, The, 48
welfare liberalism, welfare liberal governmentality, 13, 51, 52
    as governmentality, 49–50
    and pastoral power, 49
    episteme (knowledge) of, 50
    ethos (ethics) of, 49
    Keynesian political economy, 50, 51
    techne (technology) of, 50, 230
    telos (goal) of, 50

Werther, Guntram F.A., 1, 22, 31, 32, 33, 253n. 2.1.
Westbanks First Nation, *See indigenous*
Western
  democracy, 22–3, 237
  law, 18, 31
  political theory, 32, 66
  society, 2, 38
Western Australia, *See Australia*
Wet'suwet'en (Wetsueten), *See Indigenous*

"What is Enlightenment?" (Foucault), 4, 67
white settler, *See settler* 18
Wilmer, Franke, 1, 22, 24, 25, 27, 29, 72, 73, 253n. 2.1.

Y

Yanner, Murrandoo, 163
Yashar, Deborah, 254n. 2.6.
Young, Iris Marion, 12–3, 24, 249–50, 253n. 1.4.